DATE DUE

MAR 26 '98	

BRODART, CO.   Cat. No. 23-221-003

THE FI$CAL CONGRESS

Recent Titles in
Contributions in Political Science
Series Editor: Bernard K. Johnpoll

The Fall and Rise of the Pentagon: American Defense Policies in the 1970s
Lawrence J. Korb

Calling a Truce to Terror: The American Response to International Terrorism
Ernest Evans

Spain in the Twentieth Century World: Essays on Spanish Diplomacy,
1898-1978
James W. Cortada

From Rationality to Liberation: The Evolution of Feminist Ideology
Judith A. Sabrosky

Truman's Crises: A Political Biography of Harry S. Truman
Harold F. Gosnell

"Bigotry!": Ethnic, Machine, and Sexual Politics in a Senatorial Election
Maria J. Falco

Furious Fancies: American Political Thought in the Post-Liberal Era
Philip Abbott

Politicans, Judges, and the People: A Study in Citizens' Participation
Charles H. Sheldon and Frank P. Weaver

The European Parliament: The Three-Decade Search for a United Europe
Paula Scalingi

Presidential Primaries: Road to the White House
James W. Davis

The Voice of Terror: A Biography of Johann Most
Frederic Trautmann

Presidential Secrecy and Deception: Beyond the Power to Persuade
John M. Orman

The New Red Legions: A Survey Data Source Book
Richard A. Gabriel

THE FI$CAL CONGRESS

Lance T. LeLoup

Legislative Control of the Budget

Contributions in Political Science, Number 47

Greenwood Press
Westport, Connecticut · London, England

Library of Congress Cataloging in Publication Data

LeLoup, Lance T.
    The fiscal Congress.

    (Contributions in political science ; no. 47
ISSN 0147-1066)
    Bibliography: p.
    Includes index.
    1.   Budget—United States.   2.   United States.
Congress.   I.   Title.   II.   Series.
HJ2052.L443   353.0072'221   79-6823
ISBN 0-313-22009-3

Library of Congress Catalog Card Number: 79-6823
ISBN: 0-313-22009-3
ISSN: 0147-1066

First published in 1980

Greenwood Press
A division of Congressional Information Service, Inc.
88 Post Road West, Westport, Connecticut 06881

Printed in the United States of America

10 9 8 7 6 5 4 3 2 1

To
Jean W. LeLoup
and
Jean S. LeLoup

Contents

Tables and Figures

Preface

Is the Budget and Impoundment Control Act of 1974 one of the most important congressional reforms of the twentieth century? Over five years since the law was implemented, we are ready to begin to answer that question. It is a process that was born in the congressional resurgence of the Watergate era, but has come of age in the era of scarcity, stagflation, public cynicism, and Proposition 13. The politics of congressional budgeting alone are a fascinating study, but the overall significance of fiscal politics is even greater. This study of congressional budget reform will shed some light on the evolving Congress, shifting presidential-congressional power, changing fiscal policy, and the national policy-making process.

The methodology employed in this work is eclectic. It includes historical and descriptive perspectives as well as analytical and theoretical approaches. The study proceeds from a set of concerns about process and procedures, legislative politics, implementation, and policy results. Data used in the study included primary sources such as hearings, reports, and budget documents; secondary sources such as *Congressional Quarterly* and the *National Journal*, as well as the rapidly expanding professional literature; and participant observation and personal interviews conducted by the author. Interviews with members of Congress, congressional staff, and executive branch officials were conducted from 1975 to 1978. The most concerted efforts were made to interview Senate and House Budget Committee members. Interviews were held with just over one-half of the members of the House Budget Committee and one-fourth of the members of the Senate Budget Committee in this period. Also interviewed were members of the Appropriations, Ways and Means, and Finance Committees, and their staffs; members of both the House and Senate who did not serve on any of these committees; and staff of the Congressional Budget Office and the Office of Management and Budget. All interviews were semi-structured with a core of common questions, but respondents were encouraged to discuss freely all phases of the congressional budget process. Respondents were promised anonymity and are not identified in the text. All uncited or unattributed quotes have been taken from the personal interviews with the author.

It has been personally and intellectually rewarding to study the congressional budget process since its creation and implementation in 1974. It is my hope that this book will help further our understanding of congressional control of the budget and fiscal policy, stimulate further research, and convey some of the interest of budgetary politics.

Acknowledgments

Many colleagues, reviewers, and friends contributed to this study, and I am grateful to all of them. Special thanks go to Randall B. Ripley, Steven A. Shull, Eugene Meehan, Patrick Hynes, Steve Wade, Steve Ryals, Martha Lane, Mary Roberts, Bernard Johnpoll, and James Sabin. Congressman Douglas Applegate and his staff were most generous in allowing me to use his office as a base of operations. Valda Tuetken, Trish Hibler, and Mary Hines helped type and prepare the manuscript. Senator Henry Bellmon and his office were particularly helpful, as were Tom Foxwell and the staff of the Senate Budget Committee publications office. The many people who gave of their valuable time to discuss the budget process frankly with me deserve special, if anonymous, recognition. Finally, warm thanks go to Jean W. LeLoup.

Lance T. LeLoup

St. Louis, Missouri
January 1980

THE FI$CAL CONGRESS

1

Congress and
the Budget

*Money is, with propriety, considered as the vital
principle of the body politic, as that which sustains
its life and motion, and enables it to perform its
most essential function.*
— Alexander Hamilton, *Federalist #30*

Between the lofty rhetoric of statesmen and the daily tasks of bureaucrats lie money and its politics: how it is raised and how it is spent. As Alexander Hamilton noted two centuries ago, money sustains the essential functions of government. The Constitution of the United States conferred upon Congress the power of the purse, but a glance at history reveals that the executive branch gradually became dominant in the fiscal affairs of the nation.

The Constitution states that "No money shall be drawn from the Treasury, but in consequence of appropriations made by law." Mindful of the onerous taxes imposed by the British in the period before the American Revolution, the framers reserved authority to levy taxes for the legislature, specifically requiring that all bills originate in the popularly elected House of Representatives. The lion's share of the power of the purse appeared to belong to Congress.

The guidelines written into the Constitution, however, have proven to be flexible, subject to changing times and fortunes. The president and his executive officers needed some control over spending to effectively administer the laws of Congress. Even in the early years of the nation, conflicts arose with the president over money. The First Congress was embroiled over the question of executive discretion, specifically the latitude available to the secretary of the treasury to prepare estimates of revenues and expenditures.[1] Representative Albert Gallatin of Pennsylvania felt it necessary to remind his colleagues in 1798 that, "the power of granting money for any purposes whatever belongs solely to the Legislature, in which it is literally vested by the Constitution."[2]

By the twentieth century, members of Congress frequently complained about presidential usurpation of spending prerogatives and their own abdication of the power of the purse. By the early 1970s, the cries had become a chorus, and the problem had become a crisis:

I am convinced that the vast majority of Americans agree with the constitutional principle requiring that priorities of expenditure be set by the legislative branch. However, the people of this nation recognize that Congress has in reality lost control of the budget. The President has stepped forward and filled the vacuum left by our own inaction. The executive branch has . . .set its own priorities, completely independent of legislative intent. America's budgetary affairs and priorities of expenditures are now being decided by faceless bureaucrats.[3]

Senator Sam Nunn (D-G.)

Plainly it was the intent of our Founding Fathers for the Congress to make the decisions relating both to the raising and spending of money. Over the years the Congress has gradually failed in meeting this responsibility, and now we are in the awkward position of losing much of this responsibility to the executive branch.[4]

Senator Henry Bellmon (R-Okla.)

We are left, 73 years into the 20th century, with a system that belongs to the mid-19th century. We are trying to operate the largest budget in history with a system largely unchanged since the Civil War. Congress is like a giant corporation trying to operate with an accountant with a green eyeshade and a quill pen.[5]

Senator Charles Percy (R-Ill.)

In the summer of 1974, Congress passed the Budget and Impoundment Control Act, landmark legislation designed to reduce executive discretion and improve congressional procedures for dealing with the budget. It was a measure designed to restore a balance in budgetary power between Congress and the president. This book examines the impact of the 1974 Budget Act on Congress, the national budget, and the fiscal affairs of the nation.

THE EROSION OF CONGRESSIONAL CONTROL

The growth of presidential influence and the erosion of congressional control were a prelude to the major congressional reforms of the 1970s. But it was a trend that took many decades to develop. Hamilton called the power of the purse a "most complete and effective weapon."[6] As exercised by Congress through the levying of taxes and the approval of appropriations, control has rarely been effective and never complete. The initial process of handling the budget in Congress was simple compared to the complexities of today. The House Ways and Means Committee, established in 1802, initiated both taxing and spending bills.[7] In the Senate, responsibility for governmental budgeting was handled by the Finance Committee.

Although challenged periodically by the executive branch, Congress managed the nation's finances with comparative ease. Relatively few issues challenged the part-time Congress and the system remained relatively stable until the Civil War.

The spending process, under the House Ways and Means and Senate Finance Committees, faltered during the chaotic events of the war. In 1865, the House created the Appropriations Committee to consider expenditures and the Senate followed suit two years later, leaving Ways and Means and Finance with jurisdiction over taxes.[8] Another critical development that occurred in the nineteenth century was the approval of separate appropriations bills. By the end of the Civil War, jurisdiction over taxing and spending was divided, and government appropriations were approved in a number of separate actions, not in a single bill.[9]

Congressional procedures in budgeting were further fragmented in the last third of the nineteenth century, when the standing committees in Congress gained control over some appropriations and money bills.[10] This diminution of centralized control made it possible for members of Congress to secure greater benefits for their own districts, and as a result, there was less economizing in the totals. This trend helped foster the belief that the president was more "responsible" in controlling expenditures than Congress.[11] The decentralized system, in which agencies submitted spending requests directly to a dozen committees in Congress, continued until 1921 amid a growing sentiment for change.

The Budget and Accounting Act passed in 1921 established the executive budget as we know it today. The president was given the responsibility of gathering requests from all the executive agencies and submitting an annual budget to Congress. A new agency, the Bureau of the Budget (BOB), was created to assist the president. BOB was initially placed in the Treasury Department, but in 1939, along with other changes to strengthen the presidency, it became part of the Executive Office of the President (EOP). Through the 1921 Budget Act, Congress attempted to remedy the budgetary chaos that had evolved by centralizing responsibility for budget estimates with the president. It was not intended as an abdication of congressional control over the pursestrings; however, its passage was followed by an attempt to centralize congressional budget procedures as well. Congress returned control of spending to the Appropriations committees, and prohibited the other standing committees from recommending spending proposals. The standing committees were responsible for authorizing substantive legislation, while the Appropriations committees were prohibited from taking any legislative actions.[12] Beyond clarifying the jurisdiction of authorizations and appropriations, centralization of congressional procedures never came about. Appropriations bills continued to be considered individually, not as a single bill, and this pattern prevailed until 1975.

After 1921, the president's control over the federal budget continued to expand. As government became larger and more complex, it was the president and his Budget Office that kept pace. During the depression of the 1930s, control of expenditures by President Franklin D. Roosevelt increased, but a more significant shift occurred in fiscal policy. As Roosevelt was revolutionizing the American presidency, Lord John Maynard Keynes' theories about the role of government expenditures were revolutionizing capitalist economics.[13] Keynes's notions that public spending could compensate for inadequacies in the private sector emerged in Roosevelt's administration as discretionary (or compensatory) fiscal policy. The historical trends of discretionary fiscal policy and presidential government merged in the passage of the 1946 Employment Act, mandating that the president use the federal budget to maintain growth, promote full employment, and stabilize prices.

During this period, Congress continued to exercise the power of the purse through appropriations. Control was mainly in the hands of specialized and increasingly autonomous subcommittees that reviewed agency requests and made recommendations that were seldom challenged. As the federal budget became more important to the economic health of the nation, Congress became concerned with its inability to take an overview of the budget. Critics complained the appropriations process was too fragmented and fiscally irresponsible, and delegated control to the executive. In 1946, Congress attempted to deal with these problems by establishing a legislative budget.

ATTEMPTS AT A LEGISLATIVE BUDGET

Many of the defects in the congressional budget system were apparent decades earlier. Following a period of presidential expansion and growth, Congress set out to reverse the swing in the pendulum of power in the period after World War II. The Legislative Reorganization Act of 1946 instituted a number of internal congressional reforms. Section 138 of the act attempted to establish a legislative budget.[14] A Joint Committee on the Budget was set up to take an overview of the president's requests and national needs. This bulky panel consisted of all members of the House Ways and Means, Senate Finance, and the two Appropriations Committees.[15] By February 15 of each year, the Joint Committee was required to study the president's budget and report a legislative budget to both houses. The concurrent resolution was to include a ceiling on total expenditures, a figure for estimated receipts, and a recommendation on a deficit or a surplus.[16]

The movement for a legislative budget was consistent with the political tides of the postwar period. It was a recognition of congressional fragmentation and a reaction to a long period of deficit spending. With Republican party resurgence and in the spirit of the Twenty-second Amendment, it was an effort to strengthen the Congress vis-à-vis the executive. The attempts to create a legislative budget in the 1940s failed, however, and the growth of presidential power remained unchecked.

In 1947, the House approved a resolution to slash President Harry Truman's budget by $6 billion. A highly partisan controversy developed, and the House-Senate Conference Committee was unable to agree on a figure. No legislative budget was adopted for fiscal 1948.[17] The next year saw agreement on an expenditure ceiling calling for a $2.5 billion cut in the president's requests. Lacking any enforcement mechanism, the resolution proved to be a paper tiger; Congress eventually approved outlays some $6 billion above the ceiling. In 1949, reacting to the disappointing performance of the previous two years, Congress moved the deadline from February 15 to May 1. By that date, however, most spending measures had already passed and Congress did not even bother with a resolution. With barely a whimper, the legislative budget experiment faded into obscurity after only three years.

One last attempt at budget reform occurred in 1950 when the House Appropriations Committee attempted to unify appropriations into one omnibus bill. The House successfully passed the bill in May, but the Senate did not complete its action until August. Because so many supplemental appropriations were required that year, the practice was discontinued.[18]

The failure of budget reform in the 1946-1950 period was nonetheless important. Its demise was studied carefully by budget reformers in the 1970s in an attempt to learn from the mistakes from the past. There were a number of reasons that the earlier attempts failed.[19]

The Joint Committee was too large and unmanageable. With 102 members, almost 20 percent of the Congress was included, making it difficult to reach a compromise. Many Democrats, in the minority for the first time since 1932, perceived the legislative budget as a partisan tool designed to embarrass Truman. Partisan political conflicts overshadowed the larger institutional interests of improving congressional decision-making capabilities.

There was inadequate time to reach a decision. The February 15 deadline gave the Joint Budget Committee only a few weeks to consider a budget that had been nearly a year in planning. It had insufficient information to assess the merits of programs and budget components, and it lacked a professional staff to help it.

No provisions were made for amending the ceiling once it had been agreed on. Members were somewhat reluctant to lock themselves into a budget six months before the start of the fiscal year, and before their committees had formulated their plans for the session. The Joint Committee recommended spending cuts without specifying where the cuts were to be made. Therefore, even when a ceiling was set, the more difficult task of identifying items was avoided and the ceilings proved to be meaningless. Finally, the concurrent resolution was not binding. Committees could and did ignore it since no enforcement procedures existed to ensure compliance.

ATTEMPTS AT LIMITING EXPENDITURES

With the upward pressure on spending mounting in the late 1960s, Congress turned to expenditure ceilings as a device to control the budget. Between 1967 and 1972, some sort of spending limitation legislation was adopted every year except 1971.[20] In 1967, President Lyndon Johnson requested a tax surcharge to help shrink a growing deficit. After many months of dispute, committee conflicts, and bargaining, the surcharge was tied to a ceiling on expenditures. The limitation that finally passed in 1967 was of limited effectiveness because it exempted mandatory spending, trust funds, permanent appropriations, and Vietnam War costs. The surcharge failed to pass in 1967. In 1968, House Ways and Means Chairman Wilbur Mills (D-Ark.) held the surcharge proposal hostage until the president could provide a meaningful limit on spending. Both the surcharge and spending limitation were finally passed as part of the tax bill as the Revenue and Expenditure Control Act of 1968 put clamps on both budget authority and outlays.[21] But because of rapid expansion of uncontrollable categories, the actual totals exceeded the ceiling established by Congress.

In 1969 and 1970, Congress again passed statutory limits on expenditures. Mirroring the problems encountered in the previous sessions, spending exceeded the targets in both fiscal years. The futility of Congress was evident. It had no vehicle for effectively controlling spending; between 1967 and 1970, it had tried a continuing resolution, tax legislation, and supplemental appropriations to do the job. In each case, the limits were exceeded through growth of uncontrollable outlays or direct actions by Congress. The situation would get worse before it would get better.

The events of 1972 demonstrated the hapless budgetary situation of Congress and spurred the movement for reform. In July 1972, President Richard Nixon demanded that outlays for fiscal 1973 not exceed $250 billion.[22] This was above his original requests, but $10 billion below what he estimated Congress would approve without a ceiling. Nixon went on to attack budget procedures in Congress and the excesses they permitted. The Senate and House each passed spending ceilings, but could not agree on granting the president discretion to make the cuts.[23] Congress agreed on the desirability of reducing outlays but hesitated to grant any more power to the president. Congress simmered in frustration and discontent at its own budgetary inadequacies, but took a step toward finding a remedy by creating the Joint Study Committee on Budget Control.

Several trends in the 1950s and 1960s helped create the climate for reform in the 1970s. From the administrations of Truman to Nixon, the national budget grew in size, scope, and complexity. The federal government adopted new responsibilities in the areas of health, education, and social welfare. BOB became more powerful as a policy-making institution and was not seriously weakened when President Nixon reorganized it and renamed it the Office of Management and Budget (OMB).[24]

The authorizing committees, seeking to enhance their own influence, gained direct control of some spending outside the appropriations process. "Backdoor spending" was accomplished through borrowing authority, contract authority, and an expansion of entitlement programs. By the 1970s, the Appropriations committees had jurisdiction over only about 45 percent of annual outlays. This contributed to the growing feeling in Congress that it was losing what little grip it had on spending. In addition, the Appropriations committees were becoming slower and slower in completing their actions. An alarming number of agencies were forced to operate on continuing resolutions because Congress failed to pass appropriations bills by the start of the fiscal year.

Despite growth in the budget and the obvious shortcomings in congressional procedures for dealing with the budget, reform might not have come about had it not been for the impoundments of the Nixon administration. Impoundment of funds had been used occasionally by presidents in this century, but Nixon's massive impoundments infuriated the members of Congress. Arguing that Congress was fiscally irresponsible and reckless, Nixon asserted his right to establish control over the budget. By 1973, estimates of monies impounded reached $18 billion.[25] The unprecedented action by Nixon crystalized previously diffuse sentiment for congressional budget reform. In late 1972, Congress began to draft proposals to revamp the congressional budgeting system.

CONGRESS AS A POLICY MAKER

Why had it taken so long to initiate meaningful changes? Congressional procedures had remained static for half a century. It was not a partisan issue; Republicans and Democrats alike decried the erosion of congressional control of the budget. The reasons are complex and numerous, and are related to broader shifts in the relative power of the president and Congress. The notion that executive budgeting is inherently more responsible than legislative budgeting was implicit in the 1921 Budget Act, and continued to hold sway even in some quarters of Congress. Congressional procedures had been developed for a different era and were not suitable for making macroeconomic choices. Congress had no independent source of budgetary information and was dependent on the executive for such data. The powerful committees within Congress carefully protected their own prerogatives and viewed reform with suspicion. To a large extent, Congress was slow to respond because of its very nature as a policy maker.

The United States Congress is a pluralistic, decentralized institution, long on tradition if short on speed and cohesion. The House and Senate are affected by different constraints, motivations, and organizational arrangements than agencies or the presidency. Some of the same factors that help explain why Congress was slow to respond also help explain how Congress has adapted to the new budget process.

REPRESENTATION AND ROLE CONFLICT

Congress is a representative body; despite the apparent electoral security of incumbents, they must face the voters regularly. Members are elected from defined geographical constituencies, and despite the demographic similarity of those elected, their constituencies differ, and their attitudes and orientations vary. The role of representative often conflicts with the role of policy maker.[26] Senators and representatives are concerned about local problems and constituent requests as much as issues that affect the whole country. Several political scientists have suggested that in recent years, congressmen have gradually shifted away from controversial national issues toward safer tasks such as securing dollars, dams, or defense contracts for the district. David Mahew has demonstrated the decline in marginal districts since World War II, the increase in the number of safe seats, and the high success rate for incumbents seeking reelection (90 to 95 percent).[27] Morris Fiorina suggests that the phenomena of declining marginals is partially the result of a behavioral change on the part of members who more than ever emphasize constituent service.[28]

If correct, this trend magnifies a characteristic already prevalent in Congress. Compared with the diffuse constituency of the president and non-elected bureaucrats, members of Congress are interested in the budget for parochial reasons. They see it as a Christmas list as much as a blueprint for national policy, creating a tension between representation of local concerns and national issues. The old appropriations process was consistent with the local representative role of congressmen, facilitating specific, tangible allocations to the state or district. When the appropriations process failed to satisfy the demands of the members, the authorization committees went over, under, and around the Appropriations committees to create backdoor spending programs. The interest in porkbarrel legislation remains high, with evidence suggesting that in recent years there is more, not less, advocacy for local benefit programs.[29]

Representation is not limited to local concerns. By the end of the 1970s, national fiscal policy and the entire budget were dominant issues. Serious, chronic inflation and continued deficit spending gave rise to Proposition 13 in California and similar tax reduction/expenditure limitation proposals around the country. The movement to call a Constitutional Convention to draft a "balance the budget" amendment also became a national issue, creating cross pressures on Congress. The members were urged to cut taxes, hold down spending, but keep the local money rolling in. These conflicting messages from constituents make economic decisions difficult for members of Congress.

DECENTRALIZED POWER

One hundred years ago, Woodrow Wilson complained about the "impervious authority of the standing committees." Today, the committee system is still the most dominant characteristic of Congress. Committees exist as independent islands of legislative power, and maintained by the seniority system and safe seats, members are beholden to neither presidents nor party leaders. A whole range of committees deal with taxing and spending; there is no single focal point of the budget process.

Recent changes have had some impact on the committee system and the distribution of power in Congress. Many of the reforms have served to further decentralize power, such as restrictions on the number of subcommittee chairmanships a member can hold, and the increase in the number of subcommittees. More members than ever before have their own fiefdom to use as a base of operations. Successful challenges to senior committee chairmen at the start of the Ninety-fourth Congress, and the forced division of the House Ways and Means Committee into subcommittees struck at the more arbitrary exercise of power. The heralded return to "king caucus" never quite materialized, but some movement toward caucus and party leadership control was evidenced in the mid-1970s. More than any other change in recent years, the new budget process tended to centralize power more than decentralize it. But in broader perspective, budget reform did not alter the basic fragmentation of Congress. In fact, budget reformers made sure that the existing centers of budgetary power were not disturbed.

CONGRESSIONAL DECISIONS

Congress exercises the power of the purse by creating budget authority which allows agencies to obligate, commit, and disburse federal funds. The most common form of budget authority is appropriations, but it can also be in the form of borrowing authority or contract authority. Entitlements create "permanent" authority. Outlays are equivalent to the annual expenditures made by the federal government in a given year. Congress does not actually determine outlays; it approves budget authority while estimating outlays for a given year. Outlays are based both on previous budget authority and new budget authority.

Budget decisions can be conceptualized on three levels ranging from the general to the specific.[30] The priority level is the most general, consisting of decisions on the overall parameters of the budget such as total spending, total revenues, and subtotals by function. The program level consists of intermediate decisions on components of the budget, such as tax credits, agency appropriations, or the authorization of new federal activities. The most specific level is the operations level, consisting of decisions on how money is actually spent, when it is spent, and how programs are implemented.[31]

In addition to levels of decisions, the duration of decisions is important. The budget process is an annual one, but most of the decisions are multi-year: long-term projects (such as a nuclear aircraft carrier) or the commitment to spend funds for a certain purpose indefinitely into the future (such as Social Security). In a given year, the range of change is about 5 percent above or below current policy levels.[32] Budgets are stable from year to year for several reasons, the most obvious being the multiyear duration of most decisions. At any point of time, there is a general consensus over the proper scope of activities of government. In annual budgeting, changes tend to be marginal. Rapid change, either increasing or decreasing outlays would be disruptive not only to the economy, but to the orderly delivery of government services.

Concern with the inflexibility of the budget often focuses on the portion of the budget classified by the OMB as "relatively uncontrollable." In actuality, all expenditures are ultimately controllable by Congress, but in the short run, about 75 percent of outlays are mandated by current law. This includes fixed costs, such as interest on the national debt, long-term contracts and obligations, projects that take many years to complete, and entitlement programs which require the payment of benefits to all who qualify. Decision makers have some discretion over so-called "uncontrollables," but in any single year, the total changes are a relatively small proportion of the total budget. Even the controllable portion of the budget is composed of spending that is virtually locked in. Nonetheless, there is adequate flexibility within the budget for both the president and Congress to make annual changes, and over the long run, significant changes in the composition of the federal budget occur.[33]

There are basically five types of congressional decisions on the budget: establishing totals, authorization, appropriation, revenue, and oversight. Table 1-1 compares the five types of decisions by level of budgeting, key actors, type of action, and the predominant duration of actions. The table demonstrates the fragmentation and decentralization in Congress. To speak of the fiscal Congress is to speak of many committees with their own portion of the budget supervised by the Budget committees trying to accommodate the parts with the whole. Decisions range from fiscal choices

Table 1-1.
CONGRESSIONAL BUDGETARY DECISIONS

Levels of Budgeting	Congressional Budget Decision	Key Congressional Actors	Type of Congressional Action	Predominant Duration of Actions
Priority	(1) Budget totals	Budget committees ——— Congressional Budget Office (CBO)	Concurrent resolutions on the budget	Annual
Program	(2) Authorizations	Authorizing committees (standing committees)	Legislative authorizations ——— Entitlements	Annual ——— Multiyear ——— Indefinite
	(3) Appropriations	Appropriation committees	Individual appropriation bills	Annual
	(4) Revenues	House Ways and Means Committee ——— Senate Finance Committee	Permanent tax code changes ——— Surcharges, rebates	Annual ——— Indefinite
Operations	(5) Oversight and review	Appropriations committees ——— Authorizing committees ——— CBO ——— General Accounting Office (GAO)	Appropriation and authorization hearings ——— Program evaluation ——— Audits	Periodic

in macroeconomic terms to General Accounting Office (GAO) audits to determine whether funds are spent in accordance with the wishes of Congress.

The actions taken by individual committees and passed by the House and Senate are not isolated; the congressional budget process is the interrelation of these complex choices. Decisions on totals constrain subsequent actions on components of the budget. At the same time, aggregating the components of the budget puts pressure on the totals. In the past, the budget was determined simply by summing the components. The new process provides for centralized consideration of the totals, but the question remains, does it make any difference? Are the totals approved by resolution simply the sum of all the component parts of the budget or have the resolutions actually constrained and shaped the lower level decisions?

CONCLUSION

In a literal sense, Congress cannot control every dollar in the budget. It must rely on estimates of revenues, economic assumptions, and projections of outlays in entitlement programs. Imprecision is inevitable in a budget of over half a trillion dollars that is implemented by a myriad of agencies, bureaus, departments, boards, and government corporations. In addition, complete congressional control would be undesirable. Multiyear spending committments insure stability in government projects, increase the security of the aged, poor, and other beneficiaries, and facilitate planning by state and local governments. Some discretion for the president and agencies is essential in an era of rapidly changing events and conditions. "Control" is but one of many important values to be pursued in a complex political system.

Congressional control is desirable in terms of an ability to shape national priorities, determine the parameters of taxing and spending, and to review the effects of budget decisions. It was this more general control that had eroded by the early 1970s as budgeting came to be dominated by the executive branch.

NOTES

1. Robert A. Wallace, *Congressional Control of Federal Spending* (Detroit: Wayne State University Press, 1960), p. 8.

2. Charles S. Hyneman and George Carey, *A Second Federalist* (New York: Appleton-Century-Crofts, 1967), pp. 151-154.

3. Committee on Government Operations, U.S. Senate, *Improving Congressional Control over the Budget: A Compendium of Materials* (March 27, 1973), p. 37 (hereafter cited as *Compendium*).

4. Ibid., p. 45.

5. Ibid., p. 80.

6. Alexander Hamilton, "Federalist #58," in *The Federalist* (New York: Modern Library, 1937), p. 377.

7. Wallace, *Congressional Control of Federal Spending,* p. 9.

8. Ibid., p. 10.

9. Louis Fisher, *Presidential Spending Power* (Princeton, N.J.: Princeton University Press, 1975), p. 20.

10. Allen Schick, "Budget Reform Legislation: Reorganizing Congressional Centers of Fiscal Power," *Harvard Journal of Legislation* 11, no. 2 (February 1974): 306.

11. Fisher, *Presidential Spending Power*, p. 25.

12. Wallace, *Congressional Control of Federal Spending*, p. 10.

13. John Kenneth Galbraith, "Came the Revolution," *New York Times Book Review*, May 16, 1965; and Lewis Kimmel, *Federal Budget and Fiscal Policy 1789-1955* (Washington, D.C.: Brookings Institution, 1959).

14. Jesse Burkhead, "Federal Budgetary Developments: 1947-48," *Public Administration Review* 8 (Autumn 1948): 267-274.

15. Louis Fisher, "Experience with a Legislative Budget," *Compendium*, pp. 250-251.

16. Ibid., p. 249.

17. Avery Leiserson, "Coordination of Federal Budgetary and Appropriation Procedures Under the Legislative Reorganization Act of 1946," *National Tax Journal* 1 (June 1948): 118-126.

18. James P. Pfiffner, "Congressional Budget Reform, 1974: Initiative and Reaction." Paper delivered at the American Political Science Association, San Francisco, Calif., September 2-5, 1975, p. 7.

19. Fisher, "Experience with a Legislative Budget," pp. 249-251.

20. Allen Schick, "Congressional Control of Expenditures," U.S House of Representatives, Committee on the Budget, 95th Cong., 1st sess., January 1977, pp. 49-59 provides an excellent summary of statutory limits on expenditures in the 1967-72 period.

21. Ibid., p. 52.

22. *Weekly Compilation of Presidential Documents* 8, no. 31 (July 26, 1972): 1176.

23. *Congressional Quarterly Weekly Reports*, November 4, 1972, pp. 2907, 2910.

24. Allen Schick, "The Budget Bureau That Was: Thoughts on the Rise, Decline, and Future of a Presidential Agency," *Law and Contemporary Problems* 45, no. 3 (Summer 1970): 519-539.

25. Fisher, *Presidential Spending Power*, pp. 172-173.

26. Warren Miller and Donald Stokes, "Constituency Influence in Congress," *American Political Science Review* 57 (March 1963): 45-56.

27. David Mahew, *The Electoral Connection* (New Haven, Conn.: Yale University Press, 1974).

28. Morris Fiorina, *Congress: Keystone of the Washington Establishment* (New Haven, Conn.: Yale University Press, 1977).

29. John Ferejohn, *Porkbarrel Politics* (Stanford, Calif.: Stanford University Press, 1974).

30. Lance T. LeLoup, *Budgetary Politics* (Brunswick, Ohio: Kings Court, 1977), Chapter 1.

31. Lance T. LeLoup, "The Myth of Incrementalism: Choices in Budgetary Theory," *Polity* 10, no. 4 (Summer 1978): 488-509.

32. Lance T. LeLoup, "Discretion in National Budgeting: Controlling The Controllables," *Policy Analysis* 4, no. 4 (Fall 1978): 455-475.

33. Ibid.

2
Budget Reform

*I refuse to yield another iota of the dwindling
capacity of this Congress to do anything about
the crucial activities of our government. I
refuse to give to any President the right to
set aside not only the work of this Congress, but
of all its predecessors since the beginning of
our union.*
—Representative Charles Vanik[1]

Everyone agreed something was sorely wrong with congressional budget-ing procedures, but for decades Congress was unwilling or unable to do anything about it. What specifically ailed the legislative taxing and spending system? Why did Congress finally move to cure its budgetary ills? The answers lie within Congress itself, in long-term economic and political trends, and in specific events that transpired during the years of the Nixon administration.

DEFECTS IN THE OLD SYSTEM

The most pervasive failure was the inability of Congress to control the national budget. Of course, "control" is an elusive quantity that varies in meaning over time, and is but one value to be pursued in fiscal affairs. In the broadest sense, Congress simply had no handle on budget totals, could not make fiscal policy decisions, and could not shape the overall parameters of the national budget. Specific failures in control were numerous. Legislative committees as well as the Appropriations committees initiated spending committments. Congressional actions in a given year had alarmingly little impact on what the government actually spent that year. The budget was almost constantly in deficit. Congress was unable to approve appropria-tions in a timely fashion, leaving agencies in budgetary limbo for many months.

RAPID GROWTH IN FEDERAL SPENDING

The 1960s were the halcyon days of federal programs and spending. In the Kennedy-Johnson era, government expanded its role in promoting the general health and welfare of its citizens: Medicare, Medicaid, aid to education, supplemental security income, increases in cash assistance programs and assistance in kind, and other components of the so-called War on Poverty. During the same period, spending for national defense and the space program increased as well. By the late 1960s, however, inflation reared its ugly head and calls for fiscal restraint assumed their familiar ring in the halls of Congress. But the House and Senate had always found spending much simpler than cutting. Members voiced increased concern about the continued deficit and the accumulating national debt. As inflation mounted and the economy slowed, the spectre of greater deficits loomed larger in the collective mind of Congress.

Not only was deficit spending a worry, but the rate of expansion of federal spending had begun to stir complaints. Federal expenditures had increased as a proportion of the Gross National Product (although not as rapidly as state and local expenditures) throughout the 1960s. Congress was alarmed about program expansion and fiscal trends that seemed to have gathered a momentum of their own.

INABILITY TO TAKE AN OVERVIEW OF THE BUDGET

The Joint Study Committee on Budget Control, in its report of April 1973, concluded that "the failure to arrive at congressional budgetary decisions on an overall basis has been a contributory factor in the size of these deficits."[2] The problem with runaway spending was the fragmented system where no one committee had responsibility for taking an overview of the budget. This was one of the oldest complaints about the congressional budget system, heard as early as the 1920s. It was a major issue in 1946 when Congress unsuccessfully tried to centralize consideration of the totals. It was the objective in the 1960s when Congress attempted to pass expenditure ceilings.

Whether federal spending was too high or not, the fragmented process was inherently irresponsible in terms of totals. If the budget process is a battle of the whole against the parts, there were no soldiers on the side of the whole. Members could support their own pet spending projects while decrying the fiscal excesses of others. Committees and subcommittees could insure the health of programs in their own jurisdiction while lambasting the collective behavior of other committees. The inability of Congress to take an overview of the budget, as the president did, was the most pervasive complaint against the old system. In addition to rapid growth of expenditures and deficit spending, it was cited as the source of two other policy-making deficiencies.

INABILITY TO MAKE FISCAL POLICY

Because Congress could not take an overview of the totals, fiscal policy became the exclusive domain of the executive. Congressional totals for revenues and outlays were de facto aggregates of isolated taxing and spending decisions. There were no effective means of deciding how much stimulus or restraint would be provided by their actions. Economic decisions in Congress consisted of periodic tax cuts or surcharges, a new program here, a spending cut there. But the president shaped the fiscal policy of the nation.

INABILITY TO ESTABLISH NATIONAL PRIORITIES

The absence of a mechanism for making overall decisions on the budget not only was blamed for excessive spending and abdication in making fiscal policy, but it precluded Congress from assessing relative spending priorities. The question of guns versus butter was answered, but it was answered arbitrarily, almost accidentally. Between 1965 and 1975, significant reallocation from defense spending to social welfare spending took place, but it was not because Congress considered or issued such a statement of priorities. The authorizing committees increased spending for social programs by writing them into entitlement programs, avoiding the appropriations process. At the same time, as the war in Vietnam wore down, there was pressure to curtail growth of the military budget. Congress set national priorities, and it may have reflected accurately the changing sentiments of the members and their constituents. Critics complained, however, that Congress backed into them: never were they compared, debated, or approved as a whole package.

DISINTEGRATION OF THE APPROPRIATIONS PROCESS

The control exercised by the Appropriations committees was weakened by incursions from the authorizing committees. By 1974, only 45 percent of the annual budget was controlled by the Appropriations committees.[3] A large proportion of annual outlays were required by the authorizing legislation. Backdoor spending contributed to the overall loss of budget control.

One of the many symptoms of an increasingly unreliable appropriations process was the growing tendency for Congress to fail to pass appropriations bills by the start of the fiscal year. Before 1977, one would have had to go back to 1948 to find the last year in which all bills were approved in time. When regular appropriations are not enacted, agencies are forced to operate on continuing resolutions, simply extending the level of funding of the previous year. The situation grew serious in the 1970s. Between 1972 and 1975, *no* appropriations bills were enacted by the start of the fiscal year (then, July 1). In 1973 *no* bills were passed for Labor-HEW, or foreign assistance programs.[4] Many agencies had temporary funding on a permanent basis.

The gradual splintering of the appropriations process was related to the growth in backdoor spending and the increase in the share of the budget classified as relatively uncontrollable. Entitlements, contract and borrowing authority, and permanent appropriations seemed to be strangling what little control was exercised under the old system. By the 1970s, the once impermeable Appropriations committees were subject to challenge and dissatisfaction with their combined actions.

INADEQUACY OF CONGRESSIONAL INFORMATION

The erosion of budgetary power in Congress, and the growth in presidential influence, was related to the disparity in budgetary information and expertise. Congress had no OMB, no Council of Economic Advisors, no Treasury Department; it relied on the executive for nearly all of its information. Certainly Congress had tax experts, program experts, and a growing number of professional staff. But their capabilities paled in comparison with the arsenal of White House and agency experts. Congress was not able to challenge suspect data provided by a "Nixonized" OMB.

With these defects, with the dissatisfaction expressed regularly by members for decades, the question recurs: why did it take so long for meaningful reform? One reason is the inherent conservatism of Congress, the reluctance to embrace institutional change. The powerful taxing and spending committees, despite some slippage in stature, were not about to voluntarily diminish their own power, even at the cost of overall fiscal control. This was not as self-serving as it might sound, however, because the old system had been useful. The traditional authorization-appropriation process "fit" the basic nature of Congress. It was decentralized and served individual member needs. It helped members secure tangible benefits for their constituents and protect their natural allies. It allowed members to secure positions of power on money committees and develop a congressional career. The old system facilitated conflict avoidance by eliminating some tough, divisive decisions. The system minimized conflict and maximized cooperation by ignoring decisions on the whole. It let members shift the blame for fiscal problems to others. For these and other reasons the old ways were hard to dislodge, and previous attempts at reform failed. Not until the pressures mounted to the boiling point were significant changes finally pushed through. Even then, reform would have failed again without minimizing disruption to the existing power structure in Congress.

LEGISLATIVE FORMULATION

THE REFORM COALITION: COMMON GOALS, DIVERSE INTERESTS

Outraged by Nixon's impoundments, castigated by the public, and humiliated at their own impotence, Congress saw the time to be ripe for the meaningful change put off for so many years. The budget reform coalition included virtually every member of Congress, but it was an unholy alliance of diverse interests with a few common objectives. The most frequently shared goals were a desire to improve the quality of congressional information and improvement in the ability of Congress to determine fiscal policy. The visions of what that fiscal policy would be like, however, differed considerably. A majority of members were concerned about deficit spending and the growth in the budget, but this was a more salient concern to conservatives. Fiscal liberals were more interested in setting national priorities and using a national priorities debate to reallocate monies from defense to social programs. Conservatives also supported the idea of taking an overview of the budget to make the "big spenders" accountable for their votes. They reasoned that members would be reluctant to go on record and vote for large deficits.

Committee interests also varied. The Appropriations committees wanted to eliminate backdoor spending, but there was more widespread support for these proposals. It was generally recognized that growth of backdoor spending had diminished the relationship between congressional actions and actual outlays in a given year. Of course, the taxing and spending committees wanted to insure that their prerogatives were protected as fully as possible. The forces that had prevented budget reform in the past were still present, but the embarrassment of their own deficiencies and the constitutional challenge to the integrity of Congress overcame these obstacles. As is often the case with public policy, however, budget reform represented different things to different people. The architects of the Budget and Impoundment Control Act were able to arrive at a set of proposals for procedural change that the vast majority of Congress could agree on without arriving at consensus on fiscal policy goals or national priorities.

THE JOINT STUDY COMMITTEE

A few months after its formation, the Joint Study Committee issued an interim report focusing on the major weaknesses of the congressional budget process, and by April 1973, it issued a report to Congress. The interim report stressed the importance of developing procedures that would allow Congress to take an overall perspective on the budget, integrate spending and revenues, and link the actions of separate appropriations bills. The report made a number of specific proposals for reform and the recommendations were submitted as bills in both the House and the Senate.[5] The recommendations of the Joint Study Committee reflected the interests and biases of its membership, dominated by the traditional money committees. Of the thirty-two members of the Joint Study Committee, twenty-eight were members of the Ways and Means, Finance, or the House and Senate Appropriations Committee. At no time was a proposal to scrap the existing authorization-appropriations process seriously considered; from the outset, it was intended that the traditional committees would maintain their jurisdiction and a new system would be superimposed over the old one.

The Joint Committee recommended the creation of special budget committees in both houses to take an overview of the budget. These committees would be constituted with one-third of the members from the Appropriations committees, one-third from the revenue committees, and the other third from the remainder of the House or Senate. Budget committee chairmanships would rotate among members of the revenue committees and Appropriations committees. The Joint Committee recommended the adoption of budget resolutions specifying and limiting authority, outlays, revenues, and deficit. In addition, it proposed a joint professional staff be created to assist the new committees.

The self-interest of the members was reflected not only in the preservation of the traditional process but in recommendations dealing with the authorizing committees which were virtually unrepresented on the Joint Study Committee. The Appropriations members on the committee were able to get recommendations in the report to strictly curtail backdoor spending. They also prevailed in recommendations for early enactment of authorizations. Yet even the Appropriations committees were forced to accept some proposals counter to their direct interests. Since the lessons of the 1947-1949 experience convincingly indicated that no ceiling could be enforced without specifying subtotals, a recommendation to break down the budget resolution further was included.

The fact that the authorizing committees and the concerns of other congressional interests were not reflected in the Joint Committee's report led to significant changes in the final version of budget reform adopted by Congress. But the overall parameters of budget reform were shaped by the Joint Committee and part of the success of the budget process may be attributable to the basic principle they subscribed to: "no congressional committee would suffer a direct loss of jurisdiction. . . .congressional budget reform would be through an expansion of the process."[6]

HOUSE ACTION

As H.R. 7130, the Joint Study Committee proposals were referred to the House Rules Committee. The Rules Committee in the House is unusual in several respects; perhaps most significantly, it rarely has original jurisdiction over legislation, acting instead as the gatekeeper for legislation passed by other committees.[7] Members of the Rules Committee were not used to the process of detailed markup and the Rules Committee had no subcommittees. Because party leaders, by the 1970s, had considerable influence in the Rules Committee, they were able to encourage the Rules Committee to report a consensus bill. Even though direct representatives of interests were not present as they were in the Joint Study Committee, the budget reform bill passed by the Rules Committee generally protected the position of the spending committees.

There was some opposition in the House to the creation of new Budget committees. Representative David Obey (D-Wis.), a liberal member of the Appropriations Committee, argued that the new budget process should be centered within the Appropriations committees and that the goals of increased comprehensiveness, cohesiveness, and integration could be accomplished without creating new committees that would undermine the appropriations process.[8] Most members did not agree with Obey. There was scant support for the idea that the Appropriations committees could successfully engage in priority level budgeting and strong support for a separate process and new committees.

Jamie Whitten (D-Miss.), co-chairman of the Joint Study Committee and the second ranking Democrat on the House Appropriations Committee, introduced a separate bill in October 1973.[9] Whitten's bill proposed separate Budget committees, but severely limited their ability to bind subsequent appropriations actions. The Rules Committee considered both the Joint Study Committee's proposals and the Whitten bill and arrived at a compromise. They agreed with Whitten's proposal to make the figures in the first concurrent resolutions targets, not binding totals. A further concession to Appropriations was made in changing the subtotals to functions rather than administrative units, providing less direct guidance for Appropriations decisions. This also created a "crosswalking" problem in translating functions (health and agriculture) into administrative units (e.g., the Department of Agriculture and the Department of Health, Education, and Welfare).[10]

Since the House Appropriations Committee, the most powerful potential opponent of reform, was mollified, passage was virtually assured. With the sentiment for action strong among members of both parties, the revised H.R. 7130 was passed, virtually without amendment, by a substantial margin in December 1973.[11]

SENATE ACTION

The Senate Government Operations Committee began work on budget reform legislation in March 1973. Committee Chairman Sam Ervin (D-N.C.), who received national attention during the Watergate hearings, nonetheless felt that budget reform was perhaps the most important issue he had been involved with in his years in Congress. The Subcommittee on Budgeting, Management, and Expenditures, chaired by Senator Lee Metcalf (D-Mont.), had a number of budget reform bills to consider in addition to S1541, the Joint Study Committee's recommendations.

Unlike the Joint Study Committee or the House Rules Committee, the Metcalf subcommittee reflected the interests of the authorizing committees. The result was that in its report on a revised version of the bill, a number of changes were made.[12] First, the subcommittee removed the quota of Finance and Appropriations Committee members on the Senate Budget Committee, opening it up to the general membership. Second, it favored the establishment of a Congressional Budget Office that would serve all committees, rather than a single joint staff serving only the Budget committees. Finally, although the subcommittee was divided on the issue, it opted for the binding totals in the first resolution, rather than the weaker provision for targets.[13] The full committee accepted the compromises struck in committee and unanimously passed the bill in November 1973.

In December, however, Senate Majority Whip Robert Byrd (D-W.Va.) took control of budget reform and insisted that the Rules Committee consider S1541 before it went to the Senate floor.[14] As chairman of a Rules subcommittee, Byrd reopened negotiations to further balance the interests of the authorizing committees and the Appropriations committees. The compromise worked out by Byrd and the Rules Committee supported the view of the authorizing committees in loosening the provisions that had given Appropriations control over backdoor spending. The Appropriations Committee gained, however, in the compromise proposals for the second concurrent resolution and reconciliation. The Senate Rules Committee version placed equal emphasis on changing revenues, deficit, or totals instead of requiring the rescission of spending actions.[15]

The balancing of committee interests in the Senate was explicit. The Rules Committee revisions were produced by the unusual process of negotiation among representatives of ten Senate committees, four joint committees, and the House Appropriations Committee.[16] Although the revised version of S1541 differed from the proposals of the Joint Study Committee, the House Rules Committee, and the Senate Government Operations Committee, the basic premise was the same. They attempted to "add a new and comprehensive budgetary framework to the existing decision-making processes, with minimum disruption to established methods and procedures."[17] The art of compromise had been performed with dexterity; on March 21 the Senate passed S1541 by a vote of 80-0.

CONFERENCE COMMITTEE ACTION

Both the House- and Senate-passed bills agreed on the overall structure and process of budget reform. Although the final form of the bill was different from the original proposals of the Joint Study Committee, many of the changes were agreed on in the House and Senate versions and were not at issue during the conference. In general, the conference report tended to follow the more detailed Senate provisions when they differed, but followed the House bill in adopting the less specific language concerning the content of the budget resolutions.[18] A number of compromise provisions were adopted:[19]

Budget Committees: Each body deferred to the other in its preference for constituting their respective Budget committees. While the responsibilities of the committees were almost identical, their form was not. In the Senate, the Budget Committee was open to any member and was constituted as any standing committee. In the House, however, pressure from Appropriations and Ways and Means to keep the Budget Committee weak and their representation strong, resulted in a four-year limit on tenure and approximately half the members to be drawn from the other two committees. Each committee was given responsibility for reporting two concurrent resolutions to the Congress, each fiscal year. The resolutions were to specify:

1. budget authority and outlays;
2. authority and outlays for each functional category;
3. total revenues;
4. level of surplus or deficit; and
5. public debt.

The House committee was made up of twenty-three members, including five members from the Appropriations Committee, five from Ways and Means, and one each from the Republican and Democratic leadership. In contrast, the Senate committee was neither defined nor restricted in membership.

Congressional Budget Office: Title II of the conference report created a permanent office to provide analytical support and budgetary data to the Congress: The Congressional Budget Office (CBO). CBO was given responsibilities in three broad areas:[20]

1. monitoring the economy and estimating its impact on budget;
2. improving the quality and quantity of budgetary information; and
3. providing estimates of costs of budget alternatives.

Timetable: The House version prescribed fewer stages and deadlines in the process. The stricter and more detailed timetable in the Senate version was adopted with the Senate arguing that strict deadlines were essential if the process was to work.

The Budget Resolutions: The House version, establishing targets rather than binding ceilings in the first resolution, was adopted. While conservatives felt this was a major weakness that would not provide enough fiscal restraint, pressure from other participants to maintain flexibility prevailed. The conference committee also agreed that the resolutions would break down the budget targets by function, but the functional targets would be allocated by committee. The Appropriations Committee would further subdivide the totals into targets for each of the thirteen subcommittees.

Appropriations Process: To insure prompt action on appropriations bills, the conferees sided with the Appropriations Committee in requiring all authorization bills be reported by May 15. As provided in the House version of the bill, the conferees agreed to require the Appropriations Committee to complete action on *all* appropriations bills before reporting the first bill to the floor.

Backdoor Spending: In one of the most controversial aspects of the reform, the conferees agreed to follow the Senate version. Backdoor spending in the form of borrowing authority and contract authority was brought under the appropriations process, but the conference committee rejected the stricter House proposals by leaving other forms of backdoor spending outside of appropriations and creating special procedures for new entitlement legislation. The House bill would have required annual appropriations for all backdoor spending, but the conference agreement adopted the Senate position applying only new programs to this requirement.

Impoundment: The final area of compromise represented one of the major actions taken by the conference committee. Since impoundment control was not a part of initial budget reform legislation (they were separate bills), the House and Senate versions were significantly different. Expanding upon both versions, the conferees developed a hybrid process that differentiated between temporary actions (deferrals) and permanent actions (rescissions) by the president. The conferees agreed that strong provisions were necessary to protect the new budget procedures from a president who would freely alter congressional actions. Under the new law, if the president wishes to rescind budget authority approved by Congress, he must send a special message to Congress requesting a rescission. This proposal is automatically *rejected* unless Congress passes a bill to that effect within forty-five days. If the president wishes to defer budget authority, he again must submit a special message to Congress. In contrast to rescission, however, deferrals are automatically accepted unless *either* house passes a resolution disapproving it.

The legislative process, from the organization of the Joint Study Committee in 1972 until final passage in 1974, had taken less than two years. A sense of urgency pervaded the Congress as impeachment proceedings against President Nixon gathered momentum and congressional resurgence took form. Even though the basic structure and organization of the appropriations process was maintained, the bill contained some of the most radical procedural reforms adopted by Congress in thirty years. The wide-spread recognition that Congress had to revise its budgeting procedures was inescapable. In spite of the conflicts between liberals and conservatives, and between the authorizing and appropriation committees, the Budget and Impoundment Control Act passed the House by a vote of 401-6 and the Senate 75-0. President Nixon signed the bill in July 1974, less than a month before his resignation. Although the more difficult challenge of making budget reform work was yet to come, Congress had taken a critical step forward.

THE NEW BUDGET PROCESS

What kind of budgetary system had Congress created? Had reformers in the 1970s learned any lessons from the futile attempts at a legislative budget in the 1940s? Was the system overly structured or unworkable as some critics claimed?

Table 2-1 shows the timetable of the new budget process. It actually begins in January with the submission of the president's budget and current services estimates.[21] The process can be divided into four stages:[22]

1. Information gathering, analysis, and report on First Concurrent Resolution (January 15 - April 15)
2. Adoption of First Resolution: Establishing targets (April 15 - May 15)
3. Enactment of Appropriations bills (May 15 - September 14)
4. Adoption of Second Concurrent Resolution and Reconciliation (September 15 - October 1)

STAGE 1

The Budget committees begin to hold hearings soon after the president's budget is submitted to Congress. Their task is to gather information on economic conditions (employment, inflation, growth), alternative fiscal policies, and budget priorities. The committees take testimony from administration officials such as the secretary of the treasury, director of OMB, and the chairman of the president's Council of Economic Advisors (CEA). They also hear from members of Congress, outside experts, and interest group representatives, but they rely heavily on their own professional staff at this stage.

By March 15, all the standing committees in the Congress are required to submit "views and estimates" of their legislative and spending plans in the coming year, estimating the amount of new budget authority they may approve. This presents the committees with the job of crystal ball-gazing. It is difficult for them to know what actions their committee might take, particularly with sensitive or controversial programs. This information is

Table 2-1.
CONGRESSIONAL BUDGET TIMETABLE

Action to be completed	On or before
President submits current services budget to Congress	January
President submits annual budget message to Congress	15 days after Congress meets
Congressional committees make recommendations to Budget committees	March 15
Congressional Budget Office reports to Budget committees	April 1
Budget committees report first budget resolution	April 15
Congress passes first budget resolution	May 15
Legislative committees complete reporting of authorizing legislation	May 15
Congress passes all pending bills	7 days after Labor Day
Congress passes second budget resolution	September 15
Congress passes budget reconciliation bill	September 25
Fiscal year begins	October 1

Source: House Budget Committee

essential to the Budget committees' preparation of the first resolution, and forces the authorizing committees to take an early look at their agenda for the coming months. The tendency has been for the standing committees to present estimates higher than amounts actually approved to insure that they will retain flexibility in subsequent legislative actions. In addition, the views and estimates submitted by the committees range from detailed reports following committee deliberations to single page lists prepared by the chairman.

By the first of April, the CBO submits its annual report to the Budget committees. The statutory requirements call for CBO to report on alternative levels of revenues, budget authority and outlays, the levels of tax expenditures, a discussion of national priorities, and how alternative ways of allocating spending will meet national needs. [23] The form of this report has varied in the first five years of the budget process as CBO sought a format to best serve diverse congressional needs and desires. Considering the data gathered in hearings, current policy estimates, the president's request, and committee views and estimates, the Budget committees must report the First Concurrent Resolution on the budget by April 15.

STAGE 2

The layover period between April 15 and May 15 is designed to give members of the House and Senate an opportunity to consider the recommendations of the Budget committees. In practice, they must act on the reports by early May to allow time for a conference committee to resolve House-Senate differences.

May 15 is an important deadline for Congress. Standing committees must report out all legislation recommending new budget authority by that date. After May 15, legislation may be reported only if a waiver is granted. May 15 is also the deadline for adoption of the First Concurrent Resolution. Prior to its adoption, neither house of Congress may consider any revenue, spending, entitlement, or debt legislation. The figures agreed to in conference represent targets; only the figures in the second resolution are binding. The report accompanying the resolution distributes the targets by committee, translating functional totals into administrative jurisdiction. The Appropriations committees divide their targets among the subcommittees.

STAGE 3

Although the Appropriations committees begin holding hearings before May 15, the months between May and September mark the third stage of the process when spending bills are enacted. The appropriations process continues much as it has for many decades. In subcommittee hearings, agency officials defend their budget requests, justify their programs, and discuss future plans. Specialization and reciprocity are still operative at this stage and the full committee generally accepts the recommendations of the subcommittees. Under the new budget process, the subcommittees operate under more defined limits and constraints. Actions that exceed the targets cause problems for the committee and are generally opposed by the Budget committees. Because the first resolution totals are not binding, however, the committees may decide to "violate" the targets. During these months, CBO keeps track of whether the spending actions are consistent with the targets. They perform this "scorekeeping" function by issuing frequent reports comparing actions with targets.

By the seventh day after Labor Day, Congress must complete action on all spending bills. The Budget Act states that the Appropriations committees should, to the extent practicable, complete action on all spending bills before any are brought up for consideration on the floor.[24] Final action must be completed by early September so the final stage of the process can take place.

STAGE 4

The passage of the Second Concurrent Resolution on the budget and reconciliation takes place in September. Attention shifts back to the Budget committees which evaluate new information, changes in economic conditions, and approved spending actions in formulating the second resolution. This set of binding totals may be inconsistent with previous actions taken; it reaffirms or revises the targets set in the first resolution. The resolution therefore may contain instructions to certain committees to alter previous actions, including rescinding or amending appropriations, raising or lowering revenues, or it simply may change the totals. The process of reconciliation must be completed between September 15 and September 25. The fiscal year begins five days later on October 1.

The rigid timetable for September was foreseen as the most precarious time for the budget process, but practice has shown that May is more difficult; the reconciliation process has remained virtually unused except by the Senate for the fiscal 1980 budget. Congress may not adjourn *sine die* until the second resolution is approved. After it is passed, neither house may consider any legislation that would exceed the approved totals. Congress at any time may pass additional resolutions as it did to accommodate newly elected President Jimmy Carter in 1977.

IMPLEMENTING THE NEW BUDGET PROCESS

Soon after the Budget and Impoundment Control Act became law, Congress began organizing to implement the new process. Only a few weeks after it was passed, Senate Democrats named Edmund Muskie of Maine as chairman of the Budget Committee and appointed eight other Democratic members. It was possible for Muskie, who had played an important role in drafting the legislation, to become chairman when the Democratic caucus agreed not to consider seniority in picking members.[25] In early August 1974, House Democrats selected Al Ullman (D-Oreg.) as chairman of the House Budget Committee. Ullman, second ranking Democrat on the Ways and Means Committee, had been co-chairman of the Joint Study Committee. Ullman defeated Brock Adams (D-Wash.), who was backed by liberals, by a 113-90 caucus vote.[26] Democratic members from the Appropriations and Ways and Means Committees were nominated by their respective chairmen.

On the minority side, the Senate Republican Committee on Committees nominated three members of the Appropriations Committee and three members of the Finance Committee to serve on the Budget Committee. The Republican Conference, however, dropped two of these members in favor of senators who did not serve on the other money committees.[27] In the House, nine Republicans were chosen to serve on the Budget Committee. Delbert Latta (R-Ohio) became the ranking minority member on the House committee. Henry Bellmon (R-Okla.) assumed that post on the Senate committee.

The "Tidal Basin" incident late in 1974 resulted in the political demise of House Ways and Means Chairman Wilbur Mills. When Mills lost his position, Ullman opted to assume the chairmanship of Ways and Means, giving up the Budget Committee. The caucus selected Brock Adams to replace

Ullman and continue the process of assembling a staff and organizing the new committee.

In developing professional staff to serve the committees, the House and Senate proceeded somewhat differently. Senate Budget Committee staff was drawn largely from Capitol Hill veterans, familiar with Congress and the legislative process. The House Budget Committee placed a premium on expertise, gathering a group of highly competent budget and policy experts. From the outset friction developed between the two staffs; House Budget staffers suggested that the Senate staff was dominated by political "hacks," while the Senate staff considered their House counterparts politically naive to the realities of the Hill.

The Senate Budget Committee developed a closer relationship with the new Congressional Budget Office than the House Committee. The House Budget staff, focusing on expertise, seemed to perceive themselves in a competitive situation with CBO. In spite of the differences in staffing the new Budget committees, both senators and representatives were satisfied with their own personnel and organization. CBO, however, became embroiled in controversy from the start.

The creation of a Congressional Budget Office was seen as one of the most important aspects of the new budget system. It was established to provide Congress with a professional, independent source of budgetary information. Unlike the committees, CBO could not organize until a director was appointed. The Senate was looking for a person with a national reputation who would lend immediate prestige to the office. The House leaders suggested that a Capitol Hill insider might be a better choice. While the Budget committees were organizing, congressional leaders were wrangling over the CBO director. Several prominent persons were considered such as Charles Schultz and Kermit Gordon, both former budget directors under President Johnson.[28] After six months of consideration, Alice Rivlin, a senior fellow at the Brookings Institution, was appointed CBO director in February 1975.

Rivlin's background with Brookings was an anathema to many Republicans and conservative Democrats. Soon after her appointment CBO was accused of being biased, prescriptive, and liberal. Rivlin faced the task of staffing and organizing the CBO months after the Budget committees had already begun work on the fiscal 1976 budget. During 1975, several incidents (such as a request for a limousine to take CBO officials to Capitol Hill) created bad publicity for the office. An antagonistic House Appropriations Committee cut off funds for additional CBO staff when the projected number of positions was only about 80 percent filled. Other blunders by CBO officials simply added to the antagonism and accusations of political advocacy.[29]

The early difficulties of CBO were indications of the volatile political environment of the budget process. Although the vast majority of members agreed on the reform package, the unanimity cloaked the divisive splits that existed over how budget policy should proceed. Although the law required implementation in 1976, it was agreed that 1975 would be a "trial run" for the procedures in Congress. Disenchantment with the process and a lack of involvement by House Republicans quickly became apparent. Republicans announced that the first year was not important because it was just a trial run.[30] This foreshadowed a pattern of consistent opposition to the budget resolutions that would characterize the first years of implementation and make the new budget process particularly tenuous in the House.

Forced to recognize their own impotence in national budgeting, diverse elements in Congress coalesced to support major budget reform in 1974. Pressure from the existing budgetary powers in Congress to insure that their own prerogatives were protected helped to create a new system superimposed on the old. Even with the overwhelming support for budget reforms, most members recognized that the most difficult challenge was to make the new process work. Many skeptics believed the timetable was too strict; members of Congress were unlikely to change their behavior and to exert the required discipline.

In the first five years of implementation, Congress met the deadlines, produced a legislative budget, and created a new budgetary bureaucracy that has had considerable impact on Capitol Hill. The operations of the authorizing, appropriations, and tax writing committees have also been modified by these changes. The politics of congressional budgeting have been lively and provide insights into the changing character of Congress. But the key question remains: How much control has Congress gained over the management of fiscal affairs.

NOTES

1. Quoted in *Improving Congressional Control Over the Budget: A Compendium of Materials*, Subcommittee on Budgeting, Management and Expenditures, Committee on Government Operations, U.S. Senate, 93rd Cong., 1st sess., March 27, 1973, pp. 291-292 (hereafter cited as *Compendium*, 1973).

2. *Recommendations for Improving Congressional Control Over Budgetary Outlay and Receipt Totals*, Report of the Joint Study Committee on Budget Control, April 18, 1973, 93rd Cong., 1st sess., p. 8.

3. Ibid., p. 10.

4. Allen Schick, "Budget Reform Legislation: Reorganizing Congressional Centers of Fiscal Power," *Harvard Journal on Legislation* 11, no. 2 (February 1974): 310-311.

5. HR7130 in the House and S1541 in the Senate (93rd Cong., 1st sess., 1973).

6. Schick, "Budget Reform," p. 319.

7. Ibid., p. 320.

8. Committee on Rules, U.S. House of Representatives, *Hearings on Budget Control Act of 1973*, 93rd Cong., 1st sess., 1973.

9. HR10961, 93rd Cong., 1st sess.

10. James P. Pfiffner, "Congressional Budget Reform, 1974: Initiative and Reaction." Paper delivered at the American Political Science Association, San Francisco, Calif., September 2-5, 1975.

11. Two amendments on the layover period between the report and floor consideration of the budget resolutions were adopted; all others were defeated. HR7130 passed 386-23 on December 5, 1973.

12. Schick, "Budget Reform," p. 324.

13. A compromise was struck providing that totals would be binding in the first resolution, and the subtotals would serve as targets.

14. *Congressional Quarterly Weekly Reports*, February 16, 1975, p. 378.

15. *Congressional Quarterly Weekly Reports*, February 23, 1974, p. 514.

16. *Congressional Quarterly Weekly Reports*, March 16, 1974, p. 679.

17. Ibid.

18. *Congressional Quarterly Weekly Reports*, June 15, 1974, p. 1590.

19. Joel Havemann, "Conferees Approve Changes in Budgeting Procedures," *National Journal* (June 15, 1974), p. 894. See also *Congressional Quarterly Weekly Reports*, June 15, 1974, p. 1590-1595.

20. John W. Ellwood and James A. Thurber, "The New Congressional Budget Process: The Hows and Ways of House-Senate Differences," in Larry Dodd and Bruce Oppenheimer, eds., *Congress Reconsidered* (New York: Praeger, 1977).

21. The original bill specified November 15 as the deadline for submission of current services estimates.

22. Ellwood and Thurber, "New Congressional Budget Process," p. 14.

23. Public Law 93-344, Section 202. (See Appendix.)

24. Ibid., Section 307.

25. *Congressional Quarterly Weekly Reports*, August 3, 1974, p. 2041.

26. *Congressional Quarterly Weekly Reports*, August 10, 1974, p. 2163.

27. Ibid.

28. *Congressional Quarterly Weekly Reports*, September 7, 1974, p. 2417.

29. Joel Havemann, "CBO Proceeds with Work While Taking Heat on Staff Size," *National Journal* (November 1, 1975), p. 1575.

30. Joel Havemann, "Budget Report," *National Journal* (May 24, 1975), p. 761.

3

From Procedures
To Policies

*Distasteful fat is easy to trim. But frosting
presents a sore temptation to abandon the budget
diet.*
—Senator Edmund Muskie

Budget reformers were optimistic. They viewed the Budget and Impoundment Control Act as a workable vehicle to establish legislative control of the
budget. But they were also realistic. Members of both houses realized that
the process was highly structured and that the notoriously slow moving
Congress was unaccustomed to meeting strict deadlines. Some skeptics
thought that the timetable would be the downfall of the infant process and
were surprised in the first few years when the House and Senate met the
deadlines. The most serious threat to the success of budget reform in its first
years of existence was the splintering of the short-lived reform coalition in
the House. As soon as the Congress moved from a set of abstract procedures to actual decisions on fiscal policy and the allocation of budget
dollars, the difficulties became apparent. The partisan policy conflicts that
emerged in 1975 in the House carried through the rest of the decade, and
left the congressional budget process under a lingering shroud of insecurity.

THE DILEMMA OF FISCAL DECISIONS

Fiscal policy was a new arena for the Congress. For decades it had
contented itself with discreet portions of the total: tax bills, appropriations
bills, and authorization bills. The introduction of a separate but simulta-
neous set of policy choices represented a change that was inherently
conflictual; i.e., the incompatibility of economic stabilization and allocation.
Stabilization decisions were not consciously made by Congress because it
did not approve budget totals before 1975. Under the classical conditions of

scarcity, allocation decisions were made on "guns versus butter"—defense versus social spendings. The federal budget allocates billions to a multitude of programs, agencies, and activities, and Congress had played its tradition- al role in budgeting by making allocation decisions on a piecemeal basis.

Conflict arises from the fact that fiscal stabilization and allocation deci- sions are at cross purposes. In budgeting at any level, there is a tension between decisions on the whole and decisions on the parts. Demands for new monies are always greater than possible within desirable totals. The president and his Budget Office had faced this continuing dilemma for years, while Congress focused only on the components of the president's requests. With the adoption of the budget process, the House and Senate were faced with the problem of fiscal restraint versus the achievement of spending objectives.

In its struggle to establish fiscal policy and improve its control of the national budget, sharp disputes developed in Congress on the direction of fiscal policy, and differences over priorities quickly eroded the coalition that had formed to pass the Budget Act in 1974. Between 1975 and 1980, a number of issues divided the Congress. While they varied in salience from year to year, the major policy disputes formed relatively stable patterns over this period. Three major areas of disagreement can be identified:

Spending Growth: Because of inflation, the increases in uncontrollable social benefit programs, and general government expansion, the size of the budget was an issue. Conservatives criticized the rapid expansion of gov- ernment spending, cryptically noting that it now took only a few years for the budget to grow as much as it had in a century. While a majority of the members of Congress wished to restrain spending growth, they disagreed on the degree of restraint. Congressional liberals argued that spending should increase even faster to solve the social ills that remained. The issue of spending growth involved both the questions of fiscal stabilization and allocation.

The Deficit: The imbalance between outlays and revenues and the rapid accumulation of national debt was a sore point to many members. Conser- vatives believed that deficit spending was inherently evil, contributing to inflation and public cynicism about government. Although only a few of the most liberal members would go on record as favoring deficit spending in principle, the size of the deficit was a continuing dispute. As public pressure for a balanced budget grew in 1978 and 1979, a noticeable shift in sentiment was evident. By 1979, the question became how and when to balance the budget, not whether to balance it. Conflict over the size of the budget deficit revolved mainly around fiscal policy issues, but included more general questions of ideology as well.

Defense versus Social Spending: Although many programs and taxes have been disputed since 1975, the most pervasive allocation issue to divide Congress has been the relative allocation to defense and social programs. In the decade before 1975, the budget share of national defense fell from almost 50 percent to about 25 percent. Although appropriations to the military increased, there was little real growth. Conservatives were alarmed with what they saw as the erosion of the United States position in defense, and argued that despite the need for overall fiscal restraint, more resources must be allocated to defense. The liberal group continued to attack excessive military spending and pushed for further reallocation to social programs. Their position was undercut in the prodefense tide that swept through Congress after the Soviet invasion of Afghanistan and the introduction of the fiscal 1981 budget.

At different times and to different degrees, these three basic issues divided the Congress in its attempt to establish budget policy. Although political scientists have questioned the dichotomization of liberals and conservatives into two distinct groups, the degree of attitude constraint and voting consistency on fiscal issues appears greater than in other areas (foreign policy or civil rights, for example). [1] "Conservatives" tend to oppose spending growth, deficit spending, and favor defense over social welfare. "Liberals" tend to be more disposed to spending growth, deficit spending, and favor social welfare over defense.

THE ECONOMIC CONTEXT

The implementation of the budget process occurred at a particular period of our political and economic history. The policy conflicts and the effects of reform are as much a function of the particular economic situation that faced the United States during the 1970s as anything else. Economic historians may mark the decade of the seventies as one of transition, frustration, and possibly, the breakdown of the Keynesian model. The most disturbing characteristic of the decade was the pervasiveness of inflation. Traditional Keynesian theory, the paradigm of American economics since 1945, suggested that there was a tradeoff between inflation and unemployment, but "stagflation" in the 1970s showed both could exist simultaneously at unacceptably high levels. [2]

Table 3-1 shows the inflation and unemployment rates over the past two decades, and their combined rate. In the 1960s, inflation plus unemployment varied between 6 and 8 percent. By the mid 1970s, double digit inflation existed with 7 to 8 percent unemployment. Inflation proved particularly vulnerable to external pressures and no longer was simply a function of excess demand relative to the productive capacity of the economy. Reductions in supply, as in the case of the OPEC oil embargo in 1973, created a sudden inflationary surge that spiraled through all sectors of the economy. Increases in world demand, as in the case of food, following disastrous international harvests in the early 1970s, added to the inflation-

Table 3-1.
INFLATION, UNEMPLOYMENT, AND STAGFLATION

	Unemployment Rate (percentage)	Inflation Rate* (percentage)	Combined (percentage)
1961	6.0	.7	6.7
1962	4.9	1.2	6.1
1963	5.0	1.6	6.6
1964	4.6	1.2	5.8
1965	4.1	1.9	6.0
1966	3.3	3.4	6.7
1967	3.4	3.0	6.4
1968	3.2	4.7	7.9
1969	3.1	6.1	9.2
1970	4.5	5.5	10.0
1971	5.4	3.4	8.8
1972	5.0	3.4	8.4
1973	4.3	8.8	13.1
1974	5.0	12.2	17.2
1975	7.8	7.0	14.8
1976	7.0	4.8	11.8
1977	6.2	6.8	13.0
1978	5.2	9.0	14.2
1979	5.9	13.3	19.2

Source: Department of Labor, Bureau of Labor Statistics.

*December to December, unadjusted, Consumer Price Index.

ary surge. In 1973 alone, two devaluations of the dollar resulted in a 24 percent increase in the cost of imported goods.[3] While President Nixon's wage and price controls seemed to work for a short time, their rapid, unphased removal provided more upward pressure on prices.

Between 1973 and 1975, the United States economy fell into the worst recession since World War II. What the Joint Economic Committee in Congress called the "Great Recession" not only cut the real Gross National Product (GNP) more severely, but bottomed out later and failed to recover fully in more than two years.[4] Unemployment reached a postwar record of 8.9 percent in April 1975. The economy slowly recovered throughout the rest of the decade, but chronic inflation continued to be a problem, especially after the greatest postwar increase in prices that occurred in 1979.

Because of "automatic stabilizers" built into current law, the economy affects the budget as much as decision makers use the budget to affect the economy. These stabilizers are part of the so-called uncontrollable portion of the budget. On the expenditure side, transfer payments to individuals such as Aid to Dependent Children (ADC) payments, food stamps, and unemployment compensation rise automatically when GNP falls and more people are out of work. On the reverse side, the progressive income tax has the same effect. As employment falls, taxpayers may fall into lower tax brackets, and total federal revenues decline in the aggregate. Economists estimate that for every increase of 1 percent in the unemployment rate, the federal deficit increases by $20 billion (added outlays of $3 billion and lost revenues of $17 billion).[5]

Consider the situation in 1975, the first year "trial run" for the new budget process. Both inflation and unemployment were at unacceptably high levels, and traditional economic wisdom did not explain how to combat both at the same time. The United States economy had been shown to be interdependent with and vulnerable to the world economy. Outlays were automatically increasing and revenues were falling, swelling the deficit. Confusing economic problems added to the difficulties facing the congressional budget process.

BUILDING A BUDGET COALITION

FIRST YEAR TRIAL RUN—1975

Into economic confusion and political conflict the congressional budget process was born. Republican President Gerald Ford, struggling with the economic situation in his own administration, sent a fiscally conservative 1976 budget to the Congress in January 1975. Although the Budget Act did not mandate implementation until the next year, congressional Democrats felt it was essential to have an immediate impact on the fiscal policies of the nation. Liberals in particular felt Ford's budget ignored the unemployment problem, and wanted to see more spending despite increasing the deficit. The House and Senate Budget Committees realized it would be impossible to completely employ the intricate procedures in the first year. They adopted a limited implementation plan, including the first and second resolutions, but without the detail of the later resolutions. They agreed to ignore the September 15 deadline for passage of the second resolution for the first year only.

The two Budget Committees began their markup of the first budget resolution in the spring of 1975. House Republicans stated publicly that the practice run was meaningless, and they would have no inhibitions about voting against it. House Budget Committee Chairman Brock Adams suggested the committee do no more than forecast the amounts that other committees were likely to approve in the session.[6] Other committee members argued for a more forceful approach, but Adams's restrained approach prevailed. Even with this timid start, committee members had difficulty in reporting a resolution to the House. The main problem was the size of the deficit—over $70 billion—the largest in the country's history. This was simply unpalatable to conservatives who refused to go on record favoring such a sum. After some desperate negotiations, the first concurrent resolution for fiscal 1976 was sent to the House for its approval.

The House scheduled ten hours of debate on the budget resolution from April 29 to May 2, 1975. As the following excerpts from the first debate show, the major issues were deficit spending, inflation versus unemployment, and the direction of national fiscal policy. The ranking minority member of the Budget Committee, Delbert Latta, strongly opposed the resolution:

We will have acquired by fiscal year 1976 $600 plus billion in debt since the beginning of our history but we are going to acquire one-sixth of that in one single year. That is scary. . . .We are passing this tremendous debt onto our children and their children. I think that is downright immoral.[7]

Representative Jack Kemp (R-N.Y.) questioned the assumptions of the majority party sponsors that the deficit would help combat unemployment:

In 1970 unemployment was around 4.2% and the Federal budget was $193 billion. We are today debating a budget in fiscal year 1976 of upward of $390 billion and unemployment is hovering around 8.7%. . . .Why is it that as we have doubled the federal budget, we have doubled unemployment?[8]

Liberals, such as John Conyers (D-Mich.) felt the committee's proposals did not call for enough spending to tackle the record high levels of unemployment:

Congress could set no higher goal for itself than to restore the economic health of our Nation, but the Report of the Budget Committee does not foresee our doing this. . . .In fact, the committee did not even consider a budget which could have been part of a full employment economy. Although I commend the committee for its hard work . . .I feel I must vote against the resolution. The people of Detroit and of other hard pressed areas need to know that their Representatives in Congress will not abandon them.[9]

It was clear that spending and the deficit were too high for some and not enough for others, and that the budget coalition would have to be made up of a group in the middle. But faced with nearly unanimous Republican opposition, the committee had to woo potential liberal defectors while holding on to moderate Democratic supporters. As a result, the first House resolution and subsequent resolutions tended to be slightly more liberal than the Senate versions where support was garnered from both parties. In attempting to help the fledgling Budget Committee, the House leadership

urged members to support the first resolution despite their policy differences. House Speaker Carl Albert (D-Okla.) in an unusual floor speech
appealed to the members:

I am not attempting to make a brief for any particular provision or position. Never-
theless, I must assert, as the elected leader of the House, on behalf of the House and
the future of the Nation, that it is essential that we pass a budget resolution. . . .Only
by supporting a budget resolution can we reestablish . . .the principle that the
Congress will be a responsible partner, exercising its own judgement, as elected
representatives of the people, in carrying forward the economic affairs of this
Nation.[10]

Several amendments were beaten back as the committee attempted to
prevent erosion of its compromise proposals. When the final vote was
taken, the first budget resolution passed the House by a narrow 200 to 196
margin. Many of those who voted against the resolution were no longer
impressed with the process and the policy decisions that resulted. Representative Robert Bauman (R-Md.) complained:

It is truly a measure of the unreality of this entire budget process that grown men and
women stand before the House and delude themselves into thinking that we are
accomplishing something that cannot and has not been done. . . .If what we have
seen here today is any indicator, the taxpayers of this Nation will soon be just about
as bankrupt as this so-called budget reform process.[11]

House Republicans voted 3 to 128 against the resolution. They were
joined in opposition by 68 of the 265 House Democrats voting on the issue.
Virtually all of the Republican nay votes were cast on conservative grounds.
About half of the Democrats voted against it on the same basis, with at most
about twenty liberal nay votes because the budget was too small. The
issues, the partisanship, and the voting alignments that emerged were to
remain fairly stable in succeeding years.

The events of the first budget resolution in 1975 were considerably
different on the Senate side. Senator Muskie and Ranking Minority Member
Bellmon struck an alliance of bipartisanship, cooperating in formulating a
budget resolution. The Senate was more aggressive in writing the first
resolution, attempting to shape the parameters of subsequent actions,
rather than just predict actions, such as the House. Within the committee,
both Republicans and Democrats participated in determining how much
stimulus the budget should contain. With Republican participation, and
their more forceful approach, the Senate reported a budget with a deficit of
$67 billion, some $6 billion less than the House version. Although neither
Muskie, Bellmon, nor the other members of the Senate Budget Committee

were completely pleased with their final product, they agreed that the only way the process could succeed was with a united front once the committee had made its decision.

The same kind of issues were raised in the Senate as in the House. Opponents criticized the large deficit, the continued growth in federal spending, and other specific parts of the resolution. But with the bipartisan alliance forged by Muskie and Bellmon, and the seemingly more compliant confines of the Senate, the first resolution passed by the comfortable margin of 69-22. Senate Republicans favored the resolution by a 19-18 tally, in sharp contrast to their House colleagues. Senate Democrats overwhelmingly favored the first resolution, 50-4.

The House-Senate conference committee that met in May 1975 had first to work out some procedural differences, particularly the level of detail in the resolution. Within a few days the conferees agreed on a budget of $367 billion and a deficit of $69 billion, closer to the Senate version. The Senate ratified the conference by a voice vote; while the House upped its margin of victory to thirty-seven votes, it was still able to attract only five Republican votes.

Six months later, Congress adopted the second concurrent resolution for fiscal 1976. Throughout the summer, the Budget committees attempted to enforce the resolutions. In the Senate, Muskie took an assertive approach, challenging some powerful committees when legislation exceeded the targets, and won some surprising victories. In the House, Adams followed a more cautious approach, working behind the scenes to persuade committees to abide by the targets. The second resolution was passed in December 1975. The new fiscal year was not to go into effect until the next year, and there was a desire not to push the other standing committees hard in the partial implementation stage. Most of the appropriations bills had not been enacted by September, so there was no reason for the Budget committees to rush.

In developing the binding totals of the second resolution, no attempt was made to change the individual decisions that had been made or to change the priorities expressed in the first resolution. Because the targets were loose enough to encompass the bulk of the spending desires of the other committees, there was little reason for revision. During the debate on the resolution, economic issues were raised in both the House and Senate, amounting to a virtual replay of the events of May. But the second time through, Adams and the House Budget Committee had an easier time of it. The second resolution passed by a vote of 225-191, close, but more comfortable than the vote in May. The Senate again passed its version of the resolution by a comfortable margin. House-Senate conferees quickly agreed to a conference report, but the continued weakness of the House coalition again manifested itself as the compromise resolution passed by the narrow margin of 189-187. There had been some moments of doubt and several close calls, but Congress had approved a national budget for the first time in history.

MAINTAINING A BUDGET COALITION

FULL IMPLEMENTATION—1976

The congressional budget process had survived its first test, but there was little evidence that the new procedures had much impact on policy. The House did not even attempt to shape priorities, and except for Muskie's well-publicized "victory" over Senator John Stennis (D-Miss.) and the Armed Services Committee, there were few savings to point to. Although the budget process was intended to do more than trimming, it quickly became apparent that the vast majority of members of both Budget committees defined their role as such. Given the proclivity of Congress to spend, there was really no need for another spending advocate. But this troubled traditional liberals such as Muskie and Adams, who found themselves opposing programs they ordinarily would have supported. Their stands, however, helped promote the credibility of the process in both houses.

In 1976, the full set of provisions in the Budget Act were to be implemented. This meant that the March 15 deadline for views and estimates, the May 15 deadline for reporting new authorizing legislation, and the September deadlines for passage of spending bills and the second concurrent resolution would all be enforced. The problems faced in the House and Senate reflected the experience of the previous year. On the House side, Adams was concerned with survival. Across the Capitol rotunda, Muskie was concerned with having more impact on the budget totals and curbing the spending tendencies of the other committees. The economy was showing the first signs of recovery from the long 1972-1975 recession, but the deficit was still estimated to be in the range of $50 billion. The unemployment rate had begun to drop from the historic highs of 1975, and inflation had begun to moderate. But the fiscal dilemma was still apparent. Some members wanted more stimulus to reduce unemployment while others continued to complain about disastrous deficit spending. A further complication was that 1976 was a presidential election year. All the members of the House and one-third of the Senate (plus the dozen running for president) were up for reelection. The election year penchant for pork added increased spending pressures in Congress.

The first concurrent resolution for 1977 passed the Senate easily, and was passed by the House with the widest margin to that point: 221-155. Adams had been able to sway conservative Democrats and more than thirty Republicans to support the resolution. House Budget Committee members and staff were optimistic. Several suggested that this was a turning point in the process and the House was on its way towards the Senate model. Such optimism was premature, however. Only twelve months later, the committee's resolution would be unable to gain majority support on the floor of the House.

Macroeconomic concerns again dominated the debate in 1976, but defense spending became more of an issue. The sizable cuts made in President Ford's requests the previous year became much smaller cuts in fiscal year 1977. Ford even threatened to veto the defense appropriations bill if Congress cut it too much, but the election year popularity of military spending made such an action unnecessary. The sluggishness of the economy led Congress to consider a tax cut to help stimulate the economy. The House favored some additional tinkering with revenues in the form of tax reform. The issue of revenues and tax reform became particularly controversial in the Senate as Muskie and Russell Long (D-La.) were embroiled in a number of disputes. Tax expenditures were also a major issue in the Senate, as the Budget Committee attempted to restrict the creation of new "loopholes."

Several steps were taken by the House and Senate that resulted in tangible savings. The Budget committees pushed for the repeal of the 1 percent "kicker" in Social Security, the provision that increased benefits by an amount greater than the rise in the Consumer Price Index. The House also dealt with the issue of the Highway Trust Fund and a ceiling on spending was imposed.

On the whole, most of the deadlines were met with relative ease, demonstrating that Congress could indeed adapt to a strict new process. Committees cooperated in submitting views and estimates, most authorizing legislation was reported by May 15, and the first resolution passed in time. Most impressive was the fact that all the regular appropriation bills were passed by October, the first time in decades that the fiscal year began with all regular appropriations in place. On top of that, both the houses were able to agree on the second resolution in September. Procedurally, it was a success. Yet for the second year in a row, Congress failed to use the second resolution or the reconciliation process to revise the decisions made in the first resolution. They simply used the second resolution to ratify the decisions struck in May. Despite the greater security of the process in the House, the participants still proceeded cautiously.

CARTER AND THE THIRD RESOLUTION

President Ford was the first United States president to submit a budget under the Budget and Impoundment Control Act. His 1976 and 1977 budgets were altered by Congress in a substantial fashion, providing more stimulus to the economy. His lame duck fiscal 1978 budget was submitted just a few days before the inauguration of his successor, Jimmy Carter. Having shown that Congress could be independent of the executive, the Democratic Congress was anxious to show that it could cooperate with the new Democratic president. Carter and the Budget committees moved quickly to prime the economic pump. A third concurrent resolution for fiscal 1977 was drawn up and sent to both houses calling for a jobs program on the expenditure side and a $50 individual rebate on the revenue side. The net impact was to increase the deficit by about $20 billion. Republicans complained about both the proposed policy and the disregard for the process in only the second budget Congress approved. The House leadership convinced the reluctant Appropriations Committee to go along with Carter's proposals, and the third resolution was approved in March 1977.

Only a few months later, the inexperienced Carter withdrew his rebate plan in the face of growing criticism. Communication with the Budget committees was poor, and many members felt that the administration flip-flop was an embarrassment to them and their newly discovered influence in fiscal affairs. Representative Robert Leggett (D-Calif.) complained on the House floor, and echoed the sentiments of many members.

I believe our budget process must be capable of producing sound, independent judgments about the appropriate action which Congress should follow regardless of which political party occupies the White House. . . . Had President Ford done the same thing, we would not be so passive and complacent.[12]

Congress was not required to revise its third resolution, but the withdrawal of the president's proposals left considerable room in both the revenue and expenditure totals. As a result, they again revised the estimates for fiscal 1977 as part of the first concurrent resolution for the next year.

THE FIRST DEFEAT OF A BUDGET RESOLUTION

Carter's difficulties with the congressional budget process did not end with withdrawal of the stimulus package. Many members of the House blamed the president for the defeat of the first concurrent resolution for fiscal 1978. Robert Giaimo (D-Conn.) had replaced Adams as chairman of the House Budget Committee when Adams left Congress to become Carter's secretary of transportation. Defense spending became the key issue in the House in formulating the budget totals for 1978. The House Committee, continuing to be slightly more liberal than the Senate, made cuts in President Carter's requests. Carter had revised Ford's budget in March 1977, and the committee action represented a substantial cut in what both Ford and Carter had originally requested.

On the day of the House debate on the first resolution, Budget Committee member Omar Burleson (D-Tex.) offered an amendment to restore the president's figure for defense. He announced on the House floor that Secretary of Defense Harold Brown had spoken to him that day and that President Carter supported his amendment. The Burleson amendment passed by a narrow margin, and the delicate balance struck in committee began to unravel. By the end of the debate, twelve amendments to the budget resolution had been offered and six had been adopted. The result was distasteful to almost everyone. Conservatives who supported the Burleson amendment still would not support the large deficit, and liberal support had evaporated with the increases in military spending. When the final vote was taken, only 84 members supported it while 320 opposed it as amended.

Giaimo was furious with the administration. At a press conference the next day he served notice to the president:

This is the United States Congress where the Democratic majority is going to write the legislation. It is not the Georgia legislature. . . .You don't just call up from downtown and send word from the Secretary of Defense to Armed Service Committee members and others and say, "write a budget resolution."[13]

The committee regrouped and attempted to salvage a compromise budget resolution. The new House leaders, Speaker Thomas O'Neill (D-Mass.) and Majority Leader James Wright (D-Tex.) made a concerted effort to secure passage of the revised resolution. Giaimo and the leaders agreed to make a token concession to the Burleson forces by slightly increasing the target for defense, but not enough to alienate liberal support. The greatest emphasis was placed on the importance of preserving the process. A letter sent to all Democratic members of the House by Wright on May 4, 1977, included the following appeal:

I earnestly plead for your vote to sustain the committee and redeem the commitment of the House to make this budget process work. If a budget resolution should not be adopted, we'll be prevented under law from proceeding with the appropriations process. Bills of all sorts will be stymied, and Congress itself would be the victim of a self-imposed paralysis.[14]

The combined efforts of the leaderships and the committee were successful; fifty-six members changed their vote or abstained on the same Burleson amendment to increase defense spending that they had supported only a few days earlier. This time the committee was able to defeat floor amendments offered to the resolution, and the first resolution for fiscal 1978 finally passed 213 to 179.

After the crisis passed, most members of the House Budget Committee felt it actually had been helpful to their cause. It proved that defeating a budget resolution on the floor would not automatically doom the process, and it demonstrated the delicacy of committee compromises and strengthened the case against floor amendments. But in the third year of its existence, the budget process was still extremely partisan in the House, and the basic security of the system was still in question.

PROPOSITION 13 AND THE TAX REVOLT

In June 1978, an obscure California legislator was hyped into a national folk hero. Howard Jarvis was co-sponsor of California's property tax rollback—Proposition 13. When it passed by a substantial margin, the media declared that the tax revolt had begun in earnest. The events leading to the success of Proposition 13 are complex and somewhat peculiar to California. But the impact on Capitol Hill was real because senators and representatives made it real. House Republicans had already attempted to unify their opposition to Democratic budget resolution by formulating their own alternatives. Although defense spending had been the main stumbling block the previous year, in 1978, the issue was again the size of the budget and the deficit.

In considering the first resolution for fiscal 1979, Representative Marjorie Holt (R-Md.) offered an amendment to the entire budget resolution. The Holt substitute made substantial cuts in spending, some cuts in taxes, and reduced the deficit by a substantial margin.[15] The growing maturity and sophistication of the congressional participants was evident. In the first years, conservative amendments to balance the budget were simple-minded statements of principle that would not have accomplished what they claimed. But with improvements in staff and the experience of several years on the committee, Holt and the Republicans were presenting more realistic alternatives to the majority report. When the amendment was offered on the floor, the Republicans were nearly unanimous in support (only one defector). With the addition of fifty-eight Democratic votes, the Holt substitute was defeated by the narrow margin of 197 to 203. The patterns that had been established four years earlier were still very much in evidence in the House.

In the Senate, the budget process remained secure with the budget resolutions passing by comfortable margins. If 1977 had been a bad year for the Senate committee in terms of enforcing the targets, the events of 1978 helped lend support to their budget cutting and watchdog role. But it also presented a threat to the bipartisanship of Muskie, Bellmon, and the committee. The Republican party wanted to make the tax revolt a partisan political issue, and were pushing hard on the Kemp-Roth tax cut bill. Some Senate Republicans urged Bellmon to break with Muskie and push for a Republican alternative. Despite this trend, the Senate resisted the temptation to make the budget resolution a partisan issue. Democrat Sam Nunn introduced compromise tax reduction legislation linked to expenditure cuts that the Senate eventually passed. Republicans dubbed the proposal "Son of Kemp-Roth" and did not seem to mind having their issue coopted. While other Republicans flew along the campaign trail in the so-called "Tax Clipper," the Senate remained supportive of a nonpartisan budget process.

BALANCING THE BUDGET

The trends that erupted in 1978 carried into 1979. Although the deficits had fallen considerably from the nearly $70 billion that Congress approved in 1975, continued deficit spending during the economic recovery had taken its toll in the minds of many citizens. Almost everyone running for office in 1978, including those running for Congress, campaigned as fiscal conservatives. A serious movement to call a Constitutional Convention for the purpose of writing an amendment to require a balanced budget had gathered momentum in 1978. By early 1979, about thirty states had approved the call for such a convention. In the collective mind of Congress, public pressure to limit government spending was indeed a reality. What had been one of the goals of budget reform five years earlier appeared to be virtually the only goal in 1979.

Various tax cutting and expenditure limitation proposals were suggested, ranging from a constitutional amendment proposed by Congress to statutory limits on taxing and spending to more modest proposals to balance the budget. Finance Committee Chairman Russell Long, joined by Senate Appropriations Chairman Warren Magnuson (D-Wash.), Muskie, and Bellmon, proposed an amendment to the debt ceiling limitation legislation in March 1979. The Long amendment required the president to submit balanced budget alternatives in future budgets and required the Budget committees to present balanced budget alternatives with the first concurrent resolutions for fiscal 1981 and 1982.

Would this apparent consensus break the pattern of partisanship in the House over fiscal policy? Probably not. One member of the House Budget Committee in an interview with the author claimed the Republicans would even oppose a balanced budget submitted by the Democrats. "If we balanced it this year, they would oppose it on the grounds that it should be balanced at a lower level." The pressure on Bellmon to break with Muskie and support a Republican alternative in the Senate also increased. But with Bellmon's announcement that he would not seek reelection in 1980, the prospects for greater partisanship in the Senate in the future were enhanced. Although the Democrats suffered only minor losses in the 1978 elections, the dozen seats they had lost to the Republicans were greater than the margin of passage of some of the previous budget resolutions. Many of the new Democrats had campaigned for office on a platform of fiscal restraint and a balanced budget. In the face of a growing mood of fiscal conservatism, what would happen to the liberals who had supported the budget process for four years?

BUDGET BATTLES OF 1979

The fiscal 1980 budget was the scene of wide-ranging political skirmishes in 1979, from treaties to abortion to a liberal revolt. Despite President Carter's wage-price guidelines, by mid-1979, inflation was roaring at an annual rate of more than 13 percent. Economists, including those in CBO and OMB, could not agree on whether a recession was coming or had already arrived. Most members of Congress seemed to favor a restrictive budget, one that would reduce the deficit below the $30 billion figure in the president's budget.

In May 1979, the conference report on the first resolution for 1980 was defeated in the House. What was surprising was that the defeat was at least partially attributable to liberal Democrats who had decided to suffer in silence no more. Led by the congressional Black Caucus, liberals revolted against the erosion of social welfare program funding in the budget and the guaranteed increase promised to defense. House liberals, having in large part supported the budget process in the previous four years, served notice that their support was not automatic. They aligned themselves with the Republicans who perennially oppose the resolutions, and the report was defeated and sent back to conference. The revised version that finally passed was only slightly different, but another faction in the House had made itself heard.

More serious divisions emerged in September 1979 and for the first time in the five years of implementation, the fiscal year started without a congressional budget. Over the course of the summer, it became clear that Senate ratification of the Strategic Arms Limitation Treaty (SALT II) would be linked to increases in defense spending. In addition, Carter had pledged a 3 percent real growth in military outlays to NATO, one factor that had incensed liberals in May. A further complication was that runaway inflation was pushing the totals almost $10 billion above the figures in the first resolution. Finally, for the first time, Senator Muskie and the Senate Budget Committee resolved to use the reconciliation process to force committees to rescind previous spending actions.

All these events combined to put tremendous pressure on the budget process. True to the form established in previous years, the Senate was able to compromise and move while the House languished with the budget. Because the standing committees in the Senate had exceeded the targets of the first resolution, the Senate Budget Committee voted on August 2, 1979 to report a reconciliation bill requiring six authorizing committees and the Appropriations Committee to cut back $4 billion from 1980 spending. [16] For the first time, the second resolution did not simply represent the sum of committee actions. Across the Capitol, Chairman Giaimo and the Budget Committee rejected the use of the reconciliation process in the House, avoiding a direct confrontation with other committees.

The overwhelming success of Senator Muskie and the strength of the Budget Committee was reflected in the 90-6 vote approving the reconciliation action. The victory was assured however, by compromises with Senator Magnuson, chairman of Appropriations, and Senator Long, chairman of Finance.[17] Muskie also won floor battles with the Agriculture and Veterans Affairs Committees which had opposed the rollback. The result was a total cut of $3.6 billion in what the committees had recommended in the second resolution.

While imposing these cuts, however, the Senate added $4.4 billion to the defense budget and pledged an additional $33.9 billion in the next two years—reflecting the growing support for military spending. This resulted in a significant difference with the House over total expenditures for defense. The struggle in the House over defense spending and other issues led for the first time to the defeat of the second resolution on the budget.

The defeat was attributed more to poor leadership, confusion, and absenteeism because of the late hour of the vote, than to clear policy disputes. However, the presence of President Carter, the Senate, and SALT II were all felt when the amendment to raise the mark for defense was defeated.[18] A week later, a revised version of the second resolution passed the House, but not in time to start fiscal 1980 with a legislative budget. The conference committee did not approve the final figures until late November 1979, and the Senate reconciliation instructions were scrapped.

The events of 1979 resulted in the poorest performance of the budget procedures in five years, despite the first ever reconciliation action taken by the Senate. By October 1, only three of thirteen appropriations bills were enacted, and no budget resolution was approved. More seriously Congress had not even agreed on a continuing resolution threatening a financial breakdown in Washington. Split over House amendments to limit federally funded abortions and the congressional pay raise, the process resembled the disarray of the pre-1975 budget system.

In five years, Congress had shown that a legislative budget was possible, but often with great difficulty. The defeat of two resolutions in 1979 reflected the continued uncertainty in the system; even after five years, the maintenance of a budget coalition was tricky political business.

CONGRESSIONAL POLICY DECISIONS

What hath the congressional budget process wrought? How has Congress shaped the fiscal policy of the nation? Table 3-2 shows the budget totals from fiscal 1976 to fiscal 1980. The aggregate totals only provide a

Table 3-2.
COMPARISON OF BUDGET TOTALS, 1976-1980
($ in billions)

	President's Budget	First Resolution			Second Resolution		
		House	Senate	Final	House	Senate	Final
Fiscal Year 1976							
total outlays	$349.4	$368.2	$365.0	$367.0	$373.9	$375.6	$374.9
total budget authority	385.8	395.9	388.6	395.8	408.0	406.2	408.0
total revenues	297.5	298.1	297.8	298.2	301.8	300.8	300.8
deficit	51.9	70.0	67.2	68.8	72.1	74.8	74.1
Fiscal Year 1977							
total outlays	$394.2	$415.4	$412.6	$413.3	$413.2	$412.8	$413.1
total budget authority	433.4	454.1	454.9	454.2	452.6	447.5	451.5
total revenues	351.3	363.0	362.4	352.5	362.5	362.0	362.5
deficit	43.0	52.4	50.2	50.8	50.7	50.8	50.6
Fiscal Year 1978							
total outlays	$459.37	$464.5	$459.2	$460.95	$459.57	$459.9	$458.25
total budget authority	507.3	502.3	504.6	503.45	508.0	501.4	500.1
total revenues	401.62	398.1	395.7	396.3	397.93	394.8	397.0
deficit	57.75	66.4	63.5	64.65	61.64	65.1	61.25
Fiscal Year 1979							
total outlays	$499.4	$500.9	$498.9	$498.8	$489.8	$489.5	$487.5
total budget authority	565.6	569.5	566.1	568.85	561.0	557.7	555.65
total revenues	439.8	443.0	443.3	477.9	450.0	447.2	448.7
deficit	59.6	57.9	55.6	50.9	39.8	42.3	38.8
Fiscal Year 1980							
total outlays	$532.3	$529.9	$532.6	$532.0	$548.2	$546.3	$547.6
total budget authority	615.0	605.1	600.3	604.4	631.8	636.6	638.0
total revenues	503.9	509.0	503.6	509.0	519.3	514.7	517.8
deficit	28.4	20.9	29.0	23.0	28.9	31.6	29.8

Source: Congressional Weekly Reports, 1976-80.

sketch of the decisions made by Congress, but allow for some rough contrasts. Compared with the requests of the president, Congress has shown some ability to make alterations. The most significant increases were made in the first two Ford budgets, in 1976 and 1977. In both cases, Congress added about $20 billion in total outlays, reflecting the majority view that the economy needed more stimulus. In 1978, when both Ford and Carter submitted estimates, Congress approved totals much closer to Carter's proposals (to no one's surprise). Yet the Budget committees made it clear they were not about to relinquish their enhanced role in fiscal affairs. The figures for 1979 and 1980 indicate that congressional priorities were relatively close to the president's. Although attempts were made to reduce the 1980 deficit below the president's figure, it was difficult for the Congress to find palatable cuts.

Changes between the first and second resolutions were the result of changes in economic assumptions and trends more than a conscious change in congressional sentiment. Predicting outlays is an imprecise business, and economic changes can have dramatic impact on the mandatory components of expenditures. The need for the third concurrent resolution for fiscal 1979 (which was incorporated in the first resolution for fiscal 1980) arose from higher inflation which increased both revenues and outlays. Using the yardstick of current policy estimates to evaluate congressional decisions, the size of the public sector and the level of services had not been increased since 1975. If anything, there had been a slight decline. The final budget totals generally have been slightly below estimates of what a "standpat" budget would look like. The question of how much the policies were changed because of the budget process is addressed in Chapter 7.

Of greater immediate interest is the question of House-Senate policy decisions. Table 3-2 suggests that the House has tended to approve totals slightly higher than the Senate. This is consistent with the need for liberal support in the budget coalition in the House compared to the bipartisan coalition in the Senate.

Some members of the House feared that the weakness of their Budget Committee would manifest itself in negotiations with the Senate in conference. Others have noted that the Budget and Impoundment Control Act increased the power of the Senate in budgeting, making the houses equal in the budget process.

In *Power of the Purse*, Richard Fenno indicates that in spite of House preeminence in the appropriations process, the final figures are more likely to be closer to the Senate figure.[19] He suggests this may be a result of the Senate's tendency to have higher figures than the House, and that it is often easier to agree on the higher number. In examining compromises on the budget resolution, then, two questions are of interest: which house of Congress "wins," and, is the final figure closer to the higher or lower figure?

Of course, it is misleading to think of a conference agreement as a zero-sum game. Neither side wins or loses, but the position of one side may be adopted more frequently than the position of the other side. In most cases, conference committees attempting to resolve differences over the budget resolutions arrive at numbers between the House and Senate figures. Only occasionally, and because of some intervening factors, do the conferees settle on a figure above or below both of the respective versions.

Table 3-3 presents figures for the budget totals in outlays, budget authority, and revenues since 1975, and whether the higher, lower, House, or Senate figure was closer to the outcome. In the first four years, the lower figure was chosen more frequently but the final outlay figure was closer to the Senate figure only about half the time. However, the same is not true for budget authority. The House figure tended to be higher than the Senate figure, but in most cases, a number closer to the higher House total was adopted in conference. Because much of budget authority is to be spent in future years, budget authority lacks the immediacy of current outlays and revenues. It may be less of a priority for the Senate, and more important to House conferees who are anxious to keep the standing committees happy. Budget authority is more important than outlays, however, since Congress does not control outlays, only recommends appropriate levels of expenditures. On the important issue of *total* budget authority, the House is not dominated by the Senate.

Section III of Table 3-3 compares House, Senate, and conference figures for revenues. Except the first concurrent resolution for fiscal 1979, the Senate totals for revenue have been lower than the House total. This may reflect the greater generosity of the Senate Finance Committee in approving tax cuts, and the difficulty the Budget Committee has had in requiring the Senate to increase revenues through tax reform. On this dimension, the Senate appears to dominate. With three exceptions, the conference committee compromise has been closer to the lower Senate version. The first resolution for fiscal 1979 is unusual for two reasons. First, the Senate total was higher than the House total, and second, the conferees fixed revenue totals significantly higher than either chambers' version. In order to reduce the deficit, the conferees agreed to provide less of a tax cut in 1978, and added almost $5 billion to the target for total revenues. Considering outlays, budget authority, and revenue totals together, the two houses of Congress appear relatively equal in conference. The House seems to prevail more often in budget authority, the Senate more often in revenues, and they prevail equally frequently over the totals for outlays. There are also no clear patterns concerning the higher or lower figure in conference agree-

Table 3-3.
CONFERENCE COMMITTEE AGREEMENTS:
BUDGET TOTALS, 1976-1979 ($ in billions)

Item	House	Senate	Conference	Closer to House or Senate	Closer to Higher or Lower Figure
I. Outlays					
a. 1st CR FY 1976	$368.2	$265.0	$367.0	House	Lower
b. 2nd CR FY 1976	473.9	375.6	374.9	Senate	Higher
c. 1st CR FY 1977	415.4	412.6	413.3	Senate	Lower
d. 2nd CR FY 1977	413.2	412.8	413.1	House	Higher
e. 3rd CR FY 1977	419.1	415.0	417.5	House	Higher
f. 1st CR FY 1978	464.5	459.2	460.9	Senate	Lower
g. 2nd CR FY 1978	459.6	459.9	458.3	House	Lower
h. 1st CR FY 1979	500.9	498.9	498.8	Senate	Lower
i. 2nd CR FY 1979	489.8	489.5	487.5	Senate	Lower
II. Budget Authority					
a. 1st CR FY 1976	495.9	388.6	395.8	House	Higher
b. 2nd CR FY 1976	408.0	406.2	408.0	House	Higher
c. 1st CR FY 1977	454.1	454.9	454.2	House	Lower
d. 2nd CR FY 1977	452.6	447.5	451.5	House	Higher
e. 3rd CR FY 1977	477.9	467.0	472.9	House	Higher
f. 1st CR FY 1978	502.3	504.6	503.45	Split Difference	
g. 2nd CR FY 1978	508.0	501.4	500.1	Senate	Lower
h. 1st CR FY 1979	565.5	566.1	568.8	House	Higher
i. 2nd CR FY 1979	561.0	557.7	555.65	Senate	Lower
III. Revenue					
a. 1st CR FY 1976	298.1	297.8	298.2	House	Higher
b. 2nd CR FY 1976	301.8	300.8	300.8	Senate	Lower
c. 1st CR FY 1977	363.0	362.4	352.5	Senate	Lower
d. 2nd CR FY 1977	362.5	362.0	362.5	House	Higher
e. 3rd CR FY 1977	348.8	346.8	347.7	Senate	Lower
f. 1st CR FY 1978	398.1	395.7	396.3	Senate	Lower
g. 2nd CR FY 1978	397.9	394.8	397.0.	House	Higher
h. 1st CR FY 1979	443.0	443.3	447.9	Senate	Higher
i. 2nd CR FY 1979	450.0	447.2	448.7	House	Higher

Source: Congressional Quarterly Weekly Reports, 1975-1978.

FY = Fiscal year, CR = Concurrent Resolution.

ments. The higher figure for budget authority is adopted more frequently, while the lower figure for revenues is adopted more often.

Budget totals are only part of the budget resolutions and the compromises that must be struck in conference. Many times, the subtotals for budget functions are the most controversial parts of the resolution. As we have

seen, much controversy has surrounded the decision on the relative allocation to defense versus social welfare spending. Table 3-4 compares the
House, Senate, and conference committee figures on the two largest budget
functions: defense and income security. The figures tend to confirm the
hypothesis that the House tends to be more liberal than the Senate in
recommending less for defense and more for income security. In the first
four fiscal years of the budget process, the Senate recommended greater
budget authority for defense seven out of seven times, and the same
amount as the House on the eighth. Summing the differences across years,
the Senate versions of the budget resolutions recommended $8.8 billion
more for national defense. The conference committees have tended to
favor the lower House figures in the final report. In cases in which the figures
were different and they did not split the difference, the final figure was closer
to the House version in five of six cases.

The pattern of decisions on the income security function has more
exceptions. The House approved a higher figure for budget authority in six
of eight cases; the Senate was higher twice. Over the period, however, the
House approved some $15.7 billion more for income security than the
Senate. The major exception to this pattern was the first concurrent resolution for fiscal 1977 when the Senate recommended almost $7 billion more
than the House. Again, the House figure tended to dominate in conference.
The final version was closer to their totals in six of eight cases. Despite its
worries, the House has not been dominated by the Senate in conference.

It must be stressed that words like "dominate" and "prevail" are used
guardedly. Conference committee agreements are the result of many factors—personalities, intervention of leadership, actions by the president,
and a complex process of give and take. The House has not been over-
whelmed by the Senate in conference, as some feared, and may even have
a slight edge overall. Given the relatively greater strength of the Budget
Committee and the budget process in the Senate, this might not be expected. But in many cases, the weaknesses of the House committee can be
a bargaining tool in conference. The argument that certain concessions
from the Senate are essential if the resolution is to pass the House can be
persuasive. House and Senate conferees disagree to some extent on their
ability to mandate actions by the standing committees. The Senate, more
aggressive in implementing the budget process, has argued in favor of imposing its will on the other committees. The House conferees have disagreed.[20] In spite of differences on major issues, House and Senate
conferees have been able to resolve those differences, usually in a few days.
Pressured by the rigid time constraints of the budget process, this has been
the norm, even though it took almost two months for conferees to agree on
final figures for 1980.

Table 3-4.
DEFENSE VERSUS INCOME SECURITY
(Comparison of House, Senate, and Conference Agreements on Two Largest Budget Functions—Budget authority in billions)

Resolution Date	Defense					Income Security				
	House	Senate	Conference	Closer to:	Closer to Higher or Lower Figure	House	Senate	Conference	Closer to:	Closer to Higher or Lower Figure
1st CR FY 1976	$100.5	$101.0	$100.7	House	Lower	$141.3	$138.5	$140.9	House	Higher
2nd CR FY 1976	100.4	101.5	101.0	House	Lower	137.6	137.3	137.5	House	Higher
1st CR FY 1977	112.0	113.0	112.5	Split	Split	156.8	163.7	158.9	House	Lower
2nd CR FY 1977	112.1	112.1	112.1	Same	Same	155.9	156.2	155.9	House	Lower
3rd CR FY 1977	108.8	109.2	108.8	House	Lower	175.0	166.3	170.9	House	Higher
1st CR FY 1978	117.1	120.3	118.5	House	Lower	182.7	179.9	179.9	Senate	Lower
2nd CR FY 1978	116.3	116.6	116.4	House	Lower	186.8	178.8	178.6	Senate	Lower
1st CR FY 1979	127.4	129.8	128.7	Senate	Higher	192.8	192.5	193.1	House	Higher

Source: Congressional Quarterly Weekly Reports, 1975-1978.

CR=Concurrent Resolution, FY=Fiscal Year.

CONCLUSION

Congress discovered that it was easier to reform the budget process than it was to make fiscal policy and establish national priorities. In a single document, they must solve the concurrent issues of spending growth, the macroeconomic impact of budget, and the relative allocations to budget functions. Although specific issues have arisen each year, the basic cleavage in Congress has remained relatively stable since 1975. National economic conditions in the last half of the 1970s have made the decision-making process all the more difficult. The concomitant desires to spend and to exert fiscal restraint pit Congress against itself in a fundamental sense. But despite the difficulties of fiscal policy, the congressional budget process survived its early tests.

An overview of the early years of budget reform and the brief analysis of congressional decisions and conference committee compromises provide the necessary background for a more intensive analysis of both the participants and the policies that have resulted. The two Budget committees, the other taxing and spending committees, and the impact of the budget process will be examined more closely in the subsequent chapters.

NOTES

1. Aage Clausen, *How Congressmen Decide: A Policy Focus* (New York: St. Martin's Press, 1973).

2. Barry H. Blechman, Edward M. Gramlich, and Robert M. Hartman, *Setting National Priorities: The 1976 Budget* (Washington, D.C.: Brookings Institution, 1975), p. 20.

3. Ibid., p. 25.

4. *The 1976 Joint Economic Report*, Joint Economic Committee, 94th Cong., 2nd Sess., p. 78.

5. Ibid., pp. 11-12.

6. Joel Havemann, *Congress and the Budget* (Bloomington: Indiana University Press, 1978), p. 45.

7. *Congressional Record*, H 3404-5, April 29, 1975.

8. *Congressional Record*, H 3552-5391, May 1, 1975.

9. Ibid.

10. Ibid.

11. Ibid.

12. *Congressional Record*, April 26, 1977. Quoted in *Congressional Quarterly Weekly Reports*, April 30, 1977, p. 776.

13. Ibid.

14. Ibid.

15. *Congressional Quarterly Weekly Reports*, May 6, 1978, p. 1095.

16. *Congressional Quarterly Weekly Reports*, August 4, 1979, p. 1582.

17. *Congressional Quarterly Weekly Reports*, September 22, 1979, p. 2032.

18. Ibid., p. 2033.

19. Richard Fenno, *Congressmen in Committees* (Boston: Little, Brown, 1973), p. 81.

20. John Ellwood and James Thurber, "The New Congressional Budget Process: The Hows and Whys of House-Senate Differences," in Lawrence Dodd and Bruce Oppenheimer, eds., *Congress Reconsidered* (New York: Praeger, 1977), p. 178.

4

The House
Budget
Committee

*It comes down to this. We do whatever we have
to do to get a budget resolution through the House.*
—Budget Committee Member

Congress proved that it could pass a national budget, but has it demonstrated an ability to establish fiscal policy and set national priorities? Despite the centralization added by the budget process, the primary decisions on taxing and spending are still made in committees, the primary work groups of Congress. It is these participants and their decisions that demand our scrutiny, beginning with the Budget Committees.

Although the policy responsibilities of the House and Senate Budget Committees were similar in the statute, some obvious differences have become apparent. Why has transition to the budget process been more difficult for the House than the Senate? Has the House Budget Committee been able to establish a base of institutional power? How has it affected the behavior of other committees and the nature of congressional policy?

To answer these questions, the House Budget Committee must be evaluated as a functioning part of the larger Congress. Comparisons with other House and Senate committees are necessary.[1] One of the most useful frameworks for comparing committees was suggested by Richard Fenno.[2] Expanding upon his classic study of the appropriations process in Congress, *Power of the Purse*, Fenno has suggested a number of variables and relationships that help explain committee behavior and power.

The members of each congressional committee have certain goals that they want to achieve through membership on a committee. If there is a high level of consensus on goals, they will organize their committee internally in ways that seem likely to aid them in achieving these individual goals. However, each committee operates within a distinctive set of environmental constraints—most particularly the expectations of influential external groups. Committee members will, therefore, also organize their committee internally in ways that seem likely to satisfy the expectations of these groups that make up their environment. The members of each committee will develop certain strategies for accommodating the achievement of their individual goals to the satisfaction of key environmental expectations. These strategies become the proximate premises on which each committee's internal decision-making processes are based. From these strategies, operationalized as decision rules, flow committee decisions. . . .Member goals and environmental constraints are the independent variables; strategic premises (or decision rules) are an intervening variable; and decision-making processes and decisions are dependent variables.[3]

Fenno concluded that two "ideal" types of committees seem to exist in Congress. The "corporate" committee is the model of the powerful committee, characterized by integration, autonomy, consensus, expertise, orientation to the parent chamber, and greater influence. The "permeable" committee is less powerful, characterized by less integration, autonomy, expertise, greater conflict and an orientation to external actors.[4]

This framework is useful for several reasons. Particularly with regard to the relatively new Budget committees, it facilitates comparisons along defined dimensions with older, more established committees. The approach suggests key variables in explaining the development of the budget process and the conflicts between committees. We will attempt to compare the main committees in the congressional budget process on the following dimensions:

Membership and selection: the nature of members, the selection process, formal requirements, and informal practices that affect committee composition.

Member goals: the dominant values expressed by committee members and the resulting overall orientation of the committee to internal influence, constituency groups, and policies.

Committee environment: pressures, demands, and constraints from groups outside the committee, such as other members of the House or Senate, other committees, the executive branch, and clientele groups.

Strategies: prescriptions for decision-making or decision rules adopted by the committee to achieve their goals.

Decision-making processes: regularized patterns of the committee's internal operations and characteristic processes, such as partisanship, participation, specialization, and leadership by the chairman.

Decisions: the policies chosen by the committee and recommended to the full House or Senate.

A portrait of a committee, or comparisons between committees, are but imperfect snapshots caught at a single point in time. Committees are relatively stable, but over time, significant changes have occurred. For example, Fenno's description of the House Appropriations Committee in the early 1960s is clearly dated today, as is John Manley's picture of the House Ways and Means Committee only a decade after it was written.[5] If we hope to do more than chronicle the budget process, the analysis of the committees must be dynamic; it must attempt to explain the forces that shape committees and suggest alternative evolutionary paths.

MEMBERSHIP

Analysis of congressional committee assignments has suggested a number of criteria for selection: helping reelection chances, expertise, state and region, and ideology.[6] Initial appointment is critical because of the seniority system; the route to internal influence within the Congress and a committee chairmanship, is to stay on the same committee for many years. Because of direct representation of other committees and limitations on tenure, the House Budget Committee presents a different set of alternatives for members.

The congressional budget process was conceived and born in a period of reformist sentiment in the House, and was passed only a few months before the unseating of three senior committee chairmen. The tenor of these times is reflected in the establishment of the House Budget Committee. Section 101 (a) (5) of the Act states that members shall be selected to serve on the committee without regard to seniority, but more significantly, it limits service on the Budget Committee to no more than four years out of any ten.[7] Architects of the Budget Act claimed they would insure constant infusion of "new blood" into the committee by requiring a rotating membership.

In addition to the limitations on term and seniority, the drafters were pressured to give the existing taxing and spending committees in Congress representation on the Budget Committee. The Budget Act specifies that the membership shall include five members each from the Appropriations and the Ways and Means Committees, eleven members from the standing committees, and one member each from the majority and minority leadership. In anticipation of the potential conflict between these committees, the provisions were an attempt to institutionalize an overlapping membership and a direct linkage to the leadership, as well as to prevent the committee from becoming independent.[8] Two years later, the committee was expanded to twenty-five members, increasing to thirteen the "representatives" of the standing committees.

While the limitations on membership of the House committee were seen as a victory for the progressive elements in Congress, serious questions on the impact of the requirements were soon raised. Had the House institutionally insured a second rate committee? Some members complained that no sooner had they learned some of the intricacies of fiscal policy and budgeting, and began to understand econometric projections, when their tenure on the committee was over. Would the chairmen, possibly changing every Congress, be equally dedicated to the preservation of the process or equally capable of gaining consensus among the diverse elements in the committee and the Congress?

Responding to pressure from Budget Committee members and organized labor, the House Democratic Caucus changed the tenure limitations before the start of the Ninety-sixth Congress.[9] Faced with the loss of their seat on the committee after serving four years, a last minute effort was made by some members to change the rule. Labor was concerned that the seven Democratic vacancies that would result might be filled with conservatives, given the growing budget-cutting mood. The change also protected the chairmanship of Robert Giaimo who would have been rotated off the committee. The proposal, sponsored by David Obey, permits the chairman to serve four terms if not elected head until the third term on the committee.[10] The presence and vocal support of Speaker O'Neill and Majority Leader Wright helped insure the change in the caucus vote.

Besides the formal characteristics of membership on the House Budget Committee, there are important informal characteristics of the membership that affect the committee. Demonstrating the disintegration of the short-lived budget reform coalition, the members of the committee reflect deep philosophical and partisan differences. Some suggest the committee has been "stacked" with liberal Democrats and conservative Republicans, and the influence of the party leaders in constituting the committee is evident. In response to the question "Why did you seek a seat on the Budget Committee?" one minority member responded, "Because my good friend Jerry Ford asked me to go on." Similarly, a majority member appointed to the committee in the Ninety-fifth Congress answered that "the leadership wanted me to go on as a counterbalance to some of the conservative Republicans." Although most members indicate a self-selection process, there is clear evidence that the ideological cleavage on the committee has been fostered in the selection of members.

Table 4-1 examines committee "liberalism" and "conservatism" using the Americans for Democratic Action (ADA) and Americans for Constitutional Action (ACA) ratings.[11] By computing an average rating for Democrats and Republicans some rough comparisons are possible. The table suggests that in the Ninety-fourth Congress, Democratic members of the Budget Committee were close to the average for congressional Democrats, if anything, slightly "less liberal." The Republicans, however, on both rating scales, were considerably more conservative than House Republicans on the whole. This tends to confirm observations that the Republican leadership loaded the committee with fiscal conservatives, what one Democrat referred to as, "the largest concentration of right-wingers in the House." The conservative orientation of committee Republicans was re-

Table 4-1.

HOUSE BUDGET COMMITTEE LIBERALISM AND CONSERVATISM
(Ratings by Americans for Democratic Action—ADA
—and Americans for Constitutional Action—ACA)

House Budget Committee—94th Congress

DEMOCRATS			REPUBLICANS		
Name	ADA Rating	ACA Rating	Name	ADA Rating	ACA Rating
Holtzman (N.Y.)*	100	7	Latta (Ohio)*	0	100
Mitchell (Md.)*	95	0	Broyhill (N.C.)*	15	88
Stokes (Ohio)*	85	0	Clawson (Calif.)	10	79
Leggett (Calif.)*	75	4	Shriver (Kan.)	10	73
Smith (Iowa)	70	7	Cederberg (Mich.)	5	71
Adams (Wash.)	70	8	Schneebeli (Pa.)	10	71
Mink (Ha.)	70	5	Holt (Md.)*	5	84
O'Neill (Mass.)	60	8	Conable (N.Y.)*	5	63
Ashley (Ohio)*	55	13	Average	8.1	78.6
Gibbons (Fla.)	45	48			
Derrick (S.C.)*	40	57			
Giaimo (Conn.)*	40	10			
O'Hara (Mich.)	35	19			
Wright (Tex.)*	30	19			
Runnels (N.M.)	5	88			
Landrum (Ga.)	5	76			
Burleson (Tex.)*	0	93			
Committee Average, 94th Cong.	51.7	27.1			
Average for the 94th Congress	56.7	26.7		15.2	69.1

New Members on House Budget Committee—95th Congress

DEMOCRATS			REPUBLICANS		
Name	ADA Rating	ACA Rating	Name	ADA Rating	ACA Rating
Fraser (Minn.)	95	0	Duncan (Tenn.)	15	89
Mineta (Calif.)	95	0	Rousselot (Calif.)	5	88
Obey (Wisc.)	90	12	Burgener (Calif.)	15	85
Lehman (Fla.)	80	4	Regula (Ohio)	10	54
Simon (Ill.)	80	0	Average	9	80
Pike (N.Y.)	75	25			
Fisher (Va.)	70	22			
Mattox (Tex.)	—	—			
Average	83.5	9			
Committee Average, 95th Congress	66.7	16.6		8.7	81.3

Source: Ratings as published in *Congressional Quarterly Weekly Reports.*

*Remained on House Budget Committee in the 95th Congress.

tained in the new members appointed in the Ninety-fifth Congress beginning in 1977. Table 4-1 suggests that the Democrats, in turn, attempted to "liberalize" the committee in the Ninety-fifth Congress. While the four most liberal members stayed on, two of the three most conservative (Phillip Landrum of Georgia and Harold Runnels of New Mexico) did not. In addition, Omar Burleson of Texas was challenged by Pete Stark of California, and retained his seat by a narrow margin in the Democratic caucus vote.

Liberalizing becomes even more apparent in examining the new Democratic members. As a group, they were considerably more liberal than House Democrats as a whole with ADA ratings ranging from 70 to 95. As the average ratings for the committee in the Ninety-fifth Congress show, the complexion of the Democratic members changed considerably from the previous Congress. The result of the selection process left the Budget Committee clearly divided between liberal Democrats and conservative Republicans.

Changes in the makeup of the Democrat members of the committee was possible partly because of a rules change adopted by the Democratic caucus before the start of the Ninety-fifth Congress.[12] Under the old rules, the chairmen of the Appropriations and Ways and Means Committees were allowed to nominate the three Democratic members from their committees to serve on the Budget Committee. The Budget Committee was not allowed to organize until the other two committees had established their membership, which meant a delay in getting the Budget Committee started. Outgoing Budget Committee Chairman Brock Adams made the proposal to strip Appropriations and Ways and Means chairmen of this power and, instead, have the Democratic Steering and Policy Committee make recommendations to the caucus. Adams argued that this would allow the Budget Committee to organize sooner and be better prepared to receive the president's budget in January. But the move also vested more control in the Democratic leaders who have considerable influence on the Steering and Policy Committee. Opponents complained that this would allow the Budget Committee to be manipulated by the leadership, but the change in rules passed in caucus by a vote of 75 to 44.[13]

The process of selection and membership play an important role in determining the climate, goals, and decisions of the committee. The House Budget Committee is unique in several ways. Besides restrictions on tenure, there is official representation of other standing committees and the leadership. By the actions of both party caucuses, the Budget Committee is made up of representatives with starkly contrasting political philosophies.

GOALS

Although some have suggested that members of Congress have only one goal—reelection—it is probably more correct to assume they have different preferences for committee assignments because they have different values and objectives.[14] Research on committees has indicated that while each member is different in his or her own way, certain individual goals tend to predominate on certain committees.[15] Service on the Public Works or Interior Committees may help a member's chances for reelection, since they may be able to obtain tangible benefits for the district. A seat on the Appropriations, Rules, or Ways and Means Committee may increase a member's influence in the Congress. Service on committees such as International Relations or Education and Labor may provide a member with a chance to shape major national policies and develop a reputation as an expert. Richard Fenno has suggested three basic sets of goals pursued by members of Congress, and it is possible to classify the committee by the dominant goals.[16] Table 4-2 shows this classification scheme and some examples, with the addition of a fourth category to encompass the Budget Committee.

Table 4-2.
MEMBER GOALS AND TYPES OF HOUSE COMMITTEES

Dominant Member Goals	Type of Committee	Examples
1. To help foster chances for reelection	Constituency	Post Office Interior Public Works
2. To gain influence within the Congress	Power	Appropriations Rules Ways and Means
3. To help shape major national policies	Policy	Education and Labor International Relations Budget (Republicans)
4. To successfully change practices and procedures within Congress	Process	Budget (Democrats)

Source: Adapted from Richard Fenno, *Congressmen in Committee* (Boston: Little, Brown and Co., 1973).

The fourth set of member goals concerns the procedures of Congress; a committee where these objectives dominate is labeled a "process" committee. The closest analogy may be the Rules Committee, but while process and legislative procedures are subgoals of the committee, it can still be classified primarily as a power committee. Although the Budget Committee appears to be the only existing committee that fits this category, goals are defined generally on the grounds that they may be important to other committees in the future. The House Budget Committee is particularly difficult to classify, because of its partisan nature. Implicit in a categorization of committees is the assumption that the dominant goals are shared by members of both the majority and minority party. This assumption cannot be made concerning the Budget Committee. As Table 4-2 suggests, the most salient goal expressed by committee Democrats in the first few years was a process goal—implementing and protecting the stringent require-ments of the congressional budget process. Committee Republicans, in contrast, were primarily concerned with policy goals—balancing the federal budget and halting the expansion of domestic spending. While many Re-publicans express concern for the process and many Democrats express policy concerns, there exists a distinct division between the two in terms of the most *salient* objective. Taking the Budget Committee as a whole, it can be classified as a process/policy committee.

What evidence is there to support this classification? Might the other kinds of dominant member goals apply to the Budget Committee? Like all members of Congress, those on the Budget Committee are concerned with reelection. It is not an assignment, however, that provides members with a good opportunity to enhance their reelection chances. In fact, some mem-bers indicate that service on the Budget Committee is *detrimental* to re-election; support of the budget resolutions has caused problems back in the district. As one member put it after the first few years:

I have supported all of the resolutions in committee and on the floor but I can tell you that I've caught some flack back home for a budget with a deficit of $60 billion dollars. It's hard to convince people that with unemployment at 8% a sizable deficit is virtually inevitable.*

Although the Budget Committee deals with huge sums of money, unlike Appropriations or Public Works, it is difficult for members to point to tangible benefits secured for the district. At least until 1979, a seat on the Budget Committee was not sought to enhance reelection chances.

While some observers and participants agree that the Budget Committee has become relatively powerful in a short period of time, it does not qualify as a power committee. Members of the House do not seek a seat on the committee to gain power and influence within Congress. Yet, because of its "watchdog" function and continued support for the budget process by the Democratic leadership and members, it has become a force to be reckoned with. A Democratic member related this anecdote:

We have become quite influential in a very short period of time and there are dozens of behind the scenes examples of our clout. The other day a colleague said to me, jokingly but with some serious meaning, "You guys on Budget run everything—we can't even get a damned rule without your approval."

*This quote and the other unattributed quotes that follow have been taken from personal interviews given the author during the period 1975-1978.

But others still find the Budget Committee a pale reflection of the more established money committees. A senior Republican member commented:

Budget is a minor committee and is going to stay a minor committee; it is not greatly sought after. In the real world Ways and Means is a higher quality group and in terms of one's career it makes sense. I've been on Ways and Means for ten years; when the meetings conflict, naturally I go to Ways and Means where I can have a more meaningful experience.

That the Budget Committee is a process committee, for the Democratic members at least, is convincingly indicated by the consistent patterns of responses of the majority members. They stress the importance of the process per se to the Congress as a policy-making institution. Many mention the history of previous failures and are well-versed on the experiences in the late 1940s. Members claim that the procedures are absolutely essential if Congress is to gain control over the budget and demonstrate to the public that members can act with restraint and self-discipline. If Congress is to compete with the executive branch in determining national priorities, it is their job to see that the budget process does not fail. The following comments by three Democratic members are typical:

This is like a supervisory committee—the most important thing we do is manage budget forms and procedures. Our main goal is to insure that the House is responsible and disciplined in its overall expenditure of funds.

The members of this committee have an overview of what the government does and what the Congress does. We are the only ones who can make sure that Congress again becomes a full partner in fiscal policy and budgeting. We can only do this by restraining the impulses of other committees. It is absolutely essential that we protect the integrity of the process and beat back all attempts to subvert it.

The most important thing we can do in these first few years is to insure that the process works. We all have our own pet programs but individual issues must be placed second to the greater good this process can bring to the Congress.

If maintaining the budget is the primary goal of the Democrats on the committee, the responses of the Republicans just as clearly indicate that the process itself is a secondary goal. They express a high level of frustration and disillusionment with the process. Most indicate that economizing, balancing the budget, and cutting spending are their primary goals as members of the Budget Committee. Because they feel they have been unsuccessful in this, many Republican members feel their objective is to clarify party differences to show it is the Democrats who are the big spenders, not they:

Many of us [the Republicans] worked hard for its passage [the Budget Act] and supported it in anticipation that it would be a fiscal straightjacket—it hasn't worked out that way. Because of the continuation of excessive deficit spending we have been unwilling to support any of the resolutions even though we support the process. We have been forced into the situation of having to vote no on everything.

There is just one reason I'm on this committee—to cut federal spending.

Not one thing has changed [since the implementation of budget reform] and the big spenders have not been controlled one iota. We have racked up the largest deficits in the history of our country *since* this thing was passed. Why should we support the budget process for its own sake when it just means a continuation of disastrous economic policies?

In distinguishing between member goals, it is important not to overstate the differences. Republicans and Democrats articulate both process *and* policy goals; the distinction is one of emphasis and behavior. Committee members of both parties mention the importance of budgetary policy for the country in setting priorities and determining the state of the economy. Many Democrats have specific policy goals in serving on the committee: cutting defense spending, helping the cities, reducing unemployment. Like the Republicans, many of the most liberal members of the committee have been dissatisfied with the budget resolutions. Unlike the Republicans, however, most have supported the resolutions. An urban Democrat expressed it in these terms:

I have been very dissatisfied with the budget resolutions that we have approved. We're still spending too much on the Pentagon and fiscal policy that establishes unemployment of 7% is a national disgrace. But I have supported the resolutions on the floor most of the time because they would fail without our votes, and I think in the long run the budget process will work to our advantage.

Although all members express both process and policy goals, the Democratic members have been willing to place process goals over policy goals, while the Republican members have not. This pattern is in contrast to the Senate, where Republicans have worked closely with the majority, and where the budget process has had a much easier time.

If the House Budget Committee could accurately be classified as a process/policy committee on the basis of member goals from 1975 to 1979, events at the beginning of the Ninety-sixth Congress demonstrate the impermanent nature of classifications and suggest possible lines of evolution. The extension of the tenure limitation from four to six years out of ten offered the possibility that within a few years, all tenure limitations will be dropped and the committee would offer significantly greater career opportunities for members. Despite its apparent unattractiveness in terms of fostering reelection chances, the upsurge in interest in fiscal policy and a balanced budget made the committee more attractive in the Ninety-sixth Congress. The traditional measure of committee prestige is the number of requests by members to fill vacancies. At the start of the Ninety-sixth Congress, the House Budget Committee was the *most* requested committee in the House, beating out even the Appropriations and Ways and Means Committees. [17] Most of the requests were from senior members; only seven of the twenty-four requests were from freshmen.

Does this signal a major change in the committee? Not yet, but it suggests movement from its infancy to a more mature stage of development. It indicates that committee attractiveness is policy related. Members' perceptions of how assignment to the Budget Committee relates to their own goals is changing, as political trends in the nation change. The Budget Committee must remain process oriented for the present because the basic cleavage in the House is still very much present. If after several years the budget is balanced, partisanship is diminished, and the process is genuinely secure, the dominant orientation of the members may change.

ENVIRONMENT

Like other committees in Congress, the Budget Committee operates within an environment of demands and pressures from outside groups and institutions. Fenno suggests there are four prominent clusters of outsiders: members of the parent house, members of the executive branch, members of clientele groups, and members of the party leadership. [18] Because committees differ in terms of functions and member goals, they will be affected differently by outside influences. Committee members will tend to be most concerned with the outside group that can most directly affect the achievement of their goals. For example, since Appropriations and Ways and Means are concerned with internal power within the House, they are most concerned with the constraints imposed by the parent chamber. The House International Relations Committee, concerned with its impact on foreign policy, is most affected by executive branch actors (president, secretary of state, national security advisor, etc.). With the dominant goal of enhancing reelection chances, a committee such as Interior is concerned with clientele groups. While all committees in Congress share some common environmental constraints, differences in basic goals and orientation make certain aspects of the external environment most prominent for each committee.

The Budget Committee is similar to Ways and Means and Appropriations in that the other members of the House have the most direct effect on the achievement of its goals. Since the primary objective of the majority of the committee members is to insure the success of the budget process, success depends directly on the support of the rest of the House.

SUPPORT OF HOUSE MEMBERS

Only by consistently gaining the support of a majority of the members of the House can the Budget Committee be successful. Unlike other committees that might suffer some small loss of prestige at the defeat of a bill, failure of the Budget Committee to maneuver a budget resolution through the House by the deadline could lead to a paralysis of Congress and may mean the demise of the budget process itself. The Budget Committee's very existence depends on the support of the parent chamber. As was shown in Chapter 3, the process of maintaining majority support has been difficult.

Table 4-3 examines the voting alignments for the budget resolutions in the House. House Republicans have overwhelmingly voted against the budget resolutions; until May of 1977, only a handful out of the approximately 135 votes cast by Republicans were in favor of the resolutions. The twenty-nine Republican votes cast in favor of the conference resolution in May 1977 was seen as a watershed by some Budget Committee Democrats hoping to broaden the base of support for the process. But with only four Republican votes in September 1977, and only two or three in 1978 and 1979, this did not prove to be the case. In contrast to the House pattern, Senate Republicans, by a slim margin, have supported most of the resolutions (see Table 5-2, Chapter 5). In addition, House Democrats have defected on both sides; between twenty-five and forty Southern Democrats have voted against the resolutions (most because spending and the deficit were too large) and twenty to thirty Northern Democrats opposed the resolutions (about equally divided between those who felt the spending and deficit were too large and those who felt they were too small). In 1979, the process was just as partisan as it had been in 1975. The difficulty of balancing liberal and conservative demands so that a budget resolution could pass placed severe constraints on the policy choices available to the committee. The environment of conflict in the House imposes the most significant constraints on the actions of the committee.

OTHER COMMITTEES

The Budget Committee must not only deal with the House as a whole, but with the committees and subcommittees. The budget process has had a major effect on the operations and timetable of the standing committees. The most significant constraint imposed by the other committees is related to the different role orientations and functions in the budget process. Concerned with taking an overview and restricting spending, the role of the Budget Committee is in direct conflict with the policy goals of other committees. When economizing threatens defense spending, opposition from the Armed Forces Committee and Defense Appropriations Subcommittee can be expected.

Table 4-3.
HOUSE VOTES ON BUDGET RESOLUTIONS, 1975-1979

Date	Resolution	Vote Yes-No	Republicans Yes-No	Democrats Yes-No	Northern Democrats Yes-No	Southern Democrats Yes-No
5/ 1/75	Committee Report-1st, FY 1976	200-196	3-128	197-68	151-33	46-35
5/14/75	Conference Report-1st, FY 1976	230-193	5-138	225-55	164-28	61-27
11/12/75	Committee Report-2nd, FY 1976	225-191	11-124	214-67	162-31	52-36
12/12/75	Conference Report-2nd, FY 1976	189-187	3-126	186-61	147-21	39-40
4/29/76	Committee Report-1st, FY 1977	221-155	13-111	208-44	159-20	40-24
5/13/76	Conference Report-1st, FY 1977	224-170	10-125	214-45	161-21	53-24
9/ 9/76	Committee Report-2nd, FY 1977	227-151	12-113	215-38	154-16	61-22
9/16/76	Conference Report-2nd, FY 1977	234-143	21-107	213-36	156-17	57-19
2/23/77	Committee Report-3rd, FY 1977	239-169	14-119	225-50	176-15	49-35
3/ 3/77	Conference Report-3rd, FY 1977	226-173	8-122	218-51	172-16	46-35
4/27/77	Original Committee Report-1st, FY 1978	84-320	2-135	82-185	50-132	32-53
5/ 5/77	Revised Committee Report-1st, FY 1978	213-179	7-121	206-58	142-39	64-19
5/17/77	Conference Report-1st, FY 1978	221-177	29-107	192-70	122-53	70-17
9/ 8/77	Committee Report-2nd, FY 1978	199-188	4-129	195-59	139-32	56-27
9/15/77	Conference Report-2nd, FY 1978	215-187	4-132	211-55	148-33	63-22
5/10/78	Committee Report-1st, FY 1979	201-197	3-136	198-61	152-25	46-36
5/17/78	Conference Report-1st, FY 1979	201-198	2-133	199-65	134-47	65-18
8/16/78	Committee Report-2nd, FY 1979	217-178	2-136	215-42	154-25	61-17
9/21/78	Conference Report-2nd, FY 1979	225-162	7-123	218-39	158-22	60-17
5/14/79	Committee Report-1st, FY 1980	220-184	9-134	211-50	147-33	64-17
5/24/79	Conference Report-1st, FY 1980	202-196	28-116	174-80	103-70	71-10
9/27/79	Committee Report-2nd, FY 1980	212-206	0-154	185-77	122-57	63-20
11/28/79	Conference Report-2nd, FY 1980	206-186	3-140	203-46	141-28	62-18

Source: Congressional Quarterly Weekly Reports.

To some extent, the level of detail used by the House Budget Committee has aroused concern among the other committees. The Budget Committee has been "warned" not to infringe on the prerogatives of other committees on various occasions. This is the exception rather than the rule, however. The House Budget Committee has maintained the support of other committees generally by acceding to their spending desires. Through accommodation and deference to the standing committees, the Budget Committee has sacrificed policy impact for procedural protections. As will be shown in Chapter 6, the Budget Committee makes cuts in the figures submitted by the committees, but the committees have padded the requests enough to protect their options. Given the dependence of the Budget Committee on external support, and its weakness in the early years, this was inevitable. As the process becomes more institutionalized, however, the committee may attempt to limit the actions of the standing committees.

Ways and Means and Appropriations are the two most important committees in terms of the Budget Committee's environment. The nature of the Budget Act severely limits the impact that the Budget Committee can have on revenues, and Ways and Means has not perceived it as a threat to its own jurisdiction. Because expenditures are broken down into functional subtotals, the Appropriations Committee has been more affected. But, with a few exceptions, the relationship has been one of cooperation. Interviews with members of both committees generally confirmed the view of cooperation. Those with overlapping memberships perceive virtually no conflict. Most members of the Budget Committee believe they have been cautious in their dealings with the two money committees commenting that, "we have not pressed" or, "we have tread very lightly with them."

PARTY LEADERS

The situation that developed in passing the third resolution for 1977 and Carter's stimulus package indicates the essential role the party leadership plays in relation to the Budget Committee. As a new committee, and an assignment that is secondary to many members, support of the leadership is essential for its success. The Budget Committee is not nearly as independent or autonomous as the other standing committees, nor is it likely to become so as long as it has a revolving membership. The leadership in the House has been behind the Budget Committee in its efforts to pass resolutions and at other crucial junctures. Under Speaker Albert and Speaker O'Neill, the Democratic leadership has played an active role in the budget process. According to most observers, O'Neill and Wright have been more aggressive in supporting the process than Albert, and also more adept in what some members consider "using" the budget process to their advantage. One member commented:

They [the Speaker and Majority Leader] have discovered how powerful a leadership tool the budget process can be and they are beginning to use it to their advantage more and more. If they are opposed to an additional spending program, they can say, "sorry, it violates the targets." If they support it, they can lay back and let it get a waiver.

The relationship between the committee and the leaders is one of inter-dependency. Although leadership support is important to all committees, it is an even more important environmental factor for the Budget Committee.

The Republican leadership in the House has reflected the actions and attitudes of the Republican committee members. They have consistently opposed all budget resolutions for policy reasons and as a result their impact has been slight.

EXECUTIVE BRANCH

Executive requests and the president's budget are key referents for the Budget Committee. Because of an emphasis on fiscal policy, the important executive branch actors tend to be administration economic advisors and OMB officials. Despite the desire of Congress to increase its independence in budgeting, the president's figures remain a crucial element in the Budget Committee's deliberations. In committee hearings, testimony is taken regularly from the OMB director, the head of the treasury, the chairman of the president's Council of Economic Advisors, and other executive branch officials.

Congress approved spending levels some $20 billion higher than those requested by President Ford for fiscal years 1976 and 1977. They showed they could be responsive to the president in accommodating President Carter's requests for changes in the fiscal 1977 budget by passing the third resolution. Soon afterwards, however, many members were critical of the president for withdrawing the plan for a $50 tax rebate and for interference in the passage of the first resolution for fiscal 1978. The committee must attempt to balance the desire to cooperate with the president, particularly if he is a Democrat, with demands from within Congress. It was easier with Ford in the White House. But even with a Democratic president, the House Budget Committee must put the requisites of building a majority above all else. A strong president could assist them in their task, much the same as party leaders. But to date, opposing the president has been as effective as supporting him.

INTEREST GROUPS

Soon after the implementation of the budget process, interest groups descended upon the two Budget committees. Recognizing their importance in the national budget process, a variety of spokespersons have attempted to influence the targets and ceilings recommended by the committees. Organized labor has regularly testified before the committees, making suggestions not only on labor-related spending programs, but national fiscal policy as well. Labor's lobbying efforts to extend the terms of House Budget Committee members is but one example of specific issues it has addressed. State and local governments, one of the primary beneficiaries of federal spending, were particularly active in the late 1970s. The increased pressure to balance the budget and cut spending threatened revenue sharing and a variety of categorical grants. Irked at the states' passing resolutions calling for a constitutional amendment to balance the budget, Congress considered serious cuts in these programs, before reapproving them.

Business, labor, farm, and beneficiary groups have attempted to lobby the Budget committees. Groups such as the National Taxpayers Union have stressed fiscal policy goals in pushing for a balanced budget and tax cuts. Although interest groups form a meaningful part of the committee's environment, they play a less prominent role than for other congressional committees. Budget is clearly not a client-oriented committee. The attitude of the committee, in pursuing process and fiscal policy goals, is to downplay special interest concerns. It must consider the budget as a whole and attempt to minimize the specific spending appeals that are rampant in the rest of the Congress.

Given the process-orientation of the House Budget Committee, the most critical elements of its environment are the other members and committees in the House. The desires of executive branch actors and interest groups are considered, but policy advocacy from standing committees has a much greater impact on committee decisions. Given this set of environmental constraints, the House Budget Committee has developed strategies to achieve its goal of insuring the survival of the congressional budget process.

STRATEGIES

Fenno defines strategic premises as prescriptions for decision making, which allow a view of the committee as a working group, an accommodation of individual goals that can be translated into substantive decision-rules.[19] Because the Republican and Democratic members of the Budget Committee are operating under a different set of goals, the strategies they employ are also divergent.

The first two strategic premises for the Democratic members of the committee are process oriented; the first is *to write a resolution that can pass the House*. In their deliberations, members make reference to this strategy in assessing the diverse elements in the House. Attention is focused on establishing budget totals that will be acceptable to the moderate center of the Democratic party and most liberals. However, the committee clearly believes it more dangerous to be too high, alienating conservative Democrats, than to be too low, alienating liberals. This is a most delicate task that involves not only total spending and the size of the deficit, but the balance of spending between defense and social welfare programs. Since the committee Democrats were considerably more liberal than the House as a whole, this strategy is often frustrating to members' policy goals. The basic strategic premise of the committee is suggested in the following statement by a member:

The committee bill must be good because on both sides there are those who say the committee bill is too high, and others who say the committee bill is too low. The committee tried to strike a happy medium between the forces that govern this House.[20]

The defeat of the first resolution for fiscal 1978 and its revision is perhaps the best example of the delicacy of the balance necessary to get 50 percent of the House to accept a resolution. When the amendment increasing defense outlays altered the balance, the moderate-liberal coalition fell apart. The most important factor in the passage of the compromise resolution was not so much satisfying policy goals of members, but the extra effort made by the committee and the leadership to stress *process* goals.

The second process-oriented strategy of the committee is *to accommodate most of the spending objectives of the standing committees*. This strategy is not one that is suggested by committee members, but it becomes apparent in examining their behavior. Clearly there is an inconsistency between this strategy and the general budget-cutting, watchdog role. The difficulty of the committee's task and the need to safeguard the procedures in the early years made this imperative, however. Because the standing committees tend to overstate their needs, the Budget Committee is able to cut requests. But usually they do not impose cuts that threaten the programs under the jurisdiction of the other committees.

The committee attempts to make these decisions in committee, not on the House floor. In its effort to protect the process, the members consciously attempt to defeat floor amendments to resolutions. Changes of seemingly minor consequence can cripple resolutions and preclude passage. Table 4-4 examines the number and success of amendments to the budget resolutions offered on the floor. Although cases are few, it is clear why the committee attempts to defeat amendments which alter the balance it has created.

Two additional strategies of committee Democrats are policy related. Members attempt *to provide sufficient stimulus to promote growth and employment*. This fiscal policy is difficult and there is considerable disagree-

Table 4-4.
FLOOR AMENDMENTS TO HOUSE BUDGET COMMITTEE RESOLUTIONS

Concurrent Resolution/ Fiscal Year	Number of Floor Amendments Offered	Number of Floor Amendments Passed	Outcome of Resolution
1st CR FY 76	3	1	passed
2nd CR FY 76	4	2	passed
1st CR FY 77	9	2	passed
2nd CR FY 77	1	0	passed
3rd CR FY 77	1	0	passed
1st CR FY 78	12	6	*defeated*
2nd CR FY 78	4	1	passed
1st CR FY 79	7	2	passed
2nd CR FY 79	6	1	passed
1st CR FY 80	35	9	*defeated*
2nd CR FY 80	6	1	passed

Source: Compiled from *Congressional Quarterly Weekly Reports*, 1975-1979.

ment about how much is enough. But the most salient policy concern of committee Democrats has been to establish a budget that will promote jobs and growth. This was particularly evident in the first two years when the committee was responding to recession and Ford's budgets. The second policy related strategy apparent in the history of the budget process is *to restrain growth in federal spending*. Of course, this premise is often at odds with providing adequate stimulus, and one could suggest that there is a tradeoff between the two. Over the course of the first five years, there has been a discernible movement from the first to the second, as pressure to reduce spending has mounted. The latter strategy is translated into action when the Budget Committee attempts to prevent bills that violate the targets in the first resolution from reaching the floor. Because of the relative weakness and its desire to retain support from the standing committees, the House Budget Committee has not aggressively challenged bills on the floor as has its Senate counterpart. Adams and Giaimo have attempted to work behind the scenes, using persuasion and negotiation to enforce the targets.

The last policy related strategy of the majority members overlaps with the strategies of the minority. Committee Republicans indicate that their goal has been to cut and balance the budget. The main strategic premise of the Republicans has been *to clarify partisan policy differences*. In attempting to achieve their policy objectives, they have virtually excluded themselves from the process. Since the majority received no support from the minority members, the coalition is built without them; since they have little or no say over the content of the resolutions, they use their seat on the committee as a forum to demonstrate the differences between Republican and Democratic economic policy. A minority member commented:

This has not been a happy time for us [the Republicans] on the committee and we are really nonentities as far as having any say over the numbers. Most of us use the committee as a means to show the public that there is an alternative to the big spending of the Democrats. Our views have not been acted on but our voices have been heard.

All the evidence to this point has suggested some exceptionally deep divisions on the committee: a cleavage in fundamental goals and differing strategic premises. The examination of decision making further clarifies the divisions that exist in the Budget Committee.

DECISION MAKING

Even though it is a new committee, like other committees in Congress the House Budget Committee has established a "normal" decision-making process. In its short existence, the committee has stabilized the means by which it arrives at budget totals. Three aspects of committee decision-making—partisanship, participation specialization, and leadership help compare and contrast the Budget Committee to other committees in the House.

PARTISANSHIP

The dominance of partisanship has commanded a central role in the analysis to this point. Because of its pervasiveness in the committee's environment, it inevitably is a central aspect of committee decision-making. The Education and Labor Committee and the Ways and Means Committee have been portrayed in previous studies as the most partisan in the House. [21] The norm on the Ways and Means Committee, however, is what John Manley has called "restrained partisanship."

Though the two committees share a high degree of partisanship at the point of decision, the importance of partisanship during the *deliberative stage* of committee work differs radically. . . . Ways and Means members limit the play of partisanship to the final stages of decision making and do most of their work in a nonpartisan atmosphere. Education and Labor proceeds, at all stages, in an atmosphere charged with partisanship. [22]

The Budget Committee clearly more closely approximates the latter pattern of unrestrained partisanship and, in fact, exceeds it. This becomes apparent when disagreements and partisanship in committee reports are compared. Table 4-5 indicates that the Budget Commitee stands apart from other committees in the extent of committee partisanship.

The Budget Committee has responsibility for a more limited set of policy concerns than the other committees; its annual output of major legislation in normal years is the two concurrent resolutions. In every case, to date, there has been committee disagreement and each time, this disagreement has been partisan disagreement (minority views in the report by the Republican members). This stands in stark contrast to nonpartisan committees such as Appropriations and is considerably greater than even the other partisan committees. This is consistent, however, with everything that has been established about the Budget Committee in terms of conflicting member goals, a partisan environment, and strategic premises.

The partisan cleavage becomes more apparent by examining the voting behavior within the committee. In the Ninety-fourth Congress, the Budget Committee held twenty-four recorded roll call votes. As Table 4-6 shows, nineteen of these votes can be classified as party votes with a majority of Republicans opposing a majority of Democrats. This greatly exceeds that of other committees. Table 4-6 indicates the party support scores of each committee member on the nineteen party votes. Republican committee members demonstrate a high degree of party unity in their voting. They were usually joined by three Democratic members Runnels, Landrum, and Burleson. This tended to make committee votes closely divided and left Sam Gibbons of Florida and Butler Derrick of South Carolina as swing votes on the committee. Nine of the twenty-four committee roll calls were decided by a margin of one vote. Decision-making in the committee can be characterized as a constant battle; the majority can count on opposition to almost every proposal. Unlike other committees, there are no ground rules against unrestrained conflict on the committee; no precedent to attempt to present a united front to protect committee prestige. Committee members of both parties recognize the highly partisan nature of the Budget Committee. One Republican member commented: "This is a very partisan committee compared to other committees I'm on; Armed Services is nothing like this." A more senior Democratic member suggested:

This is probably the most partisan committee in the Congress. I've never seen anything like it before. And it detracts from serving on the committee because everything, even trivial things, become fights.

Republicans claim the partisanship is caused by the Democrats' ignoring their policy concerns. Democrats blame the Republicans for failing to take

Table 4-5.
COMMITTEE DISAGREEMENT AND PARTISANSHIP
(Comparison of Budget Committees, 1975-1980,
to Other Committees, 1955-1965)

Committee	Legislation	Percent of Recorded Disagreements	Percent of Party Disagreements	Party Disagree- ments as % of Recorded Disagreements
Budget	12	100% (12)	100% (12)	100%
Ways and Means	114	56 (59)	26 (30)	50
Education and Labor	96	56 (54)	25 (27)	50
Interior	78	35 (27)	8 (6)	22
Post Office	42	38 (16)	7 (3)	19
Foreign Affairs	66	24 (16)	5 (3)	19
Appropriations	154*	7 (11)	0 (0)	0

Source: Based on committee reports on major legislation. Adapted from Richard Fenno, *Congressman in Committee* (Boston: Little Brown, 1973), p. 84. Data on Budget Committee Reports on Concurrent Resolutions on the Budget, fiscal years 1976-80 (including Third Resolutions for fiscal years 1977 and 1979) have been added.

*Original appropriations bills only.

Table 4-6.
PARTY VOTING ON COMMITTEE ROLL CALLS:
HOUSE BUDGET COMMITTEE, 1975-1977

Democrats	Party Support Score*	Republicans	Party Support Score*
Adams (Wash.)	100%	Conable (N.Y.)	100%
Wright (Tex.)	100	Schneebeli (Pa.)	95
O'Neill (Mass.)	95	Broyhill (N.C.)	95
Mitchell (Md.)	95	Clawson (Calif.)	95
Mink (Ha.)	95	Latta (Ohio)	89
Giaimo (Conn.)	89	Cederberg (Mich.)	89
Leggett (Calif.)	84	Shriver (Kans.)	89
Stokes (Ohio)	84	Holt (Md.)	89
Ashley (Ohio)	79		
Smith (Iowa)	79		
O'Hara (Mich.)	79		
Holtzman (N.Y.)	68		
Gibbons (Fla.)	58		
Derrick (S.C.)	47		
Runnels (N.M.)	16		
Landrum (Ga.)	11		
Burleson (Tex.)	5		

Source: House Budget Committee.

*Two of the nineteen party votes were straight party line votes.

Party Vote: Defined as a majority of committee Democrats opposing a majority of committee Republicans (total number of recorded roll call votes, N=24; party votes, N=19, or 80%).

Party support score: Percentage of times a member voted with the majority of his or her party in committee on a party vote.

any responsibility for the committee and the budget process. As one Democrat put it, "they simply choose to ignore the realities of the House membership." Although both parties lament the situation, there is no indication it will be changed in the near future.

The Budget Committee is unique among major committees in the House, where in spite of publicized partisan disputes, the normal pattern is for members of both parties to work hand in hand. This is partially a function of the environment in the House, but is also caused by the selection of members by both parties. Further, the temporary nature of the assignment removes the major incentive for members to cooperate in establishing and preserving the reputation of the committee.

PARTICIPATION-SPECIALIZATION

The House Budget Committee has no subcommittees; the major work of the committee is done by the full committee. Because there are slack times in the calendar of budgeting, the committee has established task forces to study particular issues. Although these may be seen as *de facto* subcommittees, they do not play a significant role in committee decision making. Unlike the Appropriations Committee, subcommittee autonomy is not a significant factor. Neither are specialization and reciprocity norms of noticeable impact on the committee. Because the committee members all are members of other substantive committees, there is a tendency for members to be advocates for particular functions and programs. This behavior contradicts the basic strategic premise of the committee to balance interests and write a resolution that can pass the House. Therefore, "specialization" by committee members takes on negative connotations. The more dominant attitude is to "look at the big picture"; to be generalists rather than specialists. This norm is enforced informally by the chairman and other members who chide offenders about their "pet programs" and remind them that their main task is to balance divergent interests and the needs of all programs.

The limitation of four, then six, years service out of ten does not allow for long periods of committee apprenticeship as on other committees. A freshman member suggested that this can be advantageous for new members:

One of the reasons I tried to get on the Budget Committee is because there is no seniority here. I can have as much impact as the more senior members. I will have to wait around for years to have this much influence on other committees.

Some expertise in the area of economics and fiscal policy is necessary. But many of the Republicans do not accept the tenets of Keynesian economics and believe that most of the Budget Committee staff is partisan, biased, and does not serve their needs. The tenure limitations seem to make the staff more important on the Budget Committee than on other committees. Because many members lack expertise, the staff has played a central role in committee decision making. This sometimes affects attendance and participation at committee sessions. Since some members view the committee as a secondary assignment, attendance at other committee sessions has been a higher priority.

LEADERSHIP

The Budget Committee has had three chairmen in its first five years: Al Ullman briefly, Brock Adams, and Robert Giaimo whose term extended from 1977 to 1981. Adams attempted to act as conciliator in heading the committee but was unsuccessful in gaining Republican support. In spite of the partisanship, most of the Republicans were positive about his leadership role: "He tried hard to include us in the deliberations, we just didn't have the votes." Most felt he was fair to them but could make few concessions to them in drafting the resolutions. Democratic members also expressed general satisfaction with Adams's leadership, but some of the most liberal members felt he made too many concessions to the conservatives: "He started out as a fiscal liberal but ended up opposing things he ordinarily would have been for." Given the process-policy dichotomy on the committee, this comment may reveal the essential ingredient of Budget Committee leadership.

Adams began the practice of presenting the chairman's "mark" at the start of committee deliberations: a specific set of totals for the members to consider. This provides the committee with a starting point and tends to accentuate the chairman's role as conciliator. It also creates a trial balloon that elicits reactions from other members and acts as a vehicle for the leadership to offer conciliatory amendments. This process differs from the process in the Senate in several ways.[23] Senator Muskie does not begin with a chairman's mark and is less specific in terms of detail. In addition, the House uses the president's requests as a baseline while the Senate uses current policy estimates.

Adams trod cautiously in defending the targets established by the resolutions. Unlike Muskie, Adams avoided direct confrontation with other committees on the floor of the House. This was partly a matter of survival; neither the committee nor its chairman had an established base of institutional power. The behind-the-scenes actions, with the assistance of the leadership, proved effective on several occasions where bills and amendments that would have violated the targets never reached the floor.

Giaimo was a more established member of the House and benefited from the experience of the first two years. One member commented: "Adams walked on eggshells; Giaimo has been able to use a hammer." Like his predecessor, however, Giaimo has faced the same environment and committee cleavages and has adopted the role of conciliator in attempting to coalesce the moderate elements of the House. Since Giaimo is one of the more moderate members of the committee, his selection as chairman over several more liberal competitors is consistent with a pattern of building a moderate coalition.

Minority members have expressed less satisfaction with Giaimo's leadership and feel he has made less of an attempt to consider their views. This may be related to his stronger majority on the committee due to the changes in membership in the Ninety-fifth Congress and the feeling by many Democrats that they might as well give up on Republican support. Athough the first budget resolution under his leadership failed on the House floor, many observers believe that the success of the compromise resolution (similar to the first) was a vindication of stronger leadership style.

Republican dissatisfaction with their situation on the committee extends to their own leadership. Ranking minority member, Delbert Latta is blamed by some members for their problems. One Republican member confided:

Latta is a singularly negative fellow and generally a poor leader. This negativism has set the tenor for our relations with the other side. Part of the problem has been that our staff was so bad. These new people will be excellent. Perhaps they will infuse the ranking minority member with more alternatives and information so we will be subject to less leather lunged honkery.

The leaders of the Budget Committee have had to walk a tightrope with the committee in much the same fashion as the committee must with the House. Even though the chairmen were precluded from establishing a powerful rein over the long run, they have been relatively influential in setting the agenda and guiding the committee.

The decision-making processes in the House are in sharp contrast to the Senate. The committee in the Senate is much less partisan, with only about 50 percent of the votes qualifying as party votes. Most notable is the cooperation between the chairman and ranking minority member. Senators Muskie and Bellmon have worked together in establishing the budget process in the Senate. While Latta and Adams voted together in committee only 14 percent of the time, Muskie and Bellmon voted together exactly 50 percent of the time.

The peculiarities in the decision-making process of the House Budget Committee are most clearly revealed in comparison to other committees. The Budget Committee is characterized by unrestrained partisanship throughout decision making to an extent not seen in other committees. Traditional norms of apprenticeship, specialization, reciprocity, and subcommittee autonomy do not apply here. The situation demands a moderate leadership attempting to bring together diverse and conflicting elements. The result is a process of decision making shaped by conflicting member goals and dictated by the environmental constraints of the House.

CONCLUSION

The House Committee on the Budget is less independent in its actions, less autonomous than other committees, and has not attained integration in its highly conflictual environment. Yet, on the standard used to measure the success of other committees, it has passed budget resolutions that have begun to alter the behavior of other committees. The base of support in the House has been tenuous, but the Budget Committee has managed to build and maintain a majority.

In some ways the Budget Committee is a hybrid, unlike any other standing committee in Congress. But its unique features provide some valuable insights into the nature of congressional committees. Tenure limitations on committee membership demonstrate the importance of the incentive system that is operative in other committees. Reduced career orientation makes participation a lower priority, and makes consensus more difficult to achieve. Combined with a selection process that appears to build an ideological cleavage, the committee operates in a partisan, some-what chaotic fashion, in sharp contrast to the other money committees. A significant difference with other committees is the inherent tension on the committee between process and policy objectives.

In comparison with other committees in Congress, the Budget Committee would appear to have every reason for being weak: dependence, lack of consensus, de-emphasis of expertise, lack of career incentives for members, and relatively low member satisfaction. But while it is not powerful in an institutional fashion such as the Ways and Means or Appropriations Committees, most members and non-members have conceded that the Budget Committee is becoming influential. This developing influence suggests the importance of formal power. While it is institutionally weak, it has power simply on the basis of the legal requirements of the Budget Act. As long as it can retain the support of a majority of House members, the Budget Committee will retain and enhance that influence.

In assessing the impact of any committee, it is useful to distinguish between institutional power, and policy influence. The Rules Committee, for example, is powerful because of its formal role in the legislative process. Ways and Means and Appropriations are powerful committees as much for what they do (budgeting, revenue, etc.) as for what they are (autonomous, independent, and integrated units). All three still may be considered "power" committees in terms of member goals, but the source of their influence is closely tied to their policy and procedural responsibilities. Previous emphasis on status, autonomy, integration, and internal dynamics of congressional committees has implicitly deemphasized the importance of formal power.

Yet in the final analysis, the emphasis on protecting the process in the first few years has weakened the policy impact of the Budget Committee. An attempt to assess the impact of budget reform in a more systematic fashion is made in Chapter 7, but a few preliminary conclusions on the committee are in order here. The House committee has worked hard to pass budget resolutions, but as yet it has not tried to reshape congressional priorities. The congressional budget is still more a function of previous committments and the actions of the standing committees. This should not negate the importance of the overview that the resolutions provide. Emphasis on the process has begun to institutionalize what may later become a significant instrument of congressional policy making.

The evolution of the committee is also apparent. In five years, the Budget Committee has become more recognized, and more popular, and more powerful. If the pressure for fiscal conservatism and balanced budgets continues to grow in the 1980s, the Budget Committee may emerge as the major focal point for congressional action. The committee most likely will push for more changes that will enhance its power and stabilize the budget process. The extension of terms for six years at the start of the Ninety-sixth Congress may be only the first such step. Committee members will prob-ably push to have all tenure limitations removed. They also may seek authority to bring budget resolutions to the floor under a closed or modified closed rule, to prevent "Christmas tree" amendments. Most importantly, the Democrats will continue to seek a broader base of support, including the Republicans. The sharp partisanship forces a continued emphasis on process, and seems to greatly restrict options available to the committee. As indicated in the next chapter, bipartisan support frees the Senate committee to concentrate on budget policy, not the budget process.

NOTES

1. For example, see Richard Fenno, "The House Appropriations Committee as a Political System: The Problem of Integration," *American Political Science Review* 56 (1962): 310-324; Ralph K. Huitt, "The Congressional Committee: A Case Study," *American Political Science Review* 48 (1954): 340-365; John Manley, "The House Committee on Ways and Means: Conflict Management in a Congres-sional Committee," *American Political Science Review* 59 (1965): 927-939.

2. Richard Fenno, *Congressmen in Committees* (Boston: Little, Brown, 1973).

3. Ibid., p. xv.

4. Ibid., pp. 278-279.

5. John Manley, *The Politics of Finance* (Boston: Little, Brown, 1970).

6. Nicholas Masters, "Committee Assignments," in Robert Peabody and Nel-son Polsby, eds., *New Perspectives on the House of Representatives* (Chicago: Rand McNally, 1969). Randall B. Ripley, *Congress: Process and Policy* (New York: Norton, 1975), pp. 96-98. William L. Morrow, *Congressional Committees* (New York: Scribners, 1969), pp. 42-45.

7. *Budget and Impoundment Control Act* (1974), section101(a)(5), pp. 93-333.

8. Allen Schick, "Budget Reform Legislation," *Harvard Journal on Legislation* 11, no. 2 (February 1974): 311.

9. *Congressional Quarterly Weekly Reports*, December 9, 1978, p. 3401.

10. Ibid., p. 3404.

11. These ratings are formulated annually by the ADA (Americans for Democratic Action) and the ACA (Americans for Constitutional Action). Both are scales ranging from 0 to 100, depending upon how a member voted on roll calls selected by the group. Although computed on a different set of votes, members' scores tend to be inversely related. Members are considered "liberal" if they score high on ADA and low on ACA; and are considered "conservative" if they score low on ADA and high on ACA. These ratings only include about 5 percent of the votes cast, but they do include major issues and are easily interpreted. Although scores based on multidimensional scaling would be preferable, the ADA and ACA ratings satisfactorily demonstrate the point that is being made here.

12. *Congressional Quarterly Weekly Reports*, January 15, 1977, p. 63.

13. Ibid., p. 64.

14. Morris Fiorina, *Congress: Keystone of the Washington Establishment* (New Haven, Conn.: Yale University Press, 1977).

15. Fenno, *Congressmen in Committees*, p. 1.

16. Ibid., pp. 15-45.

17. *Congressional Quarterly Weekly Reports*, January 27, 1979, p. 155.

18. Fenno, *Congressmen in Committees*, p. 15.

19. Ibid., p. 81.

20. Representative Sam Gibbons (D-Fla.), *Congressional Record*, April 30, 1975, U.S. Senate, 94th Cong., 1st sess., Committee on the Budget, *A Compendium of Materials* (October 1975), p. 877.

21. Fenno, *Congressmen in Committees*, p. 84; Manley, *Politics of Finance*.

22. Manley, *Politics of Finance*, p. 84.

23. John Ellwood and James Thurber, "The New Congressional Budget Process: The Hows and Whys of House-Senate Differences," in Lawrence Dodd and Bruce Oppenheimer, eds., *Congress Reconsidered* (New York: Praeger, 1977), p. 198.

5

The Senate
Budget Committee

*Many "conservatives" who claim title as guardians
of the Senate's fiscal integrity are unwilling to
settle for margarine where their own bread is
buttered.*
— Senator Edmund Muskie

The House of Representatives had enjoyed constitutional supremacy over the Senate in matters of government revenue and expenditures for 185 years. But with the passage of the Budget and Impoundment Control Act, the Senate became an equal partner with the House in the realm of fiscal affairs. Instead of waiting for the House to act first, the Senate considers concurrent resolutions on the budget simultaneously with them. Our initial observations suggested that the Senate committee appears to be stronger than its House counterpart. The analysis of the Senate Budget Committee is not totally unambiguous, however. Its record is mixed, and its actions present some contradictions. While the Senate committee has clearly attempted to enforce the resolutions more aggressively than the House committee, it has also accommodated and deferred to the existing power structure in the Senate.

As in the previous chapter, the analysis of the Senate Budget Committee will focus on membership, goals, environment, strategies and decision making. Comparisons with both the House Budget Committee and other committees will assist in evaluating the impact of the committee. Changes in the Senate related to the congressional budget process must also be considered in the context of more general shifts in the Senate. The almost unanimous sentiment is that the budget process has "worked" well in the Senate, but what does that mean? What impact has it had on the Senate as an institution? Has it shifted the centers of congressional power or changed national policy?

MEMBERSHIP

The Senate did not place tenure limitations on the Budget Committee, nor did it provide for direct representation of other committees or the party leadership. Although there was initially some sentiment for direct representation of the Senate Appropriations and Finance Committees, a majority of the Senate rejected these provisions. As we saw in Chapter 2, the conference committee that resolved the details of the bill in the spring of 1974 allowed each house of Congress to constitute the committees as they had in their respective bills. Representation of other money committees was still somewhat of an issue for the Republican and Democratic caucuses in selecting members for the Budget Committee. The original plan to have half of the six Republican members from the Finance Committee was scrapped by the GOP caucus.

Although not mandated by statute, there is informal "representation" of the Finance and Appropriations Committees. Unlike the House, however, the committees are not equally represented. Of the sixteen members of the Senate Budget Committee (ten Democrats and six Republicans) in the Ninety-fourth Congress, four members were also on Appropriations and one was on Finance. This meant that the overlap in the Senate was only 30 percent compared to 43 percent in the House. In the Ninety-fifth Congress, two of the new Democrats joining the committee were on the Appropriations Committee. With six of sixteen members of the Budget Committee simultaneously on Appropriations, the Appropriations Committee had about double the representation on the Budget Committee than in the House with its five guaranteed seats. Senator Robert Dole (R-Kans.) remained the only member also on the Finance Committee.

The result is that despite the absence of statutory provisions, the other money committees had more members on the Budget Committee in the Senate than in the House; and that group clearly was dominated by the Appropriations Committee. This can be understood in the context of the Budget Act itself. The Budget Committee has greater impact on the spending side of the budget, since it specifies functional subtotals, than it has on the revenue side. This accommodation to the Appropriations Committee has helped insure cooperation on spending issues. The absence of overlap with Finance has undoubtedly contributed to the more difficult relationship between the Budget Committee and the Finance Committee.

Compared with the House, members of the Senate Budget Committee have less seniority in Congress. In the Ninety-fourth Congress, the average tenure for a Senate committee member was 8.8 years while the average for a House member was 14.8 years. [1] This suggests the Senate committee has greater career appeal for younger members. The more senior House members were already well-situated in other committees, while the more junior Senate members probably had less strident loyalties to other committees.

It was suggested in the previous analysis of the House Budget Committee that one of the causes of friction was the ideological split fostered by the selection of liberal Democrats and conservative Republicans. Can the integration of the Senate committee be explained on the basis of greater ideological consensus? Table 5-1 presents an analysis of liberalism and conservatism for the Senate Budget Committee using ADA and ACA ratings. The table includes the senators on the committee in the Ninety-fourth Congress, since only one nonfreshman joined the committee at the start of the Ninety-fifth Congress. (Hence, no ratings are available based on their past voting records.) The Democrats on the Budget Committee represent a fairly close composite of Senate Democrats as a whole. Their average ADA rating is slightly higher and their average ACA rating is slightly lower than the average for all Democratic senators. If anything, according to this measure, committee Democrats are slightly more liberal than all Senate Democrats as a group. On the Republican side, the figures look almost identical to what is found for the House Budget Committee. Senate Budget Committee Republicans are more conservative (and less liberal) than the "average" Senate Republican. Knowing that the Senate committee is more consensual than the House committee, it might be expected that the committee is a closer reflection of the Senate. The data in Table 5-1 suggest that ideological divergence on a committee does not in itself create conflict.

Because membership on the Senate committee does not rotate, the committee appears to be more stable than its House counterpart. The Senate committee is not dependent on the leadership for membership. Neither is it as dependent for support. Some members quite obviously have primary loyalty to the Appropriations Committee over the Budget Committee (Senator Magnuson, for example, who rarely attends a Budget Committee session). Dual loyalty appears to have had less of an impact in the Senate than in the House, perhaps because of the cooperation between the Budget and Appropriations Committees. It seems that in spite of an ideological split on the committee, similar to what was found on the House committee, other factors have intervened to produce a less volatile, more harmonious environment on the committee.

GOALS

The dichotomy between process goals and policy goals is clearly less pronounced on the Senate Budget Committee than on the House committee, although both are in evidence. The Senate Budget Committee most closely approximates a "policy" committee.[2] Committee Democrats placed less emphasis on the necessities of the process, and the goals of the

Table 5-1.
SENATE BUDGET COMMITTEE LIBERALISM AND CONSERVATISM
(Ratings by Americans for Democratic Action—ADA
and Americans for Constitutional Action—ACA)

Senate Budget Committee—94th Congress*					
DEMOCRATS			*REPUBLICANS*		
Name	ADA	ACA	Name	ADA	ACA
Muskie (Maine)	80	8	McClure (Idaho)	0	100
Mondale (Minn.)	75	0	Domenici (N.M.)	5	87
Cranston (Calif.)	75	4	Dole (Kans.)	10	87
Biden (Del.)	75	17	Buckley (N.Y.)	5	82
Magnuson (Wash.)	70	9	Bellmon (Okla.)	10	76
Aboureszk (S.D.)	60	14	Beall (Md.)	20	42
Moss (Utah)	55	17	Average	8.3	79
Chiles (Fla.)	45	48			
Hollings (S.C.)	40	28			
Nunn (Ga.)	20	62			
Average	59.5	20.7			
Average, Senate			Average, Senate		
Democrats	54.3	23.2	Republicans	25.7	63.3

Source: Congressional Quarterly Weekly Reports, 1976.

*Only one non-freshman joined the committee in the 95th Congress: Johnson (D-La.)—ADA=15, ACA=56.

committee concern both fiscal policy and budgetary control. As one Democratic member described it, "the main objective of the committee is to establish restraint and control, to determine priorities within prearranged limits." Others mentioned fiscal policy goals such as reducing unemployment, inflation, and the size of the deficit. Republican responses were remarkably similar in contrast to the divergent patterns identified in the House. Although Republican senators expressed different views about what *specific* policy goals should be, and some were more concerned about the deficit than their Democratic colleagues, Republicans and Democrats appeared to share the general policy goal of fiscal discipline and control. No member indicated that the process should be defended for its own sake; process was not separated from policy.

One reason for the bipartisan consensus on basic goals by members of the Senate Budget Committee may be the relative security of the process in the Senate. Because budget resolutions have enjoyed large majorities and bipartisan support, senators do not perceive the threat of imminent failure or breakdown as House Democrats have indicated. One senator has suggested that "although there was some danger in the first year, the process is secure now in the Senate. It is well accepted." This sentiment was expressed by several committee members of both parties.

Evidence supporting the categorization of the Senate Budget Committee as a policy committee comes not only from the responses of members suggesting this dominant goal, but from responses discrediting the alternatives. The committee is clearly not a constitutency committee; service on the committee offers members virtually no tangible benefits to confer on their states. In comparison with representatives, senators seem less concerned about the negative consequences of a vote in favor of the budget resolutions, and possible electoral reprisals for supporting large deficits. It is reasonable to hypothesize that because of their six-year terms, senators feel less constituent pressure than House members.

Since the Senate Budget Committee offers a member possible career advancement, deals with money (like other "power" committees), and appears to be oriented more towards the Congress itself than constituents or outside groups, it would appear to have the prerequisites for becoming a "power" committee. The evidence strongly suggests that this is not the case, however. Although many senators believe that the Budget Committee has become relatively powerful, it is not yet comparable to an established committee such as Finance. Despite its potential, the committee remains only modestly attractive to most senators. No Democrats requested membership on the committee at the start of the Ninety-fifth Congress in 1977, and three freshmen senators were "recruited" for the committee. The Senate Budget Committee does not appear to have been perceived as a route to internal influence within the Senate during its first four years of existence. Mirroring the increase in appeal in the House, however, the Senate Budget Committee was much more popular in 1979 at the start of the Ninety-sixth Congress.

The evidence suggests that the Budget Committee is attractive to a number of members who want to achieve policy goals. A Democratic member described his interest as follows:

This committee is not for everyone. The members have more of an interest in economic and fiscal affairs than most of the others. I wanted to get an overview of what the government does and the budget is a perfect vehicle for this. On Appropriations, things have become so specialized that you never see the big picture. This is an opportunity to learn about and participate in making fiscal policy and set priorities within the Congress.

The Senate Budget Committee can be classified as a policy committee on the basis of member goals, compared to the process/policy designation for the House committee. The distinction is one of emphasis and conceptualization by members. Senators on the Budget Committee are less apt to draw a distinction between process and policy at all. There is less insecurity about the procedures of the Budget Act, and Senate Republicans and Democrats express common objectives much more than in the House.

ENVIRONMENT

Noticeable changes in the Senate have occurred since the 1950s and the days of the Citadel, the Inner Club, and the Senate Establishment.[3] In the 1960s, political scientists suggested that the Senate was shifting from an already decentralized power structure to an even more individualistic one.[4] By the 1970s, Senate membership had become more Democratic, the larger Democratic majority was more regionally representative, and the Senate had become more liberal.[5] While committees continue to be important, there has been a proliferation of subcommittees, further fragmenting power. Under the Johnson rule, every senator is guaranteed a major committee assignment. Many chairmanships have been assumed by members with less seniority than was the case two decades ago. A recent analysis of changes in the Senate concludes that power is more evenly distributed in the Senate today: "The Senate is a more open and fluid and decentralized body now than it was in the 1950s. Power, resources, and decision-making authority have become more diffuse."[6]

Other characteristics of the Senate have remained constant. In his work on the "folkways" of the Senate, Donald Matthews defined six dominant norms: apprenticeship, legislative work, specialization, courtesy, reciprocity, and institutional patriotism.[7] Twenty years later, only the norm of freshman apprenticeship appears to have diminished.[8] The United States Senate still respects seniority and independence, clings to the filibuster, and does not look for strong centralized leadership. Structures and processes more than ever tend to serve individual member's needs and a fragmented power structure.

How does the budget process mesh with the Senate of the 1980s? On the surface, it would appear to run counter by imposing more centralized control of taxing and spending decisions. The Senate Budget Committee has aggressively asserted its new authority, but at the same time, the acceptance of the budget process in the Senate is partially attributable to the accommodation and deference to the existing norms and power structure.

SUPPORT FROM SENATORS

Support in the Senate for the budget resolutions and the budget process has been significantly greater than in the House. Table 5-2 shows the roll call votes in the Senate for the budget resolutions between 1975 and 1979. Over this five-year period, no committee resolutions have been defeated, and no votes have approached the razor thin margins of passage experienced in the House. The budget resolutions have enjoyed comfortable 2-1 margins of victory. The breakdown of vote by party in Table 5-2 indicates that support has been bipartisan. About half of the Senate Republicans have supported the budget resolutions and 80 to 90 percent of the Democrats have voted in favor.

Table 5-2.
SENATE VOTES ON BUDGET RESOLUTIONS, 1975-1979

Date	Concurrent Resolution/Fiscal Year	Vote	Republicans	Democrats	Northern Democrats	Southern Democrats
5/ 1/75	1st CR FY 1976 Committee Report	69-22	19-18	50-4	36-1	14-3
5/14/75	1st CR FY 1976 Conference Report	—	—	Voice Vote	—	—
11/20/75	2nd CR FY 1976 Committee Report	69-23	19-15	50-8	41-0	9-8
12/11/75	2nd CR FY 1976 Conference Report	74-19	21-15	53-4	40-1	13-3
4/12/76	1st CR FY 1977 Committee Report	62-22	17-16	45-6	32-4	13-2
5/12/76	1st CR FY 1977 Conference Report	65-29	16-20	49-9	34-6	15-3
9/ 9/76	2nd CR FY 1977 Committee Report	55-23	14-18	41-5	27-3	14-2
9/15/76	2nd CR FY 1977 Conference Report	66-20	15-17	51-3	34-2	17-1
5/ 4/77	1st CR FY 1978 Committee Report	56-31	15-17	41-14	36-3	5-11
5/13/77	1st CR FY 1978 Conference Report	54-23	17-12	37-11	29-4	8-7
9/ 9/77	2nd CR FY 1978 Committee Report	63-21	17-13	47-8	33-4	14-4
9/15/77	2nd CR FY 1978 Conference Report	68-21	19-13	49-8	36-4	13-4
4/26/78	1st CR FY 1979 Committee Report	64-27	16-19	48-8	35-4	13-4
5/12/78	1st CR FY 1979 Conference Report	—	—	Voice Vote	—	—
9/ 6/78	2nd CR FY 1979 Committee Report	56-18	14-12	42-6	30-3	12-3
9/12/78	2nd CR FY 1979 Conference Report	47-7	11-4	36-3	28-2	8-1
4/25/79	1st CR FY 1980 Committee Report	64-20	20-15	44-5	29-4	15-1
5/23/79	1st CR FY 1980 Conference Report	72-17	24-13	48-4	31-3	17-1
9/19/79	2nd CR FY 1980 Committee Report	62-36	17-22	45-14	28-12	17-2
11/ 7/79	2nd CR FY 1980 Conference Report	65-27	26-13	39-14	26-9	13-5

Source: Congressional Quarterly Weekly Reports, 1975-1979.
CR = Concurrent Resolution. FY = Fiscal Year

Chairman Muskie and Ranking Minority Member Henry Bellmon present a united front on the floor of the Senate in rebuffing challenges to the committee's figures.[9] But by no means do the resolutions sail through the Senate without opposition. The issues raised in the Senate are similar to those raised in the House: total spending is too high, the deficit is too big, defense spending is too much or too little, or some other functional category is not receiving enough money. There seems to be a noticeable difference in the tenor and the intensity of the debate, however, and the Senate has been more successful in defeating amendments to budget resolutions. The key to this success appears to be the bipartisanship and consensus-building strategies of the committee leaders. Senate debate on the conference report on the First Concurrent Resolution for Fiscal Year 1978, in May 1977, provides a hint of this consensus building.

SENATOR MUSKIE: Mr. President, I know that many members of the Senate will be less than fully satisfied with the results of the conference. With the overall spending limits set by requirements of fiscal responsibility, hard choices, compromises, and even disappointments are inevitable. In weighing national priorities, we have had to give special consideration to the conflicting needs of national defense and our domestic social responsibilities. . . .The budget process is built upon the balancing of needs, upon flexibility and compromise. I urge them to support the conference agreement.

I express my deep appreciation to Senator Bellmon, the ranking Republican on the Senate Budget Committee and in conference. Without his assistance and that of his colleagues on the Republican side of the aisle, it would have been much more difficult, if not impossible, to resolve the major issues which arose in the conference. I am most grateful to them for their help and their understanding.[10]

Speaking next, Senator Bellmon returned the compliments and urged his colleagues to support the budget resolution.

SENATOR BELLMON: Mr. President, I thank your distinguished chairman for his overly kind comments. I express my personal appreciation to our distinguished chairman [Mr. Muskie]. . . .He rendered a great service to the Senate, to Congress, and to the country by the firm, yet understanding leadership he exhibited during this most difficult time in the history of the budget process.

I strongly urge my colleagues—especially those on the Republican side of the aisle—to support this budget. It is one that has been constructed under fire and I believe deserves the wide support of the full Senate. It will prove critically important in the months ahead as we review the authorizing and appropriating bills from the other committees. As much as at any previous time, the budget process will derive its strength from Senatorial support. I sincerely hope the support is again reflected in a strong vote of approval today.[11]

A few days earlier, across the Capitol, a very different spirit was apparent in the House debate. Representative Barber Conable (R-N.Y.), speaking for the Republicans, was helping to defeat the resolution in the House.

REPRESENTATIVE CONABLE: Mr. Chairman, I am greatly disturbed by a number of rather harsh criticisms voiced by some Members of the majority's leadership and echoed on the editorial pages of some of our more respected papers which suggest that the budget process may be destroyed because some of the Republicans could not accept the decision of the majority on the Committee on the Budget. There is an underlying assumption here that the Republicans ought to support any budget resolution simply to preserve and enhance the process regardless of the results that process produces.

I remind my colleagues on the other side of the aisle that they are the majority party, by a substantial margin, and as such have been elected by the people to govern this country. You are the ones who control the legislative program for the next two years, and you are the ones who should properly be held accountable to the people for the overall performance of the Congress. [12]

The behavioral difference between House and Senate Republicans is stark; no budget resolution in the Senate has failed to gain substantial minority support. On the other hand, the House Republican conferees have signed the conference report only once (and not all of them)—and only a handful of House Republicans have ever voted for a budget resolution.

Party cohesion scores convincingly demonstrate differences between the House and Senate coalitions. Senate Republicans are much less cohesive than their House counterparts who vote as a solid bloc against the resolutions. Of the four party caucuses, House Republicans were most cohesive, Senate Republicans least cohesive. House and Senate Democrats tended to fall in between these extremes, with Senate Democrats slightly more cohesive than House Democrats. [13]

As was the case in the House, the nature of the support from other members constrains the actions and decisions of the committee. Because the Senate environment has been more supportive, Muskie and the committee have been less constrained than the House committee. But the actions of the Senate Budget Committee are very much oriented to the Senate. With Republican participation, the overall totals have tended to be lower than the House, and defense has tended to be higher. Past support should not be taken as an indication that the Senate Budget Committee has free rein over the taxing and spending totals. On the contrary, their support is a function of accommodating most of the spending desires of the Senate while attempting to restrain overall growth. Although process concerns are not paramount, support for the committee and the process could evaporate if the committee was out of step with the Senate.

OTHER COMMITTEES

The Budget Act requires Senate authorizing committees to submit their views and estimates to the Budget Committee and to report their authorization bills by the May 15 deadline. As in the House, many of the standing committees have been unhappy with the new procedures, particularly with the time crunch that has been created for them. Because they must complete their legislative action much sooner than before, some members claim that they are less able to do a thorough job of oversight.

The imposition of the new budget system over the old authorization-appropriation process was bound to cause some conflict among the many participants. As was the case in the House, standing committees feel threatened when the functional totals become too specific or begin to pry into their jurisdiction. The Senate Budget Committee has been careful about this and less specific in its subtotals than the House. Muskie has avoided considering line items, or specific programs within the functional totals. At the same time, the Senate committee appears to have been more aggressive toward authorizing committees than the House. The first conflicts between the fledgling Senate Budget Committee and the established committees of the Senate were with authorizing committees, not the Appropriations or Finance Committees.

In 1975, the Senate Budget Committee chose its first floor fight and opposed the military construction authorization bill. The bill that came back from the conference committee exceeded the targets established in the first concurrent resolution. Going up against John Stennis and the powerful Armed Services Committee, the Senate Budget Committee prevailed by a vote of 48-42.[14] Attempting to demonstrate that the principles adopted by the Budget Committee transcended liberal or conservative causes, Muskie and Bellmon next teamed up to oppose the authorization for the School Lunch Program. This favorite program of liberals also violated the targets, and was sent back to committee.[15] The conflict between the Budget Committee and authorizing committees was much more visible and dramatic than the behind-the-scenes maneuvering that took place in the House.

The Budget Committee challenged authorization bills when most observers expected it to focus on appropriations or tax bills. This served to highlight the critical importance of the authorization process to congressional budgeting, and served notice that Congress could not control the budget without first controlling authorizations.[16] The Senate committee has asserted the right to force authorizing committees to change existing law under the Budget Act, while the House has not viewed this action as being within the power of the Budget Committee.

Despite these initial successes, the Senate Budget Committee has had only a mixed record of success in confrontation with other committees. In 1977, its opposition to the energy tax bill was ignored by the Senate. A major defeat occurred when the Senate passed a costly farm bill over the protest of the Budget Committee. In March 1978, Muskie complained on the Senate floor: "I am not sure how long this budget process is going to survive, but I doubt if it can survive this kind of situation."[17] Six months later, however, the committee had completed its most successful session ever in asserting budgetary restraint over the standing committees.

Beyond periodic disagreements, relations between the Budget Committee and the Senate Appropriations Committee have been good. This is indicated first by the fact that appropriation bills have rarely been the target of Budget Committee opposition in the Senate. Second, members of both Budget and Appropriations indicate that the dominant pattern has been one of cooperation. One member, who is on both committees, commented:

From the start, there has been a mutual respect between the two committees. Unfortunately, I can't say the same for the Finance Committee. I think that Appropriations actually appreciates our efforts to hold down spending—it relieves some of the pressure on them.

A Democrat on the Appropriations Committee (and not on the Budget Committee) echoed this sentiment:

We get along with them [Budget Committee] very well and have had very few problems. At first some of my more senior colleagues were resentful—felt a little threatened—but we have moved away from this after the first year. This has been a meaningful change accomplished together, and I believe we [on Appropriations] have improved our performance.

If cooperation has been the dominant mode in relations with the Appropriations Committee, conflict has been more prevalent in relations with Senator Russell Long and the Finance Committee. One senator said, "At first he [Long] wouldn't even acknowledge the existence of the budget resolutions. At least now he criticizes them." In its report for 1976, the Senate Budget Committee included a target of $2 billion in additional revenue from tax reform.[18] Long called the target unrealistic and impractical, but his substitute amendment, opposed by Muskie, was tabled.[19] When the tax reform bill was considered on the Senate floor later that summer, however, Muskie's opposition was not sustained by the full Senate. In 1978, the Budget Committee was able to gain the upper hand in forcing Long and the Finance Committee to rewrite the tuition tax credit portion of the tax bill. One observer contrasted this 1978 victory to 1977: "It was a far cry from the previous year, when Long had walked all over the budget process during debate of the energy tax bill."[20]

Compared with the House Budget Committee, Senators Muskie and Bellmon appear to be much more assertive toward other committees. The confrontations with Stennis and Long are the stuff reputations are made of, and a reputation as guardian of spending tends to serve the goals of the Budget Committee well. In considering the episodes of conflict concerning the budget process, what is often missed is that such confrontations are the exception, not the rule. The dominant mode of interaction is cooperation. The evidence to support this view is found in members' perceptions, in the limited number of conflicts compared with routine relationships, and perhaps most importantly, in the policy recommendations of the committee. The standing committees are satisfied with the budget process, and are not unhappy with the Budget Committee because they still get most of what they want in terms of money and programs. In the one case where conflict is more prevalent (with Finance), it must be understood that the Budget Committee has very little leverage over the revenue side of the budget. The hypotheses about the policy impact of the committee will be explored more fully in the next two chapters, but in general, the Budget Committee has gained the support of Senate committees through aggressiveness in certain situations tempered by general accommodation and deference.

PARTY LEADERS

Support from the Senate leadership is important to the Budget Committee, but unlike the House, it is not as essential to its survival or success. The relationship between Majority Leader Robert Byrd and the Budget Committee is not unlike that of other Senate committees. Both former Majority Leader Mike Mansfield (D-Mont.) and Byrd supported the budget process, but they have not always supported the Budget Committee in their challenges to other committees. Missing from the Senate scene is the almost complete dependence on the leadership found in the House. Byrd and Mansfield supported all of the Budget resolutions. But in terms of enforcement, the leaders usually let the Senate work its will.

With Republican participation in the Senate, Republican leaders have had less frustration with budgeting than their colleagues in the House. As is the case with Democratic leaders, the role has been a relatively passive one in comparison to the active involvement and opposition in the House. However, Minority Leader Howard Baker (D-Tenn.) and Bellmon came under increased pressure in 1978 and 1979 from rank-and-file Republicans to clarify party differences and oppose some of the Democratic budget proposals.

EXECUTIVE BRANCH

In reacting to the president's budget, House and Senate differences are minimal. The executive budget remains the most important referent in the budgetary process, even though Senator Muskie begins markup using current policy estimates rather than the president's budget. Like the House, the Senate has demonstrated a willingness to cooperate with the president, as well as the determination to change his budget when they believe he is wrong. Loyalty to the Senate and the Congress (in that order) come before loyalty to party or to the president. Senator Bellmon joined Muskie in criticizing President Ford in 1976 for what they felt were misleading, inaccurate budget estimates. In turn, Muskie has criticized President Carter for some of his proposals. The Senate was willing to support the third concurrent resolution to accommodate Carter when he took office, but has clearly voiced its independence. Both leaders have been willing to publicly oppose a president of their own party in defense of the budget process in Congress.

The most crucial environmental constraints on the Senate Budget Committee are imposed by the senators themselves, in floor voting and in committee. Party leaders, the executive branch, and interest groups are clearly less important. The response of the committee to its environment is a complex one, including accommodation and deference to the norms and power structure of the Senate, but punctuated with aggressive confrontations with violators of the budget resolutions.

STRATEGIES

With its policy-oriented goals and more supportive environment, the strategies of the Senate Budget Committee are somewhat different than those of the House committee. The first three strategies are policy related, although they have procedural implications. The committee attempts *to write a budget resolution that restrains spending growth.* The statements and actions of the committee suggest that this is their primary strategy in the budget process, but one that can be pursued in many different ways. Fiscal restraint was only one of several policy objectives of the budget reformers, yet the policy role of the Budget Committee seems to be universally defined by the members as a budget-cutting, guardianship role. Both Senators Muskie and Bellmon articulate this value. In evaluating the performance of the committee in the Ninety-fifth Congress, Muskie defined a "victory" as the defeat of any measure that would increase spending. He went on to note:

You may not agree that the vote on all these bills constitutes a "victory." I, myself, don't relish limiting funds for worthwhie programs, but they must be done if we are to keep a grip on fiscal integrity.[21]

Interviews with other members of the Senate tend to confirm this as the first strategic premise of the committee.

A second policy-related strategy of the committee is *to provide sufficient fiscal stimulus to promote growth and employment without adding to inflation*. Based on the CBO projections and assumptions for the economy, the committee attempts to establish fiscal policy to stabilize the economy. Given the economic situation of the 1970s, this has been as trying for the Senate as for the other participants. Much of the conflict that has resulted has been over deciding what fiscal actions would be appropriate. Yet virtually all members, regardless of their specific policy preferences, agreed with the premise that they need to halt inflation, promote economic growth, and maintain strong employment.

A third policy related strategy of the Senate Budget Committee concerns specific functions and programs. It attempts *to accommodate most of the spending and program requests balancing defense and domestic needs*. While maintaining its budget-cutting premise, the committee attempts to meet the spending needs of major national programs, and to maintain the support of the standing committees. Some conflict among these three strategies of the committees is inevitable. Despite attempts to slow the profligacy of spending, the committee tries to provide room in the resolutions to meet legitimate needs. This tension between strategic premises is similar to Fenno's description of the House Appropriations Committee in the 1960s. [22] The policy choices of the committee are complex and difficult, but a majority of committee members appears to follow all three strategies in making their decisions.

In addition to the policy-related strategies of the committee, several secondary strategies related more to process objectives are apparent. The committee makes an explicit attempt *to present a bipartisan, united front on the Senate floor*. Once the tough decisions have been made in committee, most Republicans and Democrats on the committee attempt to stick together whether they won or lost in committee. This is in sharp contrast to the behavior of the House Budget Committee. The strategy tends to preserve the strength of the committee and increase its chances for continued success on the floor. Senator Bellmon's comments on an amendment to make cuts in the targets reveal this philosophy:

SENATOR BELLMON: [I] voted for an even larger cut in spending during the markup of the resolution . . .this puts me in somewhat of a dilemma. I have, since the Budget Committee was formed, consistently taken the position that we ought to work as a committee, work our wills, make the best decisions we could, and then, having come to that conclusion, we ought to support that decision as a committee so that when we came to the floor we would not each of us be going in our separate directions and, in this way, weaken the budget process. . . .So, attractive as I find the Senator's amendment to be, I must say that I feel at this time, partially because other committees will not have known in advance about the impact that such cuts might have on the areas of their concern, that the amendment should be rejected. [23]

A corollary of this strategy is to defeat floor amendments in an attempt to preserve the balance and compromises struck in committee. Table 5-3 shows the number of amendments offered to the budget resolutions and the number that have been successful. With a few exceptions the committee has been quite successful in turning back changes proposed on the Senate floor.

Table 5-3.
FLOOR AMENDMENTS TO SENATE BUDGET
COMMITTEE RESOLUTIONS*

Concurrent Resolution/ Fiscal Year	Number of Amendments Offered	Number Passed
1st CR FY 1976	4	0
2nd CR FY 1976	1	0
1st CR FY 1977	7	0
2nd CR FY 1977	0	0
3rd CR FY 1977	0	0
1st CR FY 1978	5	3
2nd CR FY 1978	4	1
1st CR FY 1979	11	0
2nd CR FY 1979	3	0
1st CR FY 1980	16	4
2nd CR FY 1980	14	6

Source: Compiled from Congressional Quarterly Weekly Reports, 1975-1979.

*All committee resolutions have passed the Senate. See Table 4-4 for comparison with House.

The final strategy of the committee is also procedural: *to oppose bills that violate the budget targets.* Most frequently, this involves opposing bills on the floor of the Senate. In contrast, the House committee has been hesitant to get itself in a position of public opposition where it would be the likely loser. The more aggressive strategy in the Senate arose in the first year of implementation when Senators Muskie and Bellmon took on some of the established committees and challenged even popular bills if they were "budget busters."

The most obvious difference in the strategies of the House and Senate Budget Committees is the relative emphasis on policy over process in the Senate. Both committees must deal with both, but with the greater security in the Senate, it has been possible for it to concentrate primarily on policy decisions. Of course, the policy-related strategies suggested for the Senate committee may be time bound. The increasing interest in fiscal restraint may be a historical accident of the decade. In another decade, the committee's strategy may be quite different. But given the spending proclivities of the other congressional committees, the strategy of fiscal restraint seems to be based on more than current public opinion. It may be that this is, in fact, a lasting premise that the committee will adopt whether money is tight or plentiful.

DECISION MAKING

The Senate Budget Committee, in its first year of existence, established a process of decision making that has generally been carried through to the present: decision making that reflects the goals, strategies, and the environment in the Senate.

PARTISANSHIP

The high levels of partisanship in the House have been contrasted with the less partisan atmosphere in the Senate. Yet one must be leery of overstating the differences or to characterize the Senate committee as nonpartisan. Significant splits, roughly along party lines, have occurred in the deliberations of the Senate committee. There often has been disagreement on basic questions of fiscal policy, defense spending, and social programs. The Senate Budget Committee most closely approximates a pattern of restrained partisanship.[24] Unlike the House committee, the Senate committee infrequently carries partisanship beyond committee deliberations. As the earlier comments of the ranking minority member indicated, there is a strong belief that once the committee has settled its differences and arrived at a compromise, it should stand united. Differences with the House Budget Committee are evident in minority reports to the concurrent resolutions. While this has been a part of every resolution in the House, it has been less common in the Senate.

The roll call votes within the committee are instructive in analyzing decision-making processes. Table 5-4 shows the extent of party voting within the committee and the party support scores of individual members. Of the seventy-two recorded roll call votes between 1975 and 1977, *none* were straight party line votes. This compares with 14 percent for the House committee. Over half (54 percent) of the votes in the Senate Budget Committee can be classified as party votes, with a majority of Democrats opposing a majority of Republicans. While this is significantly lower than the 78 percent of party votes in the House committee, the figure is still relatively high compared to other Senate committees. Democrats on the committee vary greatly in their party support scores, from 100 percent for Muskie and Alan Cranston (D-Calif.), to only 3 percent for Senator Nunn. With the presence of Ernest Hollings (D-S.C.), Lawton Chiles (D-Fla.), and Nunn, who vote with the Republicans more often than with the majority party, Muskie cannot look only to members of his own party for support on crucial committee votes. This is a further reason for full participation of the minority in committee deliberations. On many key votes, the margin for victory has been provided by Republican votes. On others, Muskie and the more liberal Democrats have lost. But they supported the resolutions later.

Although Senate Republicans, as a group, have the lowest party cohesion scores (of the four caucuses) in floor voting, in committee votes they

The Fiscal Congress

Table 5-4.
PARTY VOTING ON COMMITTEE ROLL CALLS:
SENATE BUDGET COMMITTEE, 1975-1977

Democrats	Party Support Score (percentage)	Republicans	Party Support Score (percentage)
Muskie (Maine)	100	Dominici (N.M.)	95
Cranston (Calif.)	100	McClure (Idaho)	92
Mondale (Minn.)	97	Buckley (N.Y.)	87
Aboureszk (S.D.)	87	Bellmon (Okla.)	79
Magnuson (Wash.)	62	Dole (Kans.)	74
Moss (Utah)	60	Beall (Md.)	74
Biden (Del.)	44		
Hollings (S.C.)	26		
Chiles (Fla.)	10		
Nunn (Ga.)	3		

Source: Senate Budget Committee. Compiled from committee voting records.

Note: Recorded committee roll call votes N=72
Recorded party line votes N=0 (0%)
Recorded party votes N=39 (54%)
See Table 4-6 for definitions of party votes.

have higher party support scores than the Democrats. On a number of party votes, Senator Bellmon has sided with Senator Muskie, voting against the majority of Republicans. The cooperation between Muskie and Bellmon contrasts with the pattern observed in the House on voting agreement between chairman and ranking minority member. Muskie and Bellmon voted together on thirty-six of the seventy-two recorded votes, exactly half. Agreement between leaders of the House committee was only 14 percent on all votes cast in committee. In comparison with the House, partisanship on the Budget Committee is clearly more restrained. But compared to other money committees, the Appropriations Committee, for example, there is more partisanship and more disagreement.

The Senate Budget Committee is more integrated as a political unit than the House committee. Norms to protect the reputation and prestige of the committee are present where they were missing in the House. Since members are not limited in tenure on the committee and could develop a Senate career in budget policy (as Muskie, at least, has done), the committee has a great deal more institutional power than the House committee. Although Fenno suggests that Senate committees tend to be more permeable than House committees, the Senate committee has greater integration, autonomy, consensus, and influence than the House committee.[25]

PARTICIPATION-SPECIALIZATION

The major work is done in full committee since they have no subcommittees. Compared with the House committee, there is greater interest and participation in committee sessions. Attendance for committee votes is slightly greater in the Senate as Table 5-5 indicates. Although participation for all members is only 3 percent higher in the Senate, a noticeable difference can be seen for Republican members. House committee Republicans voted on an average of 63 percent of the roll calls, while Senate committee Republicans voted 88 percent of the time. This reflects the greater integration of minority members in the budget process.

Table 5-5.
VOTING PARTICIPATION IN BUDGET COMMITTEE MEETINGS*

	House (percentage)	Senate (percentage)
Republicans	63	88
Democrats	71	67
All Members	72	75

Source: Compiled from voting records, House and Senate Budget committees.

*The percentage of votes cast on committee roll call votes out of all possible votes. Excludes proxy voting.

Members are expected to be generalists, not specialists. Since the committee must balance the desires and requests of a variety of competing interests, they must avoid being advocates of a particular set of agencies, programs, or other standing committees. This norm, also present in the House, appears to be stronger in the Senate. One member described the difference as follows:

I detect more of a constituency thing on the House side—members pushing for their pet functions. This causes problems when it is brought to the floor. We have much less of this on the Senate side. One of the reasons we have been successful is that the committee is an accurate reflection of the makeup of the Senate. Items fought out in the committee are not fought on the floor.

The committee has attempted to show the Senate that it is not an advocate of any particular point of view, rather, that it is concerned with fiscal policy and discipline.

COMMITTEE LEADERSHIP

The bipartisan leadership of Muskie and Bellmon has had a prominent role in the development of this analysis. Within the committee, the chairman and the ranking minority member established a different process of assembling the concurrent resolutions than in the House. The Senate committee operates on a higher level of aggregation, avoiding the appropriation account level of consideration found in the House.[26] Unlike Adams and Giaimo, Muskie does not begin with a specific chairman's "mark." The committee in the Senate considers a total for an entire function, often without any further specification of how the total is to be subdivided between committees. In addition, Muskie begins deliberations using the current policy estimates (projections of a standpat budget provided by the CBO) as a baseline, while Adams and Giaimo have used requests in the president's budget as a baseline.

By not establishing a chairman's mark, committee members have been more fully involved in the process of fixing totals. One of the major complaints of House committee members, especially the Republicans, is that the chairman's figures are presented as a *fait accompli*, and that the committee discussions are usually ignored by the chairman. The process of decision making adopted by the Senate Budget Committee also has reduced the number of complaints from standing committees about the incursions on their territory. It has fostered fuller participation by committee members, including minority members.

The two budget committees have approached the job of scorekeeping differently as well. On the House side, the committee informs the members of the House how much leeway remains within the budget targets based on bills enacted to date. In the Senate, the committee informs the members how much over the targets they will be if all the bills currently being considered in the Senate are passed.

COMMITTEE STAFF AND CBO

Decision making in the Senate Budget Committee is influenced by the quality of professional staff assistance. In establishing staffs for the two Budget committees in 1974-1975, the House and Senate took slightly different approaches. The House assembled a staff with extensive technical expertise. The Senate attempted to blend budgetary expertise with legislative experience, and has utilized the assistance of CBO more extensively than the House. The House staff tends to compete with CBO and in some cases, duplicates its efforts.

The Senate staff is larger than the House staff, around eighty-five persons.[27] Each senator on the committee is allowed to hire two staff people and Muskie has control of the core staff for the majority, Bellmon for the minority. Because of the expertise required, the staff tends to play a more important role on the Budget committees than on many other congressional committees. With their own staff and the assistance of CBO, the Senate has been well served. Because the House has not fully utilized CBO, CBO has been able to devote more of its attention to the Senate Budget Committee.

Although both committees express satisfaction with their staff arrangements, there may be some advantages to the Senate approach. In the individualistic Senate, member needs are satisfied by having their own staff to use in conjunction with the core staff and CBO. The political sensitivity of the Senate staff may have contributed to the ability of the committee to accurately discern the views of the entire Senate. This may have contributed to the stronger support for the budget process in the Senate. Republicans on the Senate committee have been much more satisfied with their staff than their House Republican colleagues, fostering their integration into the committee.

The Senate Budget Committee is more typical of Senate committees than the House Budget Committee is of House committees. The decision-making processes found in the internal workings of the committee are consistent with the current Senate. Power is not centralized with the chairman; Muskie often does not prevail in committee votes. Individual members have a significant impact on committee decisions, and the fluid nature of the voting alignments tends to maximize individual influence. By not establishing a chairman's mark, using current policy estimates as a baseline, and by avoiding specific program detail, the Senate Budget Committee has made sure that the budget process "fits" the Senate and serves the needs of its own members.

HOUSE-SENATE DIFFERENCES

Two questions need to be asked: How can the differences in the operation of the budget process in the House and Senate be explained? Are the differences really that significant? Clearly, the Senate has supported the budget process more than the House. Differences have been documented concerning partisanship, strategies, enforcement, and the decision-making processes. A number of factors help explain the House-Senate differences.

The tenure limitations on the House committee appear to be one explanation. Even with the extension to six-year terms, the committee is still temporary and offers no career possibilities over the long run. However, there is some chance that the restrictions will be removed in the next few years. The limitations not only affect the committee in terms of reduced careerism, but perhaps more significantly, they reduce the incentives to protect committee power and prestige. The absence of limitations on the Senate Budget Committee has allowed the more natural development of norms to reduce conflict and promote committee status.

Constituency pressures associated with the budget resolutions appear to be significantly greater in the House than the Senate. This is consistent with other research on constituency demands and legislators' responses.[28] Interviews with senators and representatives strongly suggested that the electoral consequences of voting for a budget resolution was much more salient for members of the House. Looking back to the creation of the budget process in the early 1970s, it is clear that this was one of the objectives of conservatives —to force members to go on record in support of big spending and deficits.

Members are put on the defensive without being able to show anything tangible to their constituents. Although this undoubtedly is a problem for some senators, in general, it appears to be much less of a problem than for representatives.

Personality matters in politics, and without overemphasizing, it is a significant factor in explaining House-Senate differences. Perhaps the sharpest contrast is between the ranking Republicans on the two committees. Senator Bellmon's attitudes, behavior, and style have gone a long way toward integrating Senate Republicans into the process. Representative Latta, in contrast, has attempted to rally Republicans together (very successfully) in opposition to the budget resolutions. His more vituperative style has contributed to the schism. Senator Muskie has played the role of conciliator successfully, and this has affected the success in the Senate. Many senators claim unequivocally that the success of the budget process is due to the efforts of Muskie and Bellmon. Yet it is unlikely, given the situation in the House, that a Muskie or any other Democrat could pull the House together and gain bipartisan support.

It is more likely that the Senate will become more partisan, like the House. Even if Bellmon's successor as ranking minority member is not one of the partisan Republicans, there still will be pressure to oppose Muskie and the Democrats. Yet the Senate will probably not go as far as the House in making the budget a party issue. In explaining the differences between the House and the Senate, one senator suggested, "we just do things differently over here." Despite the fact that roll call voting data indicate that there are more party votes in the Senate than in the House, the spirit of bipartisanship seems to be stronger.

The counterpoint to explanations of House-Senate differences is that the totals reached with great difficulty in the House and with relative ease in the Senate are not all that different. As noted, the House tends to be more liberal than the Senate, but the policy choices have been close. This suggests that both committees are responding to similar pressures and constraints, both in terms of the economy, the environment, multiyear spending, and the demands from other actors. Despite the fact that the process has been smoother in the Senate than the House, it has not radically altered the power structure of the Senate, and has not had a greater impact on national policy than the process in the House.

NOTES

1. John Ellwood and James Thurber, "The New Congressional Budget Process: The Hows and Whys of House-Senate Differences," in Lawrence Dodd and Bruce Oppenheimer, *Congress Reconsidered* (New York: Praeger, 1977), p. 184.

2. Richard Fenno, *Congressmen in Committees* (Boston: Little, Brown, 1973), p. 1.

3. William S. White, *The Citadel* (New York: Harper & Row, 1957). Joseph S. Clark et al., *The Senate Establishment* (New York: Hill and Wang, 1963).

4. Randall B. Ripley, *Power in the Senate* (New York: St. Martin's, 1969).

5. Norman Ornstein, Robert Peabody, David Rohde, "The Changing Senate: From the 1950s to the 1970s," in Lawrence Dodd and Bruce Oppenheimer, eds., *Congress Reconsidered* (New York: Praeger, 1977), pp. 3-20.

6. Ibid., p. 16.

7. Donald Matthews, *U.S. Senators and Their World* (Chapel Hill, N.C.: University of North Carolina Press, 1960).

8. Ornstein et al., "Changing Senate," p. 7.

9. Joel Havemann, *Congress and the Budget* (Bloomington: Indiana University Press, 1978), p. 91.

10. *Congressional Record*, May 13, 1977, S7533-34.

11. Ibid., S7535.

12. *Congressional Record*, May 5, 1977, H4066-7.

13. Ellwood and Thurber, "New Congressional Budget Process," p. 176.

14. *Congressional Quarterly Weekly Reports*, vote on August 1, 1975.

15. *Congressional Quarterly Weekly Reports*, vote in September 1975.

16. Ellwood and Thurber, "New Congressional Budget Process," p. 180.

17. Joel Havemann, "A Good Year for the Congressional Budget Process," *National Journal*, September 23, 1978, p. 1501.

18. Senate Budget Committee, *Report to Accompany the First Concurrent Resolution on the Budget, Fiscal Year 1977*, #731, 94th Cong., 2nd sess.

19. *Congressional Record*, April 8, 1976, S5295; and April 9, 1976, S5322-36.

20. Havemann, "Good Year" p. 1502.

21. Letter from Senator Muskie to the author, December 1, 1978.

22. Fenno, *Congressmen in Committees*.

23. *Congressional Record*, April 26, 1978, S6358.

24. John Manley, *The Politics of Finance* (Boston: Little, Brown, 1970). p. 84.

25. Fenno, *Congressmen in Committees*, p. 278-279.

26. Ellwood and Thurber, "New Congressional Budget Process," p. 182.

27. Ibid., p. 171.

28. Roger Davidson, *The Role of the Congressman* (New York: Pegasus, 1969). Warren Miller and Donald Stokes, "Constituency Influence in Congress," *American Political Science Review* (March 1963), pp. 45-56; Aage Clausen and Richard Cheney, "Comparative Analysis of Senate and House Voting on Economic and Welfare Policy, 1953-1964," *American Political Science Review* 44 (March 1970): 151.

6

The Taxing and Spending Committees

*If we had done our jobs properly over the past
ten years, there wouldn't have been any need
for the Budget Committees in the first place.*
—House Appropriations Committee Member

The budget resolutions and the battles over fiscal policy have been the most dramatic results of budget reform. But under the centralized umbrella monitored by the Budget committees, the authorization, appropriation, and revenue processes remain points of key fiscal decisions. To a varying degree, all had been the target of reform. The authorizing committees made inroads into the jurisdiction of the Appropriations committees, weakening legislative control of the budget. The Appropriations committees had proven incapable of taking an overview of the budget and were impossibly bogged down in their deliberations and actions. The revenue committees had never linked their decisions on taxes to decisions on spending and the total budget.

Even if the budget process has not made radical changes in the substantive decisions of other committees, it has had a major effect on how and when they act. In general, the standing committees in both the House and Senate have cooperated with the Budget committees since 1975. This chapter examines the jurisdiction and spending roles of the committees, recent changes in their power and influence, and examines the impact of budget reform on committee procedures and decisions.

SPENDING JURISDICTION AND ROLES

COMMITTEE ALLOCATIONS

Committees are not equal in terms of the money they control in the congressional budget process. Table 6-1 shows committee spending jurisdiction in the Senate, including the Appropriations Committee, Finance

Table 6-1.
SPENDING JURISDICTION BY SENATE COMMITTEE, FISCAL 1979
(New Budget Authority)
($ in millions)

Committee	Direct Spending Jurisdiction	Entitlements Funded Through Appropriations	Total	Propor- tion
Appropriations	$354,953	$(-70,453)*	$284,500	46%
Finance	$213,588	$ 34,289	$247,877	40%
Other Authorizing Committees:				
Total	$ 60,300	$ 30,200	$ 90,500	14%
Subtotals, Other Authorizing Committees				
Government Affairs	$ 26,117	—	$ 26,117	
Veterans Affairs	1,062	$ 13,752	14,814	
Foreign Relations	11,424	—	11,424	
Armed Services	-190	10,279	10,089	
Agriculture, Nutrition & Forestry	616	9,206	9,822	
Environment & Public Works	8,226	—	8,226	
Human Resources	4,237	2,613	6,850	
Commerce, Science & Transportation	1,248	199	1,447	
Energy & Natural Resources	1,038	58	1,096	
Select Committee on Indian Affairs	256	—	256	
Banking, Housing, Urban Affairs	240	—	240	
Judiciary	173	57	230	
Rules & Administration	46	—	46	

Source: Second Concurrent Resolution, Fiscal Year 1979; Senate Budget Scorekeeping Report, no 79-9, October 2, 1978.

*Since the appropriations are mandatory, they are deducted from total.

Committee, and the other authorizing committees that had allocations for fiscal 1979 (the figures are comparable for the House). Table 6-1 also shows the approximate proportion of the budget controlled by the various participants. Because of multiyear and permanent authorizations, the committee allocations vary from year to year.

There are two ways that authorizing committees have an impact on budget authority in a given year. Direct spending jurisdictions represent the portion of the budget over which a committee has control in the sense that when legislation under its purview is enacted, budget authority is created directly.[1] Entitlements funded through appropriations reflect indirect control by the authorizing committees. While legislation under their purview does not directly create budget authority and action by the Appropriations committees is required, they are mandatory actions over which Appropriations committees have no control. Therefore, the actual spending jurisdiction of the authorizing committees consists of both direct jurisdiction and entitlements funded through Appropriations. The jurisdiction of the Appropriations committees is their direct jurisdiction *minus* these entitlements.

Table 6-1 shows that in fiscal 1979, under this formulation, the Senate Appropriations Committee still had the greatest amount of money under its jurisdiction, but that it made up less than half (46 percent) of the total. It is also apparent that the Finance Committee (and the Ways and Means Committee in the House) has the greatest spending responsibilities of the authorizing committees, totals just slightly less than the Appropriations committees (40 percent). The Ways and Means and Finance Committees have a significant role in the expenditure side of the budget in addition to their tax writing responsibilities.

The spending jurisdiction of the other committees made up about 14 percent of the 1979 budget and varies from $26 billion for the Governmental Affairs Committee to $46 million for the Rules and Administration Committee. Two select committees had authorizing jurisdiction and several of the standing committees did not (in fiscal 1979). Taken as a group, it is apparent that the authorization committees have a substantial impact. When one corrects for entitlements, over half of the new budget authority created by Congress in a given year is either created directly by legislation emanating from the authorizing committees, or created indirectly by entitlements funded through Appropriations.

COMMITTEE ADVOCACY

The Budget committees were created to centralize control of the congressional budget and to take an overview of national priorities. As such, they adopt the role of guardians in the process, best exemplified by the chairman taking the floor to oppose "budget busting" legislation that violates the budget targets. The authorizing committees are primarily legislative in orientation and specialized in focus. Although they may adopt the role of guardian in dealing with executive branch agencies, within the congressional budget process, they are primarily advocates of particular programs and greater spending.

When agencies go to Capitol Hill for authorization hearings on an annual or multiyear basis, they are subjected to the scrutiny of the committees. Members attempt to assess performance, effectiveness, and to eliminate waste. They may not reauthorize programs (although in the vast majority of cases, they do) or they may not authorize as much as the agency wishes. In these activities, they are adopting the traditional role of congressional guardian of the public purse, protecting the public from the spending excesses of the bureaucracy. In spite of this professed role, the committees are usually strong advocates of the programs they oversee. There are a number of reasons for this. One reason may simply be familiarity with agencies, programs, and personnel. More important are the substantive policy goals of the committee. Members of the House Education and Labor Committee, for example, are supporters of education programs, and usually, advocates of greater spending in education. As specialists in this field, education holds a higher priority for them than most other members. The same is true for the other authorizing committees. In addition, each committee estimates its needs and its claim on the budget in relative isolation from other committees. They are not concerned with holding down spending, particularly in making initial estimates. That is the job of the Budget committees.

More surprisingly, this dual role may apply to the Appropriations subcommittees as well as the authorizing committees. The earlier work of Richard Fenno and Aaron Wildavsky portrayed the Appropriations committees as guardians whose strategic premise was to cut the executive budget.[2] As Fenno extracted from his interviews with Appropriations committee members,

The action verbs most commonly used are "cut," "carve," "slice," "prune," "whittle," "squeeze," "wring," "trim," "lop off," "chop," "slash," "pare," "shave," "fry," and "whack." The tools of the trade are appropriately referred to as "knife," "blade," "meat axe," "scalpel," "meat cleaver," "hatchet," "shears," "wringer," and "fine tooth comb." . . .Budgets are praised when they are "cut to the bone."[3]

Appropriations members still articulate the goals of a budget cutting guardian. But the overall cuts in the executive requests are small (around 1 or 2 percent), especially compared to the cuts agencies endure in the OMB.[4] In fiscal year 1977, for the first time in recent memory, Congress appropriated more than the president requested. Confronted with this apparent contradiction to their role as economizers, one House Appropriations Committee member reminded me that they had appropriated less in nineteen out of the past twenty years.

The Appropriations committees still serve as guardians when considering specific executive requests in the hearings. But within the congressional budget process, they may also act as advocates protecting their own discretion and their programs. Chairman of a Senate Appropriations subcommittee, Senator William Proxmire (D-Wis.), who prides himself on budget cutting, made the following observation about the lessons of experience:

I made a low estimate and I lived to regret it. I fought for the estimate, but I lost. Ever since then I have been a little gunshy and I have attempted to come in high rather than low. They [the estimates] can contain everything including the kitchen sink. It is easier and safer to suggest a high figure so that in the end one will look good by coming in under it rather than submitting a lower figure which may be exceeded.[5]

Committee advocacy is demonstrated in the March 15 estimates to the Budget committees. They must indicate the amount of budget authority and outlays they feel are required in the next fiscal year. The committees consistently ask for substantial increases, for more than is eventually approved in most cases. Table 6-2 shows the amount and percentage increase requested by the committees in the House of Representatives for fiscal years 1977 and 1978. Note that this table displays the increases by functional area, not by committee. This serves to show the policy areas subject to the greatest advocacy, rather than the committees that request the greatest increases. In fiscal year 1977, the committees requested a total increase in outlays of 18 percent from the previous year. In the next year, the committees requested an increase of almost 17 percent. In only two functions were there no increases or a request for a decrease. The functional areas of the budget subject to the greatest requested increase include Natural Resources and Energy (45.6 percent in 1977, 61.7 percent in 1978); Education, Employment, and Social Services (32 percent in 1977, 41.8 percent in 1978); International Affairs (46.9 percent in 1977); and Agriculture (164.6 percent in 1978).

The roles of the authorizing committees can be distinguished from the Appropriations committees by the degree of advocacy. The standing committees have not internalized budget cutting as much as Appropriations Committee members, mainly because their role in the budgetary process is different. They tend to be stronger advocates for their programs and display less guardianship. This is the case in particular with multiyear authorizations where the committees are able to lay a claim to a future share of the budget. This behavior is manifested in the "authorization-appropriations gap" where the standing committees authorize more than the Appropriations committees are willing to approve. As Allen Schick notes:

As the gap grows bigger, authorizing committees may feel compelled to behave as advocates for the programs under their jurisdiction. They may be reluctant to propose realistic spending levels lest they compromise their claims for higher appropriations in the future. When faced with escalating authorizations, members of Congress can vote for higher levels in expectation of later reductions at the appropriations stage.[6]

The advocacy by authorizing committees has several results. It creates pressure for increased spending within the Congress in addition to that from the executive branch. It may provide credibility problems as authorizations grow far beyond appropriations and is not conducive to greater congressional control. Finally, it causes direct role conflict between the authorizing committees and the Budget committees, and may reduce support for the budget process among some committee members.

THE AUTHORIZING COMMITTEES

The Budget and Impoundment Control Act affected the authorizing committees in several significant ways. Most importantly, reformers had

Table 6-2.
COMMITTEE ADVOCACY: INCREASES FROM PREVIOUS YEAR'S BUDGET REQUESTED BY HOUSE COMMITTEES
(Outlays, Current Dollars, in billions)

Function	Final FY 1976	Committee "Requests" FY 1977	Percentage Increase	Final FY 1977	Committee "Requests" FY 1978	Percentage Increase
National Defense	$ 91.9	$102.9	11.9%	$100.7	$112.6	11.8%
International Affairs	4.9	7.2	46.9	6.9	8.0	15.9
Science, Space and Technology	4.6	4.5	–2.0	4.5	4.8	6.6
Natural Resources-Energy	11.4	16.6	45.6	16.2	26.2	61.7
Agriculture	2.6	2.9	11.5	2.2	5.8	163.6
Commerce and Transportation	18.3	23.4	27.8	17.4	21.8	25.2
Community Development	7.0	7.0	0	9.1	11.7	28.5
Education, Employment, Social Security	20.9	27.6	32.0	22.2	31.5	41.8
Health	32.9	39.3	19.4	38.9	45.5	16.9
Income Security	128.2	144.1	12.4	137.2	147.8	7.7
Veterans	19.1	19.8	3.6	19.5	20.6	5.6
Law Enforcement and Justice	3.4	3.7	9.0	3.6	4.1	13.8
General Government	3.3	3.7	12.1	3.5	4.0	14.3
Revenue Sharing	7.3	8.0	9.5	7.7	9.9	28.5
Interest	35.4	44.3	25.1	39.6	41.8	5.5
Total*	$374.9	$442.0	17.9%	$431.1	$482.1	16.7%

Sources: Views and Estimates of the Standing Committees, and Second Concurrent Resolution of the Budget, Fiscal Years 1976 and 1977.
*Minus allowances and undistributed offsetting receipts.

111

succeeded in reducing backdoor spending and reinstating some of the controls of the appropriations process. Although the avenues of backdoor spending were not completely closed, the ability of the authorizing committees to avoid the regular budget process was reduced. In addition, the budget process imposed severe time constraints on the authorizing committees.

Authorizing legislation is a critical part of congressional budgeting. As established long ago in the rules of the House and the Senate, no appropriation shall be granted for any purpose not authorized by law. However, in recent years there have been an increasing number of appropriations voted without authorizations. Authorizations include both broad grants of legislative authority and specific limits on the amounts that may be appropriated. Most of the decisions made by authorizing committees and embodied by the passage of authorization bills have multiyear implications. They commit the government to expenditures for many years, often indefinitely, into the future.

AUTHORIZATIONS

Annual authorizations are a relatively recent phenomenon developing since World War II. If an agency or program has an annual authorization it must go through both the authorization and the appropriation process every year. This involves four separate hearings—two in the House and two in the Senate. The primary purpose of annual authorizations is to increase congressional scrutiny of agency programs, but may also be directed against the Appropriations Committee indicating dissatisfaction with its oversight activities. One of the first agencies to undergo annual authorization was the Atomic Energy Commission (AEC). Beginning in 1954, the Joint Committee on Atomic Energy instituted annual authorization for the construction of nuclear facilities.[7] In 1959, two major efforts were made in this direction. The first would have brought much of the Department of Defense budget under annual authorizations, including all outlays for missiles, aircraft, and naval vessels.[8] Despite the fact that the language was dropped in conference, many parts of the defense program have been authorized annually ever since. In arguing in favor of the change, proponents stressed the point that the role of the authorizing committee would be enhanced, and they would be less dependent on the Appropriations Committee.[9]

A second step taken by Congress in 1959 was to require annual authorizations for the National Aeronautics and Space Administration (NASA). This action evoked more conflict between the authorizing and Appropriations committees.[10] Appropriations Committee members complained that such a step would create needless duplication of effort. But the Science and Astronautics Committee favored the change since it would increase oversight of the new space agency as well as increase their own power vis-à-vis Appropriations.

Disagreements over annual authorizations point out some overlapping in the complex congressional budgetary system. Even before budget reform further complicated the system, authorizing committees sometimes saw themselves as "assisting in the tasks of the Appropriations Committees."[11] By establishing a dollar figure on the amount that may be appropriated, authorizing committees create a presumption of adequate funding on the part of the Appropriations committees. They feel that because of the time they spend in hearings, and the care with which they scrutinize an agency's programs, the Appropriations committees *should* allocate what was authorized. Appropriations committees usually appropriate less than what was authorized, creating the gap.

Annual authorizations increase the amount of program oversight, but they also increase the workload which may result in duplication of effort and some animosity between committees. Annual authorizations offer Congress greater short-term control than either multiyear authorizations or permanent authorizations. Congress may specify precise conditions and requirements of agencies in annual authorizations. For example, the 1976 Foreign Relations Authorization Act prohibits the State Department from implementing a computerized passport system, instructs it to undertake certain studies, authorizes employees to carry firearms, specifies requirements for security investigations, and many other precise requirements.[12]

Despite the recent popularity and the potential they offer for congressional control, only about 15 percent of the budget is authorized annually.[13] Table 6 3 lists the total annual authorizations for fiscal 1976. Recent additions include the State Department authorization, the International Trade Commission authorization for fiscal 1977, and it appears that annual authorizations for the intelligence community may soon be required.[14]

Multiyear authorizations establish the legislative basis for an agency or program for a fixed period of time, usually between two and five years. A number of federal assistance programs and grants to state and local governments have multiyear authorizations; revenue sharing is one example. Originally authorized by Congress in 1972 for a period of four years, the program was up for reauthorization in 1976.[15] This provided Congress with an opportunity to reexamine the program, its impact and operation, and the amount of funds available to it. In reconsidering revenue sharing, alternative distribution formulas were considered and changes in use restrictions were contemplated; however, the final version looked much like the original legislation. Other programs with multiyear authorizations include social services grants, water pollution programs, health programs, and various education programs.

Multiyear authorizations are a compromise between annual and permanent authorizations.[16] Because federal actions affect the budgetary cycle of state and local governments, annual authorizations can cause chaos for other units of government when they are unsure of how much federal

Table 6-3.
ANNUAL AUTHORIZATIONS, Fiscal 1976

Agency or Program	Amount (in millions)
Board for International Broadcasting	$ 65.6
Energy Research and Development Administration	5,026.5
Foreign Assistance (International Development and Food Assistance)	1,567.2
Foreign Assistance (International Security Assistance)	3,191.9
Maritime Administration	543.6
Military Construction	3,523.4
Military Procurement and Research & Development	25,513.0
National Aeronautics and Space Administration	3,562.3
National Science Foundation	791.0
Nuclear Regulatory Commission	222.9
Peace Corps	88.5
Saline Water Conversion	4.1
State Department	869.9
Coast Guard	124.9
United States Information Agency	266.8
Total	$45,361.6

Source: Allen Schick, *Congressional Control of Expenditures*, U.S. House of Representatives, Committee on the Budget, 95th Congress, 1st Sess., January 1977, p. 24.

assistance is forthcoming. Multiyear authorizations provide greater certainty for state and local governments, but allow the Congress to periodically review assistance programs.

In a single year, multiyear authorizations constitute about 10 percent of existing programs, but the proportion of the budget on a multiyear cycle is about one-fourth of the budget.[17] This type of authorization may be the wave of the future, as an alternative to "sunset" legislation. It does not provide Congress as much control as annual authorization, but it reduces uncertainty for other actors, and allows them to avoid both authorization and appropriation hearings in most years. At the same time, it allows greater scrutiny by Congress than permanent authorizations.

Permanent authorizations provide legislative authority for agencies and programs indefinitely. Although Congress may periodically review and change the authorization of a "permanent" program, it is not required to do so and does not do so on a regular basis. Permanent authorizations usually specify that sums "necessary and proper" to carry out the program should be appropriated.[18] Oversight and control of such programs is left exclusively to the Appropriations committees. One of the reasons for permanent authorizations is the need for stability and security in some federal programs. Social security, for example, should not vary in scope and operation from one year to the next, or even over five- or ten-year periods. As a major source of income for many Americans, frequent "tinkering" would have disruptive effects. Yet, as the changes made in Social Security in 1977 indicate, Congress can still make substantive changes in programs that are permanently authorized.

More than one-half of the budget is currently under permanent authorization.[19] Growth in both annual and multiyear authorizations have reduced this proportion significantly in the past thirty years. While the stability provided by these permanent programs is important, many members of Congress feel that permanent authorizations shield much of the budget from control and many programs from careful scrutiny.

Different types of program authorization are only one of the obstacles to congressional control. As discussed in the first chapter, most of the budget is locked in during the annual cycle. When Congress authorizes the construction of buildings, dams, weapons systems, ships, submarines, and bridges that take many years to complete, its discretion in a given year is limited. In most cases, once a project is underway, it is wasteful and politically difficult to discontinue the project. Although Carter's termination of various water projects in 1978 indicates that they can be stopped in midstream, this is the exception rather than the rule. Even annual authorizations do not provide Congress with complete discretion. Although NASA requires an annual authorization, the decision to implement Skylab, for example, committed the authorizing committee to a multiyear project and future funding.

For the most part, the authorizing committees consider themselves *legislative*, not *budgetary* units. Their primary function is to consider substantive policy proposals and to recommend legislation to their respective houses. Although they recognize the importance of money to their actions, their budgetary role is second to their legislative role. The authorizing committees deal with policy questions within a limited sphere. Whether it is foreign affairs, defense, health, or education, each committee has its particular area of expertise. Associated with that sphere of influence are particular subgovernments, including certain executive agencies, interest groups, and clientele groups.[20] Specialization is also characteristic of their budgetary responsibilities; they do not take an overview of the budget (except as individual members voting on the budget resolutions). These general characteristics of authorizing committees affect their roles and behavior, and differentiate them from the Budget committees or Appropriations committees.

MARCH 15 REPORTS

Accustomed to acting when they were ready and when they wished, many members of authorizing committees were disturbed with the rigid requirements of the budget process. The March 15 reports require estimates of the amount of new budget authority and outlays necessary for the coming fiscal year. Some committees make extensive reviews of their programs and include detailed staff work in preparing their reports. Others review their needs in the coming year in a superficial fashion.[21] One of the initial difficulties for the Budget committees in both houses was the erratic quality of the different reports. The Senate Armed Services Committee continued not to cooperate, claiming that it could not estimate spending needs before its hearings were held, and it submitted only a brief two-page report.[22]

There is no mystery about the divergent views of the March 15 reports held by members of Congress. Members of authorizing committees feel that the deadline is too rigid. Budget committee members, on the other hand, see the March 15 deadline as a key to the entire budget process. Compare the views of two members: Representative Jack Brooks (D-Tex.—chairman of the Government Operations Committee):

March 15 presents a real and difficult problem. Under this provision, the committees are required to set forth what we believe will be the spending decisions likely to be approved by our committees. The dilemma arises in whether or not we should include funds for new programs that may be highly controversial. Whether it is intended to or not, a recorded vote on the items in the March 15 report can be highly prejudicial to the later consideration of substantive legislation. The issue facing the Budget Committee is whether this process will give you reliable estimates from the legislative committees. Should we include every possible legislative proposal?[23]

Representative Sam Gibbons (D-Fla.—Budget Committee):

I think the March 15 deadline is a must, or you could never get the rest of the work finished that must be finished in the budget process during the remainder of the cycle. Yes, I will admit Mr. Brooks has a point. It does require us to get to work fast in committees; it does require us to make a lot of preliminary decisions, but we must think of them as preliminary decisions; as budget making. It is painful . . . but I think it is healthy. It begins to make us think earlier in the year what we are going to be doing during the whole year—to adopt a sort of agenda at least by March 15.[24]

Complaints from members of the authorizing committees have been similar on the Senate side. Senator Proxmire has suggested that the March 15 deadline be dropped and the entire timetable be advanced.[25]

Any timetable is going to impose constraints on the authorizing committees that were not present before, and their estimates are likely to be somewhat inflated in any event. The large increases projected by the standing committees are partially a function of uncertainty, but also a result of the basic advocacy of the committees for their agencies and programs. Several other results of the March 15 reports on the authorization committees can be identified.[26] Implementation of the budget process has helped to clarify the spending jurisdiction of the authorizing committees. In addition, it has helped to tie the parts of the budget process together; authorizing committees appear to have a better sense of the relationship of their decisions to appropriations. Most importantly, the March 15 reports require the standing committees in Congress to participate more regularly in at least an annual budget planning cycle. Although an annual cycle may still be inadequate because of the multiyear implications of decisions, this represents an improvement over the previous practices.

MAY 15 DEADLINE

The Budget Act requires committees to report authorizing legislation by May 15 each year, the same date for passage of the first budget resolution. Again, some of the chairmen of the authorizing committees felt this was too great a limitation on the time they spend considering legislation. If a committee reports authorizing legislation after May 15, the Budget committees may require a change in the effective date until the next year.[27] As will be shown in the next chapter, the Budget committees have been accommodating and generous on requests for waivers of the deadline.

The deadline for legislation tends to create a logjam in the congressional calendar, since many bills are reported just before the deadline. In 1976, forty house bills and seventy-five Senate bills were reported the few days before May 15.[28] In addition, the authorizing committees reported more bills than previously, even before extensive hearings were held. This is another outcome of the uncertainty caused by the timetable and the desire of the standing committees to preserve their options. As a result, the percentage of authorizing bills that are finally enacted is somewhat less than before the budget process was implemented.

RELATIONS WITH OTHER COMMITTEES

The first real tests of the Budget Committee in the Senate arose in challenges to authorizing committees. Although the House Budget Committee has shown more deference to the authorizing committees in floor votes, their specificity in line items and programs has irritated some of the standing committees.

In 1975, Representative Thomas Morgan (D-Pa.), chairman of the International Relations Committee, complained that the Budget Committee was intruding on the jurisdiction of his committee.[29] In 1976, Representative Charles Wilson (D-Calif.) stated that when the Budget Committee took positions on authorizing legislation, it involved itself in line item budgeting not within its jurisdiction and unacceptable to members of the authorizing committees.[30] The basic clash between the authorizing committees and the Budget committees takes place within the context of program versus priority budgeting. Committees generally support overall fiscal control, but object to reductions in their own discretion and power.

In the first years of the budget process, some authorizing committees continued to report legislation creating new contract and borrowing authority. The Budget committees monitored these developments closely and, allied with the Appropriations committees on this issue, were able to defeat these attempts. For example, a bill reported by the House Merchant Marine and Fisheries Committee in 1975 would have created permanent authority to spend license fees. The House Appropriations Committee amended the bill to subject it to the appropriations process.[31] A similar action by the House Banking Committee to create new authority was also brought under the appropriations process. Although the authorizing committees could continue to report existing entitlement legislation, new entitlements were subject to appropriations. Most authorizing committees have cooperated, recognizing the strong sentiment against backdoor spending. But when discipline is imposed, the reaction may be negative. When the House Budget Committee successfully imposed a ceiling on highway spending, the chairman of the subcommittee complained it had accomplished a "willful, deliberate and destructive maneuver . . .to accomplish by subterfuge what it had been unable to accomplish on the floor of the House."[32]

Conflicts have not been limited to authorizing versus Budget committees. Besides their opposition to backdoor spending, the Appropriations committees sometimes find their roles and responsibilities at odds with the authorizing committees. Instead of extending the May 15 deadline, the Appropriations committees believe the standing committees should report legislation sooner. The House Appropriations Committee made the following observation about the authorization process:

If the authorizing committees wait to report legislation until the deadline of May 15, it will have a minimal impact or no impact on appropriation bill markups. . . .If the new budget process is to succeed, the legislation machinery of the House must be timed to produce authorizing legislation in advance of the May 15 date. . . .The Committee notes that during this session very few bills containing major authorizations for 1977 appropriations have come to the House floor.[33]

The differences in perception and prescriptions for the budget timetable are clearly a function of the various roles of participants. Balancing the authorization, appropriation, and budget process is a delicate and difficult task.

THE APPROPRIATIONS COMMITTEES

APPROPRIATIONS

Historically, legislative control of the budget has been accomplished through appropriations. Congress has fluctuated between line item and lump sum allocations.[34] During periods of national emergency, Congress has been more willing to appropriate lump sums. Line items provide Congress with a greater opportunity for control, but as the budget has grown in complexity, the categories have been merged into larger and larger accounts. Although committees may still refer to their actions as line item review, it has become essentially lump sum budgeting. This is not the equivalent of surrendering control, however. The Appropriations committees have other devices to assert control over executive branch actions.[35] First, the committees may write program or financial restrictions into the appropriations bills. These provisions can set limits on what agencies can do with their funds in very specific terms. Second, the committees may write specific policy directives into the appropriations bills. They may require the agency to take certain actions or may forbid them to take others. Third, the committees may require the agencies to submit more detailed budget estimates than those supplied in the president's budget. This allows the committee to scrutinize a particular area more closely and provide additional controls on agency actions. Although the committee reports do not have the same legal impact as line item actions, they do impose significant limits on agency actions.[36]

Although most of the decisions made by the committee are fiscal decisions, there is evidence that the Appropriations committees are increasingly concerned with programmatic decisions. Arnold Kanter found that the Defense budget is subjected to a differential review: different parts of the requests are treated in different fashions.[37] Research and Development receive more programmatic consideration than other, less controllable, portions of the budget. Robert Bledsoe and Roger Handberg, also examining the Defense budget, found that the Appropriations committees have intensified their programmatic actions in comparison to the fiscal emphases identified in earlier studies.[38]

Despite changes that suggest more careful scrutiny of executive requests and various forms of control imposed by the Appropriations committees, the growth and complexity of the budget mitigate against this trend. Louis Fisher has detailed the many forms of spending discretion in the hands of the president and the bureaucracy, techniques that may undermine congressional control.[39] The decisions of the Appropriations committees must be made within a complex set of external constraints, many imposed by the budget process.

The House and Senate Appropriations Committees, broken down into subcommittees, consider the requests of executive agencies and make recommendations to their respective bodies. This basic task remained the same after budget reform. The amount of budget dollars under the jurisdiction of the various subcommittees varies considerably, as Table 6-4 indicates. Defense and Labor-Health, Education, and Welfare subcommittees control about half of the Appropriations committees' allocation. As has been the case for decades, each subcommittee holds hearings on the agencies and programs under their purview. But a number of changes have occurred both in the actions of the committees and in their institutional power.

Table 6-4.
APPROPRIATIONS SUBCOMMITTEES AND ALLOCATION,
U.S. SENATE, 1979 ($ in billions)

Subcommittee	New Budget Authority	Share
Defense	120,300	34.1%
Labor; Health, Education and Welfare	73,687	20.8%
Housing and Urban Development; Independent Agencies	70,356	19.9%
Agriculture	22,184	6.2%
Interior	11,962	3.5%
Public Works	10,462	2.8%
Transportation	9,873	2.7%
Treasury, Post Office, General Government	9,714	2.7%
Foreign Operations	9,273	2.6%
State, Justice, Commerce, Judiciary	9,192	2.6%
Military Construction	3,881	1.0%
Legislative Branch	1,127	.3%
District of Columbia	287	.05%
Total,* Appropriations Committee	353,076	100. %

Source: Senate Budget Scorekeeping Report, No. 79-11, November 13, 1978.

*Totals may vary due to rounding.

"CLASSICAL" VIEW OF THE COMMITTEES

The view of the House Appropriations Committee provided in the 1960s was that of a well-integrated political unit, responsive to the demands of the parent chamber, and concerned with protecting their prestige and reputation.[40] Fenno characterized the Appropriations Committee as a "power" committee: the primary goal of the members in seeking a seat on the committee was to enhance their power within the House of Representatives.[41] The most salient environmental constraints were imposed by the other members of the House; Appropriations was hypothesized to be a House-oriented committee. To achieve its goals, Fenno suggested that the committee pursued several concomitant strategies: to reduce executive budget requests, and to provide adequate funding for programs. The general ideological consonance between Republicans and Democrats over their budget-cutting rule tended to facilitate consensus on the committee.

Appropriations was described as a decentralized committee with semi-autonomous subcommittees doing most of the work. Fenno reported that 96 percent of the total meetings were subcommittee meetings.[42] The full committee met to ratify (occasionally to modify) the decisions of the subcommittees. Of the committees Fenno studied, the House Appropriations Committee was one of the least partisan. Members of the two parties worked closely together with a sense of common purpose. The norms of specialization and reciprocity were dominant on the Appropriations Committee. Members sat on several subcommittees and developed expertise in those areas of the executive budget. In recognizing the specialization of other committee members, they expected their own to be respected. Committee Chairmen Clarence Cannon (1955-64) and George Mahon (D-Tex.; 1964-78) functioned as consensus chairmen, without dominating decision making.

The Senate Appropriations Committee, according to Fenno, differed from the House committee in several ways.[43] Some senators sought the committee because of its power, but others valued the position's advantages for constituent service. Senators indicated an equal interest in the benefits that could be secured for their home states. Decision making in the Senate is more individualistic than the House, and committees are less dominant. One senator contrasted the differences between the two committees:

The Appropriations Committee isn't nearly as important over here as it is in the House. Over there, it's life or death for a member. He has to get his project approved by the Appropriations Committee and they're very tough. Over here it's much looser. It's much easier for the individual Senator to get his projects in the bill.[44]

Because of the salience of the House and the timing of appropriations, the Senate committee had been considered a "court of appeals," restoring reductions in agency requests made in the House. Senators followed more individual goals than House members concerned with constituency-based requests. In general, Fenno portrayed the Senate Appropriations Committee as less specialized, more constituency oriented, but like the House committee in maintaining a decentralized structure, avoiding partisanship, and responding to consensus chairmen.

COMMITTEES IN DECLINE?

In 1962, a dispute between the House and Senate held up all appropriations bills for a period of months. Columnist Drew Pearson wrote:

The seniority system permitted two octogenarians, Senator Carl Hayden (D-Ariz.) and Clarence Cannon (D-Mo.) to hold up all appropriations bills for three months because they wouldn't agree on which would walk across the Capitol to meet the other.[45]

The dispute involved more than a personal disagreement, and actually arose over basic differences in the role of the House and Senate in the appropriations process.[46] The appropriations process has come a long way since then; if the protagonists in the 1962 dispute could come back and watch the activity around the May 15 and September 15 deadlines, they surely would be astounded. But the appropriations process did not change under its own momentum fast enough in the 1960s. A majority of the members of Congress felt they had fallen short in their role of guardian of the public purse. The decentralized system of budgeting could not provide the overview that was seen as essential in the 1970s. In 1962, the chairmen of the Appropriations committees could almost bring much of the business of government to a halt. By the late 1970s, the committees were scrambling to protect their role in the budget process.

A subtle shift may have occurred in members' goals in serving on the committees. As David Mayhew has shown, marginal districts in the House have declined significantly since 1948.[47] Incumbents are more effective than ever at getting reelected, and fewer who seek reelection are defeated. Morris Fiorina proposes that this is partially a function of a behavioral change on the part of congressmen.[48] He argues that congressmen can effectively assure reelection by concentrating on constituent service, performing an ombudsman role, rather than by focusing on major national issues. Service on an Appropriations subcommittee allows a member to secure and protect district projects. What Fenno identified as a significant goal for Senate Appropriation Committee members may now apply to House committee members as well. A second reason to suggest the movement of the House Appropriations Committee from a "power" committee to a "constituency" committee is relative influence and prestige. To be sure, the Appropriations committees are still among the most powerful in Congress, but they are weaker vis-à-vis other committees than they were in the previous decade. Therefore, the lure of increased influence within the Congress is reduced from past years.

These trends are consistent with a change that occurred in the late 1960s. Prior to that time, members of the Appropriations subcommittees were not supposed to be directly interested in the programs for which their committee was responsible. The intention was to reduce self-interest and advocacy. In the last decade, that appears to have changed. Farmers sit on the Agriculture Subcommittee, hawks sit on the Defense Subcommittee, urban liberals sit on the Labor-Health, Education, and Welfare Subcommittee. The increase in committee advocacy, a reduction in the guardianship role, and a shift toward a constituent orientation are related to this change.

Reputations often live on beyond the terms of performance, but the retreat from preeminence is clearly visible for the Appropriations committees. Despite the fact that the committees still consider themselves guardians of the public purse—budget cutters—it is clear that a large faction of Congress is dissatisfied with their efforts. In June 1978, the House considered a number of across-the-board cuts in appropriations bills. This so-called "meat-axe" approach simply reduces the total appropriation by a fixed percentage.[49] A 2 percent across-the-board cut was approved for the controllable portion of the Health, Education, and Welfare budget and the State, Justice, and Commerce appropriations bill. A 5 percent cut was approved for legislative appropriations a few days later.

The concurrence of these votes with the passage of California's Proposition 13 was no coincidence, but the budget-cutting mood was more than a passing fad. Similar attempts have been applied to the budget resolutions, and a $2.5 billion across-the-board reduction was approved in May 1979 in the House for the first resolution for fiscal 1980.[50] Such slashes are more onerous to the Appropriations committees: the Budget committees deal with budget aggregates but the Appropriations committees look at the details of the budget. An across-the-board cut is a repudiation of this role for it does not specify where the savings can be found, and it leaves discretion with executive branch agencies. The Senate, too, was vulnerable to the budget-cutting mood in 1978. The Treasury, Postal Service, and general government appropriations bills were subjected to a 2 percent cut and the committee, showing fragmentation where unity once prevailed, split 10 to 9 on the floor vote.[51]

Members of both the Budget and Appropriations committees in the House agree that the Appropriations Committee is weaker. One Democrat who sits on both committees commented:

Appropriations is still a strong committee, but it's nothing like it used to be. Everbody in the Congress is becoming an expert on spending and they are less likely to defer to us. It's a whole new ball game with the Budget Committee and Appropriations just isn't top dog anymore.

One of the indicators of the power of the Appropriations committees was their record of floor-success—preventing amendments. Although reduced, this continues to be high. But is it really a good indicator of success? Allen Schick questions this measure:

Certainly the ability to prevail against floor challenges is an important consideration, but a high success rate might simply mean the reporting committee has little choice as to what it recommends. Legislative power must entail the discretion to decide what to do and what not to do. The 1977 public works employment bill suggests this discretion is not always held by the Appropriations Committee.[52]

Other observers support the claim the actions of the Appropriations committees are increasingly bounded by external constraints. Some more cynical Capitol Hill observers claim that the only way the Appropriations committees can revive their tarnished image as budget cutters is to act as strong advocates early in the process. By setting the targets as high as possible, they can still protect their pet programs while appearing to make cuts in the budget. Internal changes, the climate in Congress, and the mood of the country combined with the new budget process have significantly altered the classical view of the Appropriations committees.

CHANGES IN TIMING

The Appropriations committees had perhaps the most to lose with the budget reforms, despite the provisions included to mollify their opposition. Ironically, of all the participants, the Appropriations committees have had the least problems and the appropriations process is well-integrated with the budget process.

The most immediate impact was on the operating procedures of the committees. The committees had to supply views and estimates of budget authority and outlays for the March 15 report. The totals have to be allocated by subcommittee, as Table 6-4 has shown for fiscal 1979. The Budget Act stipulated that appropriations bills cannot be considered until the first resolution is approved and action on the appropriations bills must be completed by the seventh day after Labor Day. This actually forces the committees to report bills in the middle of the summer since Congress usually recesses in August. The subcommittees begin markup in April and May which causes two problems. Neither the first resolution nor the authorizing legislation is yet approved leaving gaps in guidance. The Appropriations committees usually rely on the Budget committee reports, but the versions differ in the House and Senate. The speedup in procedures has raised questions about the adequacy of time available for review in the hearings. One member of the House Appropriations Committee complained:

The subcommittee did not have time to hold a detailed hearing which has been customarily held in the past. We covered the entire budget request. Much of our deliberation was more general and less detailed than has been the case in recent years.[53]

The committees have, however, been able to accomplish something that eluded them in the past—the passage of appropriations before the start of the fiscal year. In the first four years, almost all the regular appropriations bills have been approved on time. The exceptions were delays caused by non-financial issues such as federal funding of abortions.

The Appropriations committees, under the statute, have the jurisdiction to limit entitlement authority for a fiscal year in another committee's jurisdiction, if it exceeds the most recent allocation.[54] The scorekeeping reports issued by CBO have helped coordinate the appropriations bills and the budget resolutions. Despite the tendency for advocacy (or perhaps because of it), the actions of the committees have been consistent with the resolutions. It became apparent, early in the implementation process, that the first resolution "targets" were to be interpreted as ceilings. The generosity in establishing the subtotals in the first resolution have made this possible. This has also left the reconciliation process unused, until the Senate attempted it in 1979.

RELATIONS WITH THE BUDGET COMMITTEES

Because of the House Budget Committee's periodic incursions into line item budgeting, relationships with the Appropriations committee have been subject to more conflicts than in the Senate. Chairman George Mahon warned the Budget Committee against intruding in areas reserved to the Appropriations committees. An Appropriations Committee report noted:

The Committee notes with concern the tendency to identify and make recommendations for specific line items. While these line item recommendations have no actual effect, they do tend to obscure the overall macro-economic responsibilities of the Budget Committee and to needlessly duplicate much of the hearings and deliberations that are the responsibility of the authorizing committees. The Committee urges that the content of the reports on the Concurrent Resolutions to the Budget be confined to the purposes set forth in the Act.[55]

The House Budget Committee took steps to keep Mahon as an ally, which was essential. It hired Bruce Meredith, a trusted former Appropriations staffer, as one of its directors.[56] It also sided with the Appropriations Committee on several important issues.

In the Senate, Appropriations Chairman John McClellan (D-Ark.) was originally skeptical but soon became a strong ally of Muskie and the Budget Committee. Despite the challenge by Muskie over impoundment jurisdiction, Senate Appropriations was not threatened by line item estimates by the Budget Committee. Muskie commented.

We do not go into the program detail that the Appropriation committee does. If we were to do the actual allocation by appropriation bill, we would be doing the Appropriations Committee's work. That is not our responsibility.[57]

The Senate Appropriations Committee had more to gain than its House counterparts. Always a second class citizen as the "Appeals Court," the strict timetable enabled the committee to approach parity with the House. One observer concluded that the budget process assisted McClellan in consolidating his power as chairman by giving him more control over the subcommittees.[58] For these reasons, the relationship emerged into an alliance.

One of the most divisive incidents occurred in the House over President Carter's stimulus package in early 1977. The third resolution, formulated by the House Budget Committee and leadership, called for $3.7 billion in new spending. The House Appropriations Committee approved only half this figure. During a meeting of Budget and Appropriations Committee leaders in his office, Speaker O'Neill made clear the policy of the leadership, and the Budget Committee's figures were to be upheld. The Appropriations Committee's bill was rewritten, but it left the committee somewhat embittered about the loss of discretion apparent in the steamrolling job that had occurred.

The members of the Budget committees in both houses generally characterized the relationship with the Appropriations committees as good. Words like "friendly," "allies," "cooperative," "constructive" dominated; one House Budget Committee member said, "there were a few problems at first, but now we're working hand in hand." Budget reform altered the power and autonomy of the Appropriations committees, but recognizing that the Budget committees perform an essential task that they were unable to do, the committees have developed strong working relationships.

A number of significant changes in the Appropriations committees have occurred in the last twenty years. They tend to be less stringent guardians of the public purse than they once were, with evidence of advocacy appearing more frequently. Consistent with growing decentralization in Congress, the committees have lost some of the institutional power they once enjoyed. Members appear to be increasingly oriented to constituent concerns rather than institutional power. The Senate Appropriations Committee is more nearly the equal of its House counterpart than was previously the case. The budget process itself has reduced the autonomy the committees once had on the spending side of the budget. Because change was gradual, however, and carried out with the acquiescence of the Appropriations committees, major institutional conflicts between committees have not occurred.

THE WAYS AND MEANS AND FINANCE COMMITTEES

JURISDICTION

The Ways and Means and Finance Committees are unique in having a key role in both the revenue and expenditure sides of the budget. The convenient label, "tax-writing committees" is a misnomer. As Table 6-1 showed, they have jurisdiction more than 40 percent of federal expenditures, just slightly less than the Appropriations committees. The committees retain almost complete control of the revenue side of the budget, leading some other observers to conclude that the Ways and Means and Finance Committees have excessive control. Senator Muskie commented only half humorously:

The Finance Committee now controls the entire revenue side of the budget, which is 50 percent of it, and then if you look at the spending side, Medicare, Medicaid, Social Security and so on—You add it altogether, yes, and I expect it is close to 75 percent of the whole budget which goes through the Finance Committee. We don't focus on it, we let it grow, and I don't blame Russell [Long] for not wanting the budget process; he has got 75 percent of the budget now, why should he give to anybody else any part of it? [Laughter].[59]

Table 6-5 examines the spending jurisdiction of the Finance Committee (jurisdiction of the Ways and Means Committee is similar). They control some of the largest expenditures in the federal budget, including income maintenance and health care. Both the House and Senate have turned back efforts to carve up the jurisdiction of the two committees. Recent budget battles, such as the change in Social Security taxes and benefits, have focused on the tax-writing committees. They are likely to become more important rather than less important in the coming decade if the national health insurance debate heats up—and unless Congress makes some changes.

Table 6-5.
FINANCE COMMITTEE SPENDING JURISDICTION
FISCAL YEAR 1979
(new budget authority in billions)

Programs	Direct Spending Jurisdiction	Entitlements Funded Through Appropriations
Social Security	$102,727	
Federal Hospital Insurance	21,894	
Federal Supplementary Medical Insurance	9,751	
Unemployment Insurance	15,994	$ 885
Social Service		2,578
Medicaid		11,253
Aid to Dependent Children (ADC)		6,663
Supplemental Security Income		5,558
Revenue Sharing	6,855	
Interest on Debt	54,700	
Refundable Earned Income Credit	841	
Other	524	
Total – Fiscal 1979*	$213,588	$ 34,289
Grand Total†		$247,877

Source: Senate Budget Scorekeeping Report, no. 79-11, November 13, 1978, p. 47.

*Allocation in the second resolution FY 1979.

† Does not reflect certain actions completed in the second session of the 95th Congress.

The policy influence of the Ways and Means and Finance Committees on the budget is not limited to the big expenditure items. Their control of revenue affects policy in a myriad of ways besides total revenue and deficit. Taxes are increasingly used as social incentives and disincentives. One of the elements of the committees' decisions that have growing impact are tax expenditures. Tax expenditures are defined as the loss of revenue resulting from special tax provisions such as exclusions, exemptions, deductions, preferential tax rates, tax credits, or tax deferrals. They can be assigned a dollar figure, representing the equivalent of a direct outlay to the taxpayer. Tax expenditures have grown rapidly in the last decade, largely a result of actions taken by the Ways and Means and Finance Committees. Between 1967 and 1977, tax expenditures increased 178 percent, more than the 146 percent increase in federal spending.[60] Table 6-6 shows tax expenditures to corporations and individuals from 1974 to 1983. By the end of this period, they are projected to reach almost $200 billion. If the past growth in *new* tax expenditures is continued, the total will exceed this figure.

Table 6-6.
TAX EXPENDITURES ($ in billions)

Fiscal Year	Corporations	Individuals	Total
1974	$19,345	$ 61,770	$ 81,115
1975	21,335	66,880	88,215
1976	23,195	75,785	98,980
1977	27,050	87,420	114,420
1978	31,815	92,600	124,415
1979	34,425	101,750	136,175
1980*	36,356	110,215	146,571
1981*	37,620	121,420	159,040
1982*	37,740	133,525	171,265
1983*	39,820	147,690	187,510

Source: *Report to Accompany First Concurrent Resolution on the Budget, Fiscal Year 1979*, U.S. Senate, Budget Committee 95-739, 95th Cong., 2nd Sess., p. 46.

*Current policy projections.

Reforms to reduce tax expenditures have been relatively minor. Congress has reduced the oil depletion allowance, limited some shelters, enacted new carry-over rules, and increased the minimum tax. These actions have been more than offset in the 1970s by expansion of the investment tax credit, corporate surtax exemption, employment tax credit for elderly and child care, and employee stock ownership credit.[61] While the goals and results may be laudable for groups and individuals, the impact on the already fragmented tax structure is not. These actions represent an expansion by the Ways and Means and Finance Committees (sanctioned by Congress) into new policy areas. The committees are using tax expenditures to implement national policy goals in a variety of areas unrelated to fiscal policy.

COMMITTEE TRANSITIONS

Like the Appropriations Committee, the House Ways and Means Committee was considered a "power" committee; members desired appointment to gain internal influence in the House. John Manley concluded that House members were not on the committee to improve their reelection chances—they could do more on other committees.[62] In contrast, members of the Senate Finance Committee made little mention of internal influence and instead voiced policy and reelection goals.[63] Ways and Means was seen as more partisan than Appropriations, but to preserve its influence, restrained partisanship. It also attempted to preserve its influence by reporting bills that would pass the House; floor changes were perceived as detrimental to member goals. Of course, the use of closed rules fostered the floor success of the committee. At the same time, Manley emphasized the ties between Ways and Means and the party leaders. Committee members purposely attempted to follow partisan policy choices when necessary.[64]

Unlike Appropriations, the Ways and Means Committee was more centralized with strong leadership; the committee had no subcommittees and conducted all work in full committee sessions. With only twenty-five members compared to more than fifty on Appropriations, the task of centralized control was considerably easier. Wilbur Mills's role as chairman and leader was much analyzed. Although the press often portrayed Mills as a czar, Manley's assessment focused on Mills's abilities as a consensus leader. With profound technical expertise and experience, Mills was able to keep the members satisfied through compromise and accommodation, while dominating decision making.[65]

With Senate committees less dominant than House committees, the Finance Committee was not considered as powerful as its House counterpart. Interest groups and the administration were identified as important parts of the environment of the Finance Committee. Finance Committee members would help themselves by serving clientele groups and their home state. They were less subject to institutional constraints (and prerogatives) than the Ways and Means Committee. Their secondary position (the House originates all revenue bills) made them more reacting than initiating. Manley found the Finance Committee to be more conservative than the Ways and Means Committee, and less partisan.[66]

The transformation of the Ways and Means Committee began in the 1970s. As the House Democratic caucus emerged as a powerful force, a number of procedural reforms were adopted. The caucus voted to open most committee hearings, a change aimed directly at the Ways and Means Committee.[67] In 1973, the caucus put restrictions on the committee's ability to use a closed rule to prevent floor amendments. Next, the caucus adopted a rule requiring all committees greater than twenty members to break down into at least four subcommittees. This was, again, aimed specifically at Ways and Means. Mills had abolished subcommittees in the 1950s and had refused to reinstate them until the caucus mandate.

The most significant changes occurred in late 1974, before the start of the Ninety-fourth Congress. The caucus stripped the committee of its role as the Democratic committee on committees—the power of the Democratic members to make committee appointments. The committee was enlarged from twenty-five to thirty-seven members and a fifth subcommittee was required.[68] All of these changes were made easier by the personal demise of Mills. The scandal of the "Tidal Basin" incident and the public admission of his alcoholism led to his resignation in December 1974, and the selection of Al Ullman as the new chairman. The reforms were intended to democratize the procedures and weaken the autonomy of the Ways and Means Committee. Significantly, the committee was able to protect its substantive jurisdiction from encroachments proposed by the Bolling Committee, which proposed reassigning several big expenditure programs to other House panels.[69]

Although the Senate Finance Committee has not been "reformed" to the extent of the Ways and Means Committee, it has felt a trickle of reform while turning away the tides of change. Committee sessions, once closed with no public records, are now largely open, and Finance Committee markup sessions produce transcripts available to the public. But most attempted reforms have been turned back by Senator Russell Long and his committee. The Finance Committee was not considered excessively powerful as was Ways and Means under Mills, and the reform sentiment was much weaker in the Senate than the House. The Finance Committee had stable leadership through the critical period of the middle 1970s, while the Ways and Means Committee was evolving from Mills to Ullman. Long successfully defended the jurisdiction of the Finance Committee at the start of the Ninety-fifth Congress from proposals to remove Social Security, Medicare, and other social programs from its control. Despite pressure to give Finance subcommittees a greater role, their lowly status has not changed, sustaining Long's personal control.

THE LIMITED IMPACT OF THE BUDGET COMMITTEES

Despite reforms on the House side to reduce the power of the Ways and Means Committee, both the Ways and Means and Finance Committees have expanded their policy domain since the implementation of the budget process in 1975. The Budget Act requires the Budget Committees "to devise methods of coordinating tax expenditures, policies and programs with direct budget outlays," but the Act did not equate tax expenditures with direct outlays. The Budget committees must list tax expenditures, but they are not approved in the resolutions. There is no provision for Congress to directly control tax expenditures, nor integrate decisions with other budget choices. To date, the Budget committees have been unable to curb the expansion of these individually popular measures. Unlike the other authorizing committees and the Appropriations committees, budget reform has meant few additional constraints for the tax-writing committees, and an increase rather than a reduction in their jurisdiction and influence.

Both Al Ullman and Russell Long have resisted attempts by the Budget committees to bring their own committees' actions under closer scrutiny and centralized control. They are assisted by the weak provisions in the Budget Act dealing with revenues. Senator Muskie described the root of the problem:

Our problem with Finance is that there is only one number in the budget resolution that affects revenues, and that is the overall revenue floor. If we adjust that to accommodate some total of tax expenditure reform, as we did two years ago, $2 billion, you see Russell [Long] is astute enough so he can put together a totally unanticipated package of offsetting changes in the revenue code that would fit under the $2 billion restriction. . . .Russell plays the game superbly. He is defending his committee's jurisdiction and no committee in the Senate has expanded its jurisdiction over more substantive program areas . . .than Finance.[70]

The relations between the House Budget Committee and the Ways and Means Committee had been more harmonious than the Muskie-Long battles in the Senate. One reason is the caution that Adams and Giaimo have displayed in dealing with the other committees, compared to the more aggressive strategy of Muskie and Bellmon. In the first budget resolution in 1976, the Senate Budget Committee included a figure of $2 billion in revenue gained from tax reform—eliminating tax expenditures. Long opposed this on two grounds: first, that tax reform legislation usually does not take effect immediately, and second, that the Budget Committee had no right to instruct the Finance Committee.[71] Muskie and the committee held their position and took the fight to the Senate floor, where Long prevailed in a number of votes. In 1977, the Finance Committee met the *totals* of the first resolution for fiscal 1978, but contrary to the directions included in the accompanying report.[72] The Budget Committee urged the Senate to change the Finance Committee's bill. Senator Lloyd Bentsen (D-Tex.) argued for the Finance Committee:

If it [the Budget Committee] can deal with specificity and detail as to which taxes should be raised and which taxes should be lowered, then it has taken over the responsibility of the Senate Finance Committee. . . .If that happens, you are going to see this same pattern followed in the Appropriations Committee and finally, in the other authorizing committees, and you will have seen the destruction, I think, of the budget reform act.[73]

The Senate upheld the position of the Finance Committee in a close vote. Enough other committees were concerned about the encroachments of the Budget Committee to vote against it.

The Senate Budget Committee suffered some of its sharpest defeats in attempting to control tax expenditures. In 1977, the Senate approved a string of new tax expenditures that exasperated Muskie:

Its quite clear to me that as far as the Internal Revenue Code is concerned, the Senate has indicated the budget process is meaningless. . . .May I say to my colleagues, you kicked the biggest hole in the budget process that you could conceivably kick.[74]

Although the House-Senate conference committee provided a vehicle for reversing Senate decisions and upholding the original Senate Budget Committee provisions, it demonstrated the continued independence of the Finance Committee and the support Long could draw on in the Senate. Consideration of the Finance Committee's energy tax bill produced a similar result. Long kept the bill consistent with the budget resolution by changing the effective date of legislation. This, again, removed an important tax decision from review under the budget process.

In 1978, the issue of tuition tax credits provided a victory for Muskie in his series of continuing confrontations with Long.[75] The Finance Committee's bill needed waivers and appropriations. The Budget Committee recommended against the waivers and the Senate Appropriations Committee voted down the spending. The Finance Committee rewrote the bill and attempted to restore it to its original form by floor amendment. Muskie raised a point of order and was sustained by a 75-21 vote.[76]

Relations have been smoother on the House side and there is greater consensus over the need to curb tax expenditures. However, Chairman Al Ullman has taken care to warn the House Budget Committee against intrusions into the jurisdiction of Ways and Means. On several occasions Ways and Means has opposed the Budget Committee when it attempted to constrain its actions. In 1976, Representative James Corman (D-Calif.) requested a waiver on behalf of his Ways and Means subcommittee on unemployment compensation. The Budget Committee opposed the waiver on the grounds that the emergency was not sufficient to justify waiving the timetable. Corman lashed out:

I think the Budget Committee staff was trying to tell the Ways and Means Committee that it doesn't have much power anymore. The whole game up here is power and the staff of the Budget Committee would like to see the committee have a veto over all the other congressional committees.[77]

But with the dependence on leadership and passive strategies of the House Budget Committees, such confrontations have been noticeably absent.

Interviews with both senators and representatives tend to confirm the fact that the budget process has had little impact on the tax-writing committees.

Although the House has not seen the equivalent of Muskie-Long disputes, both Republicans and Democrats state that the impact on revenue committees is slight. One Democrat on the House Budget Committee commented:

We have had good relations with Ullman and Ways and Means, but very little impact on what they do. The means to influence substantive tax policy is simply not there. But at least he [Ullman] is not fighting the process like Long is on the other side. Ullman has been more supportive all along since he helped get this committee organized.

Budget reform concentrated on the expenditure side of the budget. Substantial changes in the authorizations and appropriations process have occurred, evidence of the impact of the Budget committees. The Budget Act, however, is noticeably weak in integrating the revenue process except at the highest level of aggregation. Tax expenditures, tempting in the benefits they provide, escape systematic evaluation and consideration. The taxing and spending committees have played a significant role in implementing the budget process. But in terms of overall centralization of congressional control, some serious gaps remain.

NOTES

1. U.S. Senate, Committee on the Budget, *Senate Budget Scorekeeping Report*, October 2, 1978, no. 79-9, p. 2.

2. Richard Fenno, *Congressmen in Committees* (Boston: Little, Brown, 1973), p. 48. Aaron Wildavsky, *The Politics of the Budgetary Process* (Boston: Little, Brown, 1964).

3. Richard Fenno, "The Appropriations Committee as a Political System," in Robert Peabody and Nelson Polsby, eds., *New Perspectives on the House of Representatives* (Chicago: Rand McNally, 1969), p. 129.

4. Lance T. LeLoup and William Moreland, "Agency Strategies and Executive Review: The Hidden Politics of Budgeting," *Public Administration Review* 38, no. 3 (May/June 1978): 232-239.

5. U.S. Senate, Committee on the Budget, "Can Congress Control the Power of the Purse," Hearings, 95th Congress, 2nd sess., March 6, 1978.

6. Allen Schick, "Congressional Control of Expenditures," U.S. House of Representatives, Committee on the Budget, CP 95-1, January 1977.

7. Harold P. Green, "The Joint Committee on Atomic Energy: A Model for Legislative Reform," in Ronald Moe, ed., *Congress and the President* (Pacific Palisades, Calif.: Goodyear, 1971), pp. 166-179.

8. Richard Fenno, *The Power of the Purse* (Boston: Little, Brown, 1966), p. 72.

9. Ibid., p. 72.

10. John S. Saloma, "Legislative Effectiveness: Control and Investigation," in Moe, *Congress and the President*, pp. 192-194.

11. Fenno, *Power of the Purse*, p. 73.

12. Schick, "Congressional Control."

13. Ibid., p. 22.

14. Ibid., p. 23.

15. Richard Nathan and Charles Adams, *Revenue Sharing: The Second Round* (Washington: Brookings Institution, 1977).

16. Schick, "Congressional Control," p. 24.

17. Ibid.

18. Ibid., p. 19.

19. Ibid.

20. Randall B. Ripley and Grace Franklin, *Congress, The President, and the Bureaucracy* (Homewood, Ill.: Dorsey Press, 1976).

21. Joel Havemann, *Congress and the Budget* (Bloomington: Indiana University Press, 1978), pp. 164-165.

22. Ibid.

23. U.S. House of Representatives, Committee on the Budget, "Oversight of the Congressional Budget Process," Hearings, 95th Congress, 1st sess., October 5-6, 1977.

24. Ibid., p. 51.

25. U.S. Senate, "Can Congress Control," p. 22-23.

26. Schick, "Congressional Control," p. 21.

27. Havemann, *Congress and the Budget*, p. 165.

28. Schick, "Congressional Control," p. 27.

29. Louis Fisher, "Congressional Budget Reform: The First Two Years," *Harvard Journal on Legislation* 14, no. 3 (April 1977): 433.

30. Ibid.

31. Havemann, *Congress and the Budget*, p. 168.

32. Fisher, "Congressional Reform," p. 434.

33. U.S. House of Representatives, Committee on Appropriations, *Views and Estimates on the Fiscal Year 1977 Budget*, 95th Congress, 1st sess., p. 3-4.

34. Louis Fisher, *Presidential Spending Power* (Princeton, N.J.: Princeton University Press, 1975), pp. 59-63.

35. Schick, "Congressional Control," pp. 33-35.

36. Ibid., p. 35.

37. Arnold Kanter, "Congress and the Defense Budget 1960-1970," *American Political Science Review* 66 (March 1972): 129-143.

38. Robert L. Bledsoe and Roger B. Handberg, "Congressional Decision-Making in the Post Vietnam Era: Continuity or Change Concerning the Defense Budget." Paper delivered at the Southwestern Political Science Association, Dallas, Texas, March 30, 1977.

39. Fisher, *Presidential Power*.

40. Fenno, *Power of the Purse*.

41. Fenno, *Congressmen in Committees*, pp. 2-5.

42. Ibid., p. 95.

43. Ibid., p. 142.

44. Ibid., p. 149.

45. Jeffrey L. Pressman, *House vs. Senate* (New Haven: Yale University Press, 1966), p. 1.

46. Ibid.

47. David Mayhew, *The Electoral Connection* (New Haven: Yale University Press, 1974).

48. Morris Fiorina, *Congress: Keystone of the Washington Establishment* (New Haven: Yale University Press, 1977).

49. Timothy B. Clark, "Appropriations Committees Losing Their Grip on Spending," *National Journal* (July 22, 1978): 1170.

50. *Congressional Quarterly Weekly Reports*, May 19, 1979, pp. 944-945.

51. Clark, "Appropriations Committees," p. 1171.

52. Schick, "Congressional Control," p. 41.

53. *Congressional Record*, June 17, 1976, p. 122, H6068.

54. John Ellwood and James Thurber, "Some Implications of the Congressional Budget and Impoundment Control Act for the Senate." Paper delivered at the American Political Science Association, Chicago, Ill., September 1, 1976.

55. U.S. House of Representatives, House Budget Committee, *Views and Estimates of the Standing Committees on the Fiscal Year 1977 Budget*, 94th Congress, 2nd sess., March 22, 1976, pp. 59-60.

56. Havemann, *Congress and the Budget*, p. 147.

57. Quoted in Ibid., p. 150.

58. Ibid., p. 151.

59. U.S. Senate, "Can Congress Control," p. 45.

60. U.S. Senate, *Tax Expenditures*, 94th Congress, 2nd sess., March 17, 1976.

61. U.S. Senate, *Report to Accompany First Concurrent Resolution on the Fiscal Year 1979 Budget*, 95-739, 95th Congress, 2nd sess.

62. John Manley, *The Politics of Finance* (Boston: Little, Brown, 1970), p. 82.

63. Fenno, *Congressmen in Committees*, p. 144.

64. Manley, *Politics of Finance*, p. 154.

65. Ibid., pp. 98-151.

66. Ibid., p. 297.

67. Catherine Rudder, "Committee Reform and the Revenue Process," in Lawrence Dodd and Bruce Oppenheimer, eds., *Congress Reconsidered* (New York: Praeger, 1977), p. 119.

68. Ibid., pp. 120-121.

69. Ibid., p. 119.

70. U.S. Senate, "Can Congress Control," p. 45.

71. Havemann, p. 59.

72. Ibid., p. 67.

73. Quoted in Ibid., p. 68.

74. Ibid., p. 69.

75. Joel Havemann, "A Good Year for the Congressional Budget Process," *National Journal* (September 23, 1978): 1502.

76. Ibid.

77. Havemann, *Congress and the Budget*, p. 170.

7

The Impact of
Budget Reform

*The most glaring weakness of the congressional
budget process is the failure to consider
national priorities. It has fallen prey to
the inherent conservatism of budgeting and
insured the maintenance of the status quo.*
—A Member of the House

In reforming the congressional budget process, a large majority agreed on significant procedural changes without ever arriving at a consensus over specific policy objectives. Conservatives wished to reduce spending and balance the budget. Liberals hoped to debate and restructure national priorities. The Appropriations committees wanted to eliminate backdoor spending. Most members agreed that Congress needed greater centralized control over the budget to prevent further erosion to the president.

There can be no single judgment about the impact of budget reform. Its impact can be more fairly judged by examining a number of dimensions that range from more clearly defined effects to more abstract and subjective judgments. The dimensions and some of the key questions to answer are as follows.

Procedures and Timetable. A precondition for any other assessment was the survival of the process. Given the failures of the late 1940s, the ability of Congress to adapt to a new set of procedures was by no means assured. Many skeptics predicted that Congress could not muster the discipline necessary to make the complicated law work. On this fundamental point, the budget process has succeeded. But the more critical question is what difference has it made. Have the deadlines been met? Have the appropriations and authorization processes adapted successfully? How have the waiver provisions been employed? Is the budget process now secure? In general, how have the procedural changes worked?

Impoundment Control. The titles of the act dealing with impoundment control were an important part of the legislation. Faced with the evidence of President Nixon's impoundments, many members were more enthusiastic about restricting impoundments than they were about the new budget process. How effectively has Congress controlled impoundment of funds by the president? Has the system proved to be workable? How have presidential requests for deferrals and rescissions been acted on by Congress?

The Quality of Budget Information. Budget reformers recognized that information was a key to gaining control of the budget. As the budget grew in size, scope, and complexity in previous decades, Congress became increasingly dependent on the executive branch for information. An independent source of budget data and information was seen as essential. The Congressional Budget Office was created to fill this need, and both the House and Senate Budget Committees were allowed to establish staff support. Has the quality of information improved and are members more knowledgeable about budgeting than before? Has the information provided by CBO been "independent"? Has it been used effectively by the Congress? What impact has the CBO had on Congress and the budget?

Taxing, Spending, and National Priorities. Perhaps the most critical dimension of evaluation is the impact of budget reform on national policy. These questions are also most vulnerable to subjective judgments based on differing objectives. One of the questions most commonly asked is, has spending been less than it would have been without the process? Are decisions on taxes and spending more integrated than before? Has Congress increased its impact on fiscal policy? Has the budget process resulted in any realignment of national priorities?

Legislative Versus the Executive. The last major element in the evaluation of budget reform is the question of the balance of budgetary power between the president and Congress. One of the objectives of reformers in the early 1970s was more independence from the president and executive branch agencies. Has Congress redressed the imbalance in power? Has the president's power been reduced? Judgments about these matters will in part rest on the four process and policy dimensions listed above, so the broader question of influence in national fiscal affairs is taken up in the final chapter.

Some claim that it is too early to evaluate the impact of the congressional budget process, that the results will not be fully understood for several decades. Certainly we will know more in twenty years, but there is a great deal that can be said at this point. The patterns that have been established in the House and Senate have shown remarkable stability. While some changes have taken place, the coalitions, leadership, and decision-making processes have demonstrated ample consistency to draw conclusions on the impact of budget reform.

PROCEDURES AND TIMETABLE

It became clear during the first attempt to pass a budget resolution that the overwhelming bipartisan support for the Budget Act would break down when faced with actual numbers and choices. But defended by the Budget committees and the House leadership, the budget process had survived controversy, and with only a few exceptions, met the deadlines.

The first budget resolution was passed May 14, 1975, one day before the statutory deadline. The September 15 deadline was waived in the first year of partial implementation, and the resolution was finally approved in December. In the ensuing years, Congress has generally met the May and September deadlines for the budget resolutions. The House, on several occasions, has passed resolutions a few days late, but the only significant delay occurred in 1979, when the conference committee could not agree on a number of major issues including the Senate's reconciliation instructions. The budget was not approved until late November 1979. With this exception, timely approval has been critical for the budget process since the subsequent stages depend on timely passage.

The March 15 deadline for committee views and estimates has been met, but the quality of the reports has varied sharply. The information provided in these reports is important to the Budget committees, but is it not as critical to the timing of the process as is the May 15 deadline for passing the resolution, for example. Since the standing committees have a vested interest in staking their claim on limited resources in the formulation of the congressional budget, they have complied with the March 15 deadline, despite grumbling about the short time available to them.

APPROPRIATIONS BILLS

In 1976, the second year of the budget process and first year of full implementation, all regular appropriations bills were passed by October 1, the start of the fiscal year. One had to go back to 1948 to find the last time all appropriations were passed prior to the beginning of the fiscal year. This was a significant accomplishment for Congress given the increasing delays in appropriations prior to 1975. The change in the fiscal year from July 1 to October 1 gave Congress more time, but this is only a small part of the explanation. Between 1972 and 1975, *no* appropriations bills were enacted by July 1, and the last time all spending bills were enacted by even October 1 was 1961.[1] In 1977, three regular appropriations bills were delayed late into the first session of the Ninety-fifth Congress. The House and Senate had agreed upon the dollar figures in the budget, but were deadlocked on extraneous issues, the most controversial being federal funding of abortions. In 1978, most bills were passed by October 1 and all regular appropriations were enacted by the middle of October. Given the dismal record of delays and the prevalence of continuing resolutions in the 1960s and 1970s, the budget process has had a substantial impact on the timely enactment of appropriations. This provides a significant benefit to agencies which can develop more accurate operating budgets by October 1, rather than continuing at last year's funding level.

WAIVERS

The May 15 deadline for authorizing bills has been enforced less stringently by the Budget committees than it might have been. Section 402 of the Budget Act allows the May 15 deadline to be waived under special circumstances. Although most authorizing committees have been able to meet the May 15 deadline, the waiver provisions have been used extensively. This provision is necessary but can weaken the process when used too frequently or without good reason. In the Senate, authorizing committees must report a waiver resolution that is referred to the Senate Budget Committee for its recommendation to the full Senate. These requirements were not implemented until 1976, and in the next three years, 101 waivers were requested.[2] Only two of these requests were not recommended favorably by the Senate Budget Committee, although in several other cases, the requests became moot. In general, the Senate Budget Committee has been very flexible in granting waivers of the May 15 deadline to the authorizing committees.

One might expect that the number of requests for waivers would decline as the Congress adjusts to the budget timetable, but this has not been the case. In 1976, twenty-one waivers were requested. This increased to forty-three in 1977, and thirty-eight in 1978. Table 7-1 lists the most common reasons given by the authorizing committees for reporting legislation after the deadline. The two most prevalent reasons, delay caused by the administration and unforeseen needs, appear consistent with the justification for

Table 7-1.
REASONS FOR WAIVER OF BUDGET ACT, 1976-1978

Reason	No. of Cases
Delay caused by administration	23
Emergency; unforeseen needs	20
Committee workload, inadequate time, other priority legislation	19
Committee reorganization, adjournment, staff problems	13
Other congressional delays	12
Committee error, unfamiliarity with procedures	5
No reason given	4
Other	6
	N=101

Source: Compiled from records of Senate Budget Committee, on section 402 waiver requests.

the 402 waiver procedures. Other reasons, however, reflect delays that should be correctable through better planning, such as workload, staff problems, and unfamiliarity with procedures. To some extent, they reflect the difficulties in the authorization process caused by the timetable.

Certain committees in the Senate have used the waiver procedures more frequently than others. Table 7-2 reveals that about 70 percent of the waivers were requested by eight Senate committees. The Foreign Relations Committee heads the list with eleven requests. Both Foreign Relations and the Select Committee on Energy have a greater problem with administration-caused delays. Others, such as Environment and Public Works, Agriculture, and Judiciary Committees, seem to have less valid reasons for frequent waiver requests.

Table 7-2.
BUDGET ACT WAIVERS: FREQUENCY BY SENATE COMMITTEES,
1976-1978

Committee	Waivers Requested
Foreign Relations	11*
Energy (Select)	10†
Environment and Public Works	9
Agriculture	9†
Judiciary	9
Indian Affairs (Select)	8
Banking and Currency	6
Armed Services	6
	68
Others (4 or less each)	33**
Total	N=101

Source: Compiled from records of Senate Budget Committee.

*One request received an unfavorable recommendation from the Senate Budget Committee.
†One request was not acted on by the Senate Budget Committee.
**Three requests were from individual members, not committees.

Even with its infrequent opposition to waivers, the Senate Budget Committee has shown that spurious requests can be opposed and defeated. In 1976, the Budget Committee opposed a request from the Interior and Insular Affairs Committee to waive the May 15 deadline. It argued that there were no exceptional circumstances to justify the waiver, and that the legislation was duplicative and too expensive.[3] The Interior Committee objected to the Budget Committee making substantive judgments on legislation in its purview, but the Senate leadership backed the Budget Committee and the waiver resolution was never sent to the floor for a vote.

Waivers have also been prevalent on the House side where the Rules Committee has jurisdiction over them. The Rules Committee consults with the House Budget Committee and has usually followed its recommendation. In the Ninety-fifth Congress, the Budget Committee supported thirty-four waivers, many tied to the third resolution for fiscal 1977. Many of these were technical or emergency in nature. House Budget Committee Chairman Giaimo rejects the notion that the House has been too generous in granting waivers:

Because the Budget Committee has been reluctant to support substantial numbers of waivers, only the most compelling cases are ever considered by the Committee. In my view, the Committees' waiver policy has worked well to date. We have achieved widespread compliance with the procedural requirements of the Budget Act, and we have buttressed that compliance by exercising a limited degree of flexibility where dictated by unusual or pressing circumstances. [4]

To keep the question of waivers to the budget act in perspective, one must recall that most of the authorizing committees have complied with the May 15 deadline; the waivers requested in the Senate and the House represent a small fraction of all authorizing measures. Many of the waiver requests were justified, and flexibility is often needed to deal with emergencies. Finally, the cost of antagonizing the standing committees is not worth the benefits of cleaning up some of the procedural loose ends. The record of action on waivers generally supports the notion that the Budget committees have attempted to accommodate the legislative committees. As the Budget committees gain institutional power in the coming years, they may wish to oppose waiver requests more frequently. It may only take a few refusals per year to remind the rest of the committees to take the May 15 deadline seriously.

In assessing procedural impact, budget reform has been successful. Most deadlines have been met with regularity. If the occasional confusion associated with congressional budget does not yet conjure up the image of a "well-oiled machine," it is nonetheless a remarkably well-orchestrated process. Most of the credit for this implementation success lies with the Budget committees and Democratic party leaders. They did what skeptics said could never be done: disciplined an undisciplined Congress. After five years, the process appears secure. But adaptation to the forms is only a necessary first step to budget control.

IMPOUNDMENT CONTROL

The impoundment control provisions of the Budget Act (Title X, the Impoundment Control Act) were never "used" on their main target, Richard Nixon. The former president resigned before the procedures for rescission and deferral took effect. Both Ford and Carter, however, have tested the Title X requirements. Under the 1974 Act, the president could request that Congress permanently rescind budget authority, or temporarily defer outlays. Congress must approve legislation for a rescission, but a deferral is possible unless Congress specifically forbids it.

Presidents impounded funds without much controversy until Nixon began to systematically substitute his spending priorities for those of Congress. Gerald Ford, the first president to operate under the impoundment restrictions, proposed a number of rescissions and deferrals in 1975 and 1976. For fiscal 1975, Ford requested $43 billion in rescissions and $24.6 in deferrals. The House and Senate rejected most of the rescissions, but were more generous with deferrals. Table 7-3 summarizes the president's requests in fiscal years 1975-1977.

Table 7-3.
RESCISSIONS AND DEFERRALS, FISCAL 1975-1977
($ in billions)

	Number	Amount	Percent
Rescissions			
– Proposed	152	$ 8.949	100%
– Approved	52	$ 1.241	14%
– Rejected	101	$ 7.708	86%
Deferrals			
– Proposed	328	$40.736	100%
– Approved	284	$31.009	76%
– Rejected	44	$ 9.727	24%

Source: Office of Management and Budget, reported in Joel Havemann, *Congress and the Budget* (Bloomington: Indiana University Press, 1978), p. 182.

The pattern that has been established suggests that impoundment control has worked. The president can no longer impound funds at will. Congress has been willing to accept more routine requests (usually deferrals) that represent genuine savings or changes that make the expenditure unnecessary. But they have rejected rescissions that have major policy consequences.[5] For example, Congress turned down Ford's requests to rescind funds for education of the handicapped and community development planning grants, and his proposal to defer highway construction funds in 1976.

Impoundment control procedures created some new problems of their own. The language in Title X was unclear in places; the two Budget committees disagreed over the exact nature of rescissions and deferrals.[6] The General Accounting Office (GAO), the congressional agency which monitors executive impoundments and has the power to take the president to court, concluded that the act had given the president *new* authority, in the form of deferrals, to impound funds.[7] An additional problem arose with the number of rescissions and deferrals sent to Congress by the president. Ford began the practice of submitting rescission requests in the amount that Congress had exceeded his requests. This created a backlog of work and threatened to overload the system.[8] No limits had been placed on the number of rescissions or deferrals that the president could propose. Part of this problem was a result of the carryover of funds impounded under the Nixon administration. The number of presidential requests has declined since 1976.

On several occasions, GAO reclassified deferrals as rescissions because there would have been insufficient time to expend the funds once the deferral had expired. GAO sued the administration in 1975 over home-ownership funds in the Housing and Community Development Act.[9] Ford and OMB refused to spend funds after forty-five days had elapsed since GAO classified the request as a rescission. Even after Congress disapproved the impoundment as a deferral, OMB refused to spend the money. It argued that since the money was impounded under Nixon, the provisions were not retroactive, and further, challenged the legality of GAO's ability to sue the executive branch. The funds were released before the judge could rule on the merits of the case.

Other disputes arose during the Ford administration. It became clear that a great deal of confusion surrounded Title X and that the president would act to preserve as much power over impoundments as possible. By the beginning of the Carter administration in 1977, most of the procedural haggling had ended, with both branches generally agreeing on the process.

Since 1977, most of the requests from the president have concerned economies and unnecessary expenditures. It is ironic that this is how the presidential power of impoundment was mainly used until 1969. Despite the problems that occurred in the first two years of implementation, the impoundment control procedures have proven workable. Congress has shown that it will exercise its authority to prevent the president from arbitrarily altering its spending priorities by withholding funds. At the same time, although the process is occasionally burdensome, the flexibility to control unnecessary spending has been retained.

IMPROVING CONGRESSIONAL INFORMATION

Information is power, or so some of the congressional budget reformers thought. By the 1970s Congress had grown increasingly dependent on OMB and the executive branch for all its information on the budget. With Nixon in the White House, there was increased skepticism on Capitol Hill that Congress was receiving either accurate information or complete information. But there was no way to tell; the president had a monopoly on budget experts and data. One of the main objectives of the Budget Act was to improve the quantity and quality of congressional information, and develop an independent source of budgetary data. Three main organizations were created for this purpose: the House Budget Committee staff, the Senate Budget Committee staff, and the Congressional Budget Office. We will concentrate on the latter in an attempt to evaluate the impact of reform on congressional information.

THE CONGRESSIONAL BUDGET OFFICE

Director Alice Rivlin disliked the characterization of CBO as a "congressional OMB." CBO was not to formulate the congressional budget as OMB formulates the executive budget—that was the job of the Budget committees. But like OMB, CBO was to provide budget projections, estimates, and economic data. Title II of the Budget Act detailed the duties and responsibilities of the CBO: to assist the Budget, Appropriations, Ways and Means, and Finance Committees by providing information on budget authority, outlays, tax expenditures, revenues, and related topics. To the extent practicable, they are to provide assistance to other committees and members when requested. CBO is required to submit an annual report to the Budget committees on budget alternatives, and in addition, periodic reports on specific topics. Title II gave CBO authority to secure budget data directly from executive agencies and departments.

The main tasks of CBO developed in response to workload and congressional demand. CBO is required to provide both budget analysis and policy analysis in various forms:

Scorekeeping: Comparisons of pending and enacted legislation with totals specified in the budget resolutions.

"Costing-out" bills: Projections of the five-year costs of House and Senate authorizing bills to help clarify the long-term spending implications of current legislation.

Five-Year Projections: The annual report of current policy levels of taxing and spending projected for five years.

Report on Budget Alternatives: The report on alternative levels of taxing and spending, analyzing fiscal choices and priority choices.

Policy Analysis Reports: Special studies of current issues that affect the budget.

The scorekeeping function turned out to be a time-consuming activity that drew time and resources away from other activities. At the outset, it was impossible for CBO to cost-out all the legislation pending in Congress, but this improved as they expanded their capacity to perform this function.

The CBO was organized and began operation in an atmosphere of controversy, beginning with the selection of Rivlin as director. When she was finally chosen in early 1975, CBO was already half a year behind the Budget committees. CBO had little impact on the first trial run in the spring of 1975, but managed to anger a number of congressmen.

The CBO was not intended to be a policy advocate; its role was to provide information. But within months, it acquired the reputation of liberal advocacy. Republicans and conservatives faulted the staff selection process, and criticized the Keynesian slant of its staff economists. The first CBO economic report was criticized for favoring stimulus and expansion rather than restraint to combat inflation. Also in 1975, CBO was accused of bias against the military and the defense budget.[10] These problems were exacerbated by the publicity given the CBO and Rivlin, and the lack of congressional experience of its staff.

The problem came to a head when the CBO was confronted by an antagonistic House Appropriations Subcommittee on the Legislative Branch. The committee considered a proposal to slash CBO personnel in half, but finally voted to freeze the staff at 193 persons, some fifty less than had been planned.

Was this simply an instance of congressional arrogance and jealousy? Much of the criticism of CBO was unfounded and unfair, but much of it was avoidable and the result of poor judgment by CBO officials. Like the other participants, CBO was attempting to carve out its own turf in the congressional budget process, and offended some other participants. The difficulties of CBO in its first year are of interest insofar as they affected its performance.

With its limited staff, CBO has been unable to do as much as originally anticipated. The annual report on budget alternatives had been particularly troublesome. The first report was heavily criticized and was largely ignored by the Budget committees. Subsequent attempts have been slightly better, but CBO is still searching for an optimum formula.

Despite the demands of scorekeeping and bill costing, CBO has produced a number of analytic studies. By mid-1977, it had issued nine major reports, twenty-eight issue papers, thirty-five background papers, and 105 other studies.[11] The largest category of these published studies was in the area of human resources, followed by defense, paralleling the amount of federal resources committed to these areas. CBO produced these documents either in responding to requests or by its own initiative (under the authority of the Budget Act). Table 7-4 shows the source of CBO requests through mid-1977. The requests were almost equally divided between the House and Senate, with about 20 percent of the studies originating within CBO. But this data is not consistent with other information about relative House-Senate utilization of CBO. Most observers conclude the Senate uses the CBO much more than the House does. Although the number of requests may be similar, it is suggested that the Senate uses the analysis more thoroughly in its decision-making processes. The staff of the House Budget Committee has been more critical of CBO, in contrast to the more open and enthusiastic embrace of CBO work by Senate Budget staffers. The Senate uses CBO scorekeeping work and five-year projections on a regular basis. The Appropriations committees and other standing committees have not yet relied on CBO to any great extent.

Table 7-4.
REQUESTS TO THE CONGRESSIONAL BUDGET OFFICE (CBO)

Senate	28.2%
House	26.5%
Joint House and Senate	25.4%
CBO initiated	19.9%
	100%

Source: "CBO Oversight" Hearings, House Budget Committee, 95th Congress, 1st sess., June 3, 1977, p. 8.

The difficulty of estimating the cost of spending bills became apparent as CBO first attempted to perform this function in 1976. That year, the cost of 29 percent of the Senate bills and 59 percent of House bills was estimated. This improved to 65 percent for the Senate and 72 percent for the House in 1977.[12] This is one of the most important functions of CBO and it has raised the awareness of legislators regarding the long-term cost implication of substantive proposals. Part of the improvement since 1976 is the result of greater cooperation from the authorizing committees and an appreciation of the usefulness of this information.

How have the committees rated the perfomance of CBO in improving the quality of congressional information? A study by the House Commission on Information and Facilities surveyed committee staff members in an effort to evaluate CBO.[13] Table 7-5 shows that the cost estimates of authorizing bills are assessed most favorably by committee staff, while the five-year projections are evaluated least favorably. The acceptance of this budget information by the committees is important to the continued success of the CBO. Overall, its performance in providing high quality, independent budget analysis is good. The standing committees know how the legislation under consideration relates to the targets in the resolution, they are aware of the cost implications of their bills, and they have an idea of overall spending trends in the future. All of this material represents an improvement in the quality of information used in decision-making, and considerable progress over past practices.

This essential budget analysis is only one component of the information supplied by CBO. Despite its importance and acceptance, budget analysis is generally mundane compared with policy analysis, the second major product of CBO. On this dimension, the record of CBO to date is much less impressive. Part of the difficulty is in the nature of the CBO product.[14] The Budget Options Reports are still of minor importance in

Table 7-5.
EVALUATION OF CBO FUNCTIONS BY COMMITTEE STAFFS

Function	% Favorable	% Neutral or Unfavorable	Number of Responses
Projecting costs of authorizing bills	79%*	21%	19
Scorekeeping	73%	27%	26
Projecting impact of spending and tax bills	58%	42%	19
Five-Year Projections	42%	58%	24

Source: Adapted from House Commission on Information and Facilities: *Congressional Budget Office*. Reported in Joel Havemann, *Congress and the Budget* (Bloomington: Indiana University Press, 1978), p. 114.

*Results have been averaged from responses on two questions (timeliness and accuracy) of projecting costs of authorization bills.

formulating the first concurrent resolution. Some of the issue papers and studies have been of high quality, but they did not always suit the needs of the clients on the congressional committees. The other problem with CBO policy analyses lies not with the producer, but with the consumer: Congress simply has not used even some of the best studies to a great extent. This is not a new phenomenon in Congress. Many legislators prefer to rely on their own political instincts and reject policy analysis in general. Although Congress now uses analysis to a greater extent than before, the progress has been slow.[15]

IMPROVING THE RELEVANCE OF CBO

The Congressional Budget Office, despite its occasional unfavorable publicity and political difficulties, has compiled a good record. Without question, the quality of congressional information has improved, and CBO can be credited for much of the progress. Yet, if CBO is to have a greater impact on budgetary decision making, further changes are necessary.[16] CBO should clarify its information gathering functions from those of the Congressional Research Service, GAO, and Office of Technology Assessment. The independence of congressional information is important, but the duplication is not necessary. CBO, in cooperation with OMB and the executive branch, is currently trying to integrate budget data systems. This should allow continued scrutiny by Congress, but assure a common base of accurate budget data for both the legislative and executive branches.

The problem with CBO's policy analysis is more difficult. If the House and Senate are to increase their use of policy analysis, CBO must be more savvy in selecting issues and identifying clients. If CBO studies continue to be good, acceptance will gradually increase. CBO publicity and advocacy are probably overemphasized as problems for the organization. It is unlikely that a timid director would have had any more impact and probably would have had less. Because "neutral" analysis is virtually impossible, segments of the Congress always will be critical of studies. In the long run, only a tradition of accuracy and quality will assure a significant impact for CBO.

TAXING, SPENDING, AND NATIONAL PRIORITIES

Has the budget process in Congress had an impact on the federal budget since 1975? Would the federal budget look much different had Congress not passed the Budget Act? The latter question may be impossible to answer since there is no "control budget" to show what congressional decisions would have been under the old system. But it is possible to examine different kinds of evidence and offer some tentative conclusions.

THE IMPACT ON SPENDING

When budget reformers in the early 1970s said the budget was out of control, many meant that federal spending was growing too rapidly and that Congress seemed powerless to stop it. Conservatives, and many moderate Republicans and Democrats, felt the first objective of budget reform was to halt the growth in spending. Has the budget process in Congress resulted in less spending than would have otherwise been approved? There are several ways to attempt to answer the question, none totally satisfactory. Figure 7-1 shows the percentage increase in federal spending for ten years—five before and five years after the budget process. Unfortunately, this data allows us to draw few implications about the effect of the budget process, except that growth in spending was not dramatically halted. The average percentage change for the five years prior to implementation of the process was 10.6 percent; in the five years following, it was 10.4 percent. Of course the reasons for growth in annual outlays are varied. Inflation, recession, entitlement programs, and other factors must be considered.

In the first few years of the budget process, holding down spending was subrogated to economic recovery from the severe 1973-1975 recession. In contrast to President Ford's proposed restrictive budgets, the Congress was somewhat more expansionary. But by 1978 a subtle shift in emphasis was apparent. With the economy recovering, unemployment down to 6 percent, but inflation unchecked, sentiment to hold down spending grew in Congress. No longer just a conservative, Republican objective, budget control increasingly meant spending restraint. Proposition 13 in California, the balance the budget amendment, and the popularity of "fiscal conservatism" dominated the 1978 mid-term elections. So by the fifth year of the budget process, the dominant concern had become fiscal restraint. But what of the budgets in fiscal years 1976-1980? If the aggregate figures do not reveal that the budget process had an impact, many House and Senate members mentioned specific instances of spending reductions. A majority

Figure 7-1.
PERCENTAGE OF INCREASE IN OUTLAYS FROM PREVIOUS YEAR

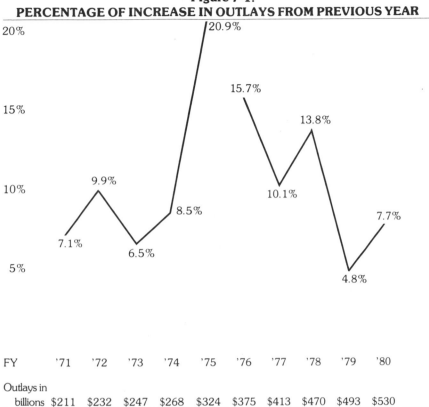

Source: *Budget of the United States Government,* Fiscal Year 1980.

of members felt that spending was less than it would have been without the budget process. A member of the Senate Budget Committee:

There is no question that the budget process has resulted in reducing spending below current services by $15 billion in the first two years. We took the one percent kicker out of federal retirement, we won floor fights over nutrition, milk programs, veterans, and armed services. These are concrete evidence of a real impact.

A member of the Senate Appropriations Committee:

Federal spending would have been significantly higher [without the budget process]. I have voted against certain domestic social spending programs that I would have voted for five years ago and always did. And there are many who will tell you the same thing.

A member of the House Appropriations Committee:

The Budget Committee claims that we have reduced spending by $14-20 billion below what it would have been. I'm not sure if it's that much, but there's no question that it [the budget process] has helped hold down spending.

A high ranking staff member on the House Budget Committee:

It is absolutely unassailable that significant amounts of spending have been saved. The budget process has changed members' behavior. It was easy for them to vote for individual spending items but much more difficult to approve the totals.

A member of the House Budget Committee:

It's clear that the budget process has reduced overall spending. It's much tougher now to vote for these attractive programs that violate the targets.

Most Democrats interviewed felt that the budget process had resulted in at least some reductions in outlays, but some were more tempered in their assessment than others.

Total federal spending would have been somewhat higher but not a great deal. The impact has been relatively minor. We have a long way to go before we really control spending. I guess that some reductions have been realized, but it's infinitesimal given the scope of the problem. A few billion don't [sic] mean much when you've got a half a trillion dollar problem.

Only a few members claimed that the budget process had not reduced total expenditures at all.

This process has been a bust. We haven't saved a dollar, although some of them are claiming we've cut billions. Just look at how much more we're spending this year than last year if you want the answer.

Members' assessments of the results of the budget process are closely related to their perceptions of what the budget process was intended to accomplish, and their own disposition towards fiscal policy. Those who want to see massive cuts and the budget balanced immediately are the most disappointed. It is ironic, though, that the fiscal conservatives have actually been the big winners. What was only one of several objectives for the budget process in 1974, to reduce spending growth, became the dominant objective five years later. The liberal revolt in 1979 was the result of frustration over the sweep of fiscal conservatism coming at the expense of social programs. Of course, the swing towards restraint was not the result of budget reform. Public pressure to cut spending in 1978 and 1979, and the surge in support for defense spending in 1980 would have been as great without the process. The congressional budget process simply provided a vehicle for responding to economic trends, public pressure, and international events.

The evidence of specific spending measures indicates that if expenditures have been reduced, there were still strong spending pressures in Congress. The Senate Budget Committee's compilation of "test votes" on the budget process in 1977 can be used as an example. Table 7-6 shows how the deficit was increased by $6 billion through Senate actions that increased outlays and reduced revenues.

Table 7-6.
BUDGET IMPACT OF KEY VOTES, U.S. SENATE, 95th CONGRESS,
1st SESSION ($ in billions)

Vote	Budget Authority	Outlays	Revenue	Classified as "Victory" or "Defeat" for Targets by Senate Budget Committee
1. Increase Agriculture Outlays		$+0.7		Defeat
2. Increase SBA Loans	$+1.4	+1.4		Defeat
3. Add Energy Tax Credit for the Elderly			$-1.2	Defeat
4. Cut Inter-city Bus Tax Credit*			-0.2	Victory
5. Table Residential Energy Tax Credit			-1.7	Defeat
6. Add Tuition Tax Credit			-1.1	Defeat
7. Extend Unemployment Benefits*	+0.5	+0.5		Victory
8. Increase Corn Target Price*	+0.5	+0.5		Victory
9. Reduce Agriculture Target Price	+0.5	+0.5		Defeat
Total	+2.9	+3.6	-4.2	
Less Votes #4, #7, #8*	-1.0	-1.0	+0.2	
Net Budget Impact	+1.9	+2.6	-4.0	
Addition to Deficit				$6.6 billion

Source: Senator Henry Bellmon, Senate Budget Committee.

*Votes on which the Senate upheld previously established budget targets.

The figures suggest that in 1977, the Senate Budget Committee suffered more "defeats" than "victories." In 1978, however, the record appeared more successful. The Budget Committee was defeated on the Emergency Agriculture Act, but was successful in votes on child nutrition, the Witteveen facility, housing authorization, Conrail reorganization, tuition tax credits, education amendments, and CETA reauthorization among others.

The budget process was responsible for some reductions in spending in its first half decade of operation, but in terms of the overall budget, they are minor. The trend toward a balanced budget and reducing federal spending as a proportion of GNP was a result of economic and political trends, not the process itself. The Senate Budget Committee adopted fiscal restraint as its main objective, but the House had to place survival of the process first. Reflecting on the evidence presented throughout this study, it is extremely difficult to make a convincing case that the process has resulted in significant savings. The legitimate needs of programs and the pressures from standing committees have not been ignored. The success of the process may in fact be attributed to the fact that some restraint has been exercised by Congress without gutting important programs. What can be concluded with some certainty is that the budget process provided a more workable vehicle for the Congress to use in responding to economic and political trends.

THE IMPACT ON NATIONAL PRIORITIES

If the conservatives wanted the budget process to reduce spending and balance the budget, liberals were anxious to debate the budget as a whole and reevaluate national priorities. Many objected to the coziness of the appropriations process, where vested interests remained insulated from overall judgments. Some liberals envisioned a process whereby Congress would reallocate defense dollars to social programs when members had a chance to look at the whole budget. Some members evidenced a belief that the old budget didn't reflect the true priorities of Congress: that the piecemeal appropriations process concealed hidden priorities.

Like the silent Republican majority predicted by Goldwater's strategists in the 1964 presidential debacle, no hidden priorities have emerged, nor have national priorities been restructured. Some would go so far as to say that the nation's priorities have not even been subject to a critical analysis under the budget process. Although "national priorities" refers to the relative allocations to functions and even programs within the budget, the most common yardsticks are defense and social welfare—guns versus butter. Table 7-7 reveals that in the five years since implementing the budget process, the two main categories of federal expenditures have been virtually fixed in their relative shares. Ironically, the five years preceding budget reform witnessed significant reallocation from defense to income security. If one looks back to 1966, defense spending made up 43 percent of outlays, compared to only 24 percent for social welfare expenditures. In the decade between 1966 and 1976, significant reallocation occurred, with the two categories reversing their relative shares.

The lack of a centralized budget process in Congress no more explains this reallocation than the existence of the process explains the lack of

Table 7-7.
RELATIVE BUDGET SHARES: DEFENSE VERSUS SOCIAL WELFARE, BEFORE AND AFTER BUDGET REFORM

	Before Reform					After Reform				
	1971	1972	1973	1974	1975	1976	1977	1978	1979	1980
Relative Share of Defense	36%	33%	30%	29%	26%	24%	24%	23%	23%	24%
Relative Share of Income Security	35%	37%	39%	41%	44%	46%	45%	43%	43%	45%

Source: Budget of the United States Government, Fiscal Year 1980, p. 578.

reallocation between 1976 and 1980. If one extrapolates the 1966-1976 trends, it is understandable why some members of Congress expected the shift in priorities to continue under the new process. But Table 7-7 shows that budget composition has been remarkably stable since 1975. Members' perceptions of the impact of the budget process on national priorities are consistent with the data.

The following are responses of four members of the House and Senate Budget Committees to the question of reallocation:

Although some members saw this as an opportunity to take away from the defense budget and give to social programs, this has not happened. Actually, defense has fared rather well. This may be simply an education process, learning about the increases in the Russians' spending and the limitations of ours.

There hasn't been much reallocation, but the hawks have tried to fit the defense budget into certain social programs. They are using aggregate comparisons to increase defense spending that weren't possible before the [budget] act.

There may have been a very marginal transfer from defense to social programs but not very much has changed. The budget process should have a greater impact in the future in terms of altering the composition of federal spending.

There has been no reallocation of national resources but the decline in defense spending has been halted. One of the things I've been surprised with is the lack of redistribution in the budget process. With the scarcity of resources, I thought there would be more debate over where money would go, and this would be a big plus.

Liberal Democrats who anticipated establishing new national priorities through the budget process were the most disappointed. Representative John Conyers conveys this viewpoint:

The most serious shortcoming of the budget process has been the neglect of its priority-setting purpose. We have not done nearly enough to define and order priorities according to national needs; or to anticipate and plan for future needs so that we may judge the desirability and effectiveness of existing programs.

The goal of fiscal discipline and of budget control is a conservative's overriding concern, and the goal of setting and revising priorities . . .is an overriding concern of liberals. This latter goal has been shortchanged, in my view, both because of the inherently conservative nature of budgets, and the far greater difficulty of implementing change through the budget than maintaining the status quo.

Obviously, there will always be several priorities, reflected in the budget. But unless we focus on concrete goals and targets, we will not be in a position to determine what has to be traded off, sacrificed, and how the several priorities are related to one another.[17]

Is this a failing in one of the goals of the Budget Act? To the extent that the process has not really examined the question of overall priorities, it may be. But one must conclude that a majority of members are satisfied with current allocations, or view other alternatives as worse. The process, per se, cannot restructure priorities. Only a majority of members, using the budget process, can do so. The problem may not be in setting priorities; the problem is whose priorities are being set. The stability of budget allocations between 1975 and 1980 indicated that a majority supporting reallocation does not exist.

On the other hand, taking an overview of the budget may have rigidified current allocations. With the scarcity of resources for new programs in the period, participants may have fought all the harder to keep their current share. The overview provided by the concurrent resolutions may have helped advocates of greater spending for defense make their case. The problem faced by Congress is now more like the problem that has faced the OMB and the president for years: Where does one make cuts? Budget reform has not changed the political nature of budgeting. Reallocation tends not to occur by taking from one and giving to another; it tends to occur by allocating new resources on a differential basis. Advocates of reallocation will probably remain dissatisfied until new resources become available for federal programs, and pressures for tax cuts, balanced budgets, and increased military spending have waned.

There remains some validity in the charge that the budget process has not forced Congress to establish priorities. The reconciliation process was virtually unused in the first five years. Although Congress has made hard choices in constituting resolutions, perhaps the harder choices have been avoided. This is understandable given the tenuous support for the process in the House, but reconciliation remains an element of unused potential.

House Budget Committee Chairman Robert Giaimo, reflecting on the problem of underspending and growing pressure in Congress for across-the-board cuts, commented on the reconciliation process:

Maybe we have been living too cautiously in this Committee in our early years. Maybe we have to live dangerously. The Budget Act provides for a reconciliation process. . . .You realize what a controversy that [using the reconciliation process] will stir up. But it will test the committment of the Congress to its budget process.[18]

If the budget process has helped reduce spending, its impact on overall budget priorities has been negligible. But perhaps proponents of this goal had expectations far above what was possible. Nonetheless, one can conclude that the process itself still represents an improvement. When a majority of Congress is disposed to alter national priorities and the composition of the budget, it will have a much more workable vehicle to employ than was available before 1975.

IMPACT ON TAXES

When Congress issued a chorus of complaints about the president and its own outdated budget procedures, most of the attention focused on the spending side of the budget. No one discussed the crisis in the ability of Congress to affect the tax laws. Aside from his questionable use of the Internal Revenue Service, Nixon did not dominate Congress in this area. At the time of the Budget Act, the last monumental revenue battle between the executive and legislature was the Johnson-Mills struggle over LBJ's tax surcharge proposal in 1968. The objectives of budget reform in terms of taxes were less salient.

Nonetheless, the Budget Act attempted to improve the coordination of taxing and spending, and to bring revenues under the new centralized budget system, without reducing the jurisdiction of the tax-writing committees. The most significant proposal was not included in the act: the provision to include tax expenditures in the budget resolutions.

One can assess this exclusion in two ways. It could be persuasively argued that this may have saved the budget process in the House in its early years. The inclusion of an additional set of highly controversial issues might have been too much for the new system, already strained to obtain majority support. On the other hand, one can also argue that the exclusion of tax expenditures from the resolutions precluded meaningful integration of revenue decisions into the budget process, and allowed (if not insured) the continued autonomy of the Ways and Means and Finance Committees.

The report issued by the Joint Study Committee on Budget Control included relatively few recommendations on tax procedures. It suggested that a tax surcharge bill would be appropriate if revenues were too low.[19] Other recommendations were general, such as to "review proposed revenue legislation in the President's budget" and their own proposals. The Budget Act mandated that the Budget committees "request and evaluate continuing studies of tax expenditures, to devise methods of coordinating tax expenditures, policies and programs with direct budget outlays."[20] The only constraint imposed on revenues was a target for receipts. In the first five years, the target has been more a function of economic assumptions than policy decisions. There is no mechanism to control the way that revenue is raised within the budget process. A further constraint on the Congress is that no bill raising or lowering the amount of revenue agreed to in the resolution may be considered. This has been circumvented by moving the effective date of the legislation to the next fiscal year. Russell Long commented after the Senate approved a string of new tax expenditures, "Think of the fun you're denying yourself next year."[21]

The impact of budget reform on the revenue process has been negligible. The revenue process is no more manipulable for fiscal policy than it was before. Taxes have not been used significantly to alter the deficit. Taxes have been used to accomplish an ever-increasing number of non-financial goals, as the proliferation of new tax expenditures bears witness.

Participants in the budget process now recognize the weakness of the provisions dealing with taxes. Respondents indicated that the Budget committees and the process had very little impact on what the revenue committees did. While almost all the members interviewed felt the budget process had affected authorizations and appropriations, the comments in the House and Senate were nearly unanimous about the tax-writing committees and their chairmen.

A Democractic member of the Senate Budget Committee:

When you consider our record over the past few years, we have really been quite successful. The only area where we have been consistent losers is with Long and the Finance Committee. We have tried on numerous occasions to influence the tax side, but we haven't even gotten half a loaf. There are really two reasons for this. One is Long; he's shrewd and has a lot of clout in the Senate. But we've beaten other powerful Chairmen. The real reason is that we don't have the statutory authority to mandate that level of specificity in the first place.

A Republican commented:

We [on Budget] want them [on Finance] to close tax loopholes. They want to write more. So far, they've won.

A House Democrat:

There has been very little impact on Ways and Means. More and more the Budget Committee is using a double standard with Appropriations and Ways and Means. They've done much too little imposing on tax matters.

The members with seats on both the House Budget and Ways and Means Committee are the first to acknowledge that they are not very much affected by the budget process. Unlike their colleagues on the Budget Committee, however, they see no problem in this. The oversight hearings on the budget process revealed a similar assessment about revenue policy.

I would like to direct my efforts to . . .the revenue side of the budget. Something is very untouchable about the revenue side of the budget. In a sense, we just rubber stamp what the Ways and Means Committee comes up with. We don't spend time . . .to really be sure that their actions don't undercut what we're trying to do in the budget.[22]

Budget reform in Congress has actually been expenditure reform; the revenue side has escaped and remains only partially integrated in the budget process. This reflects the low salience of this issue among budget reformers, and the resulting lack of emphasis in the act. It also is a function of the natural tendency of committees to protect their own interests. The Ways and Means and Finance Committees have done this effectively. The lack of an impact on the revenue side weakens the overall budget process. As congressional decision makers contemplate a multiyear budgeting system, taxes will be more important for short-term fiscal adjustment. That responsiveness in revenue matters is currently missing. In addition, the uncontrolled proliferation of special interest tax provisions is a growing problem. Congress approves the new tax expenditures, just as it used to approve attractive spending measures, without taking an overview. Until a mechanism for taking an overview of tax expenditures like one that now exists for spending is imposed, it is unlikely that tax expenditures will be "controlled."

CONCLUSION

What is the verdict on the success of budget reform in Congress? Those who hoped for drastic cuts in spending were disappointed; those who hoped to see national priorities restructured were disappointed. But those who had less precise policy objectives were generally more satisfied with the results. Although determinations of the success of reform are subjective, we can draw some general conclusions about its impact.

The policy impact of budget reform has been relatively slight. Some savings have been realized, but the relative allocation within the budget has been more stable than in the decade that preceded. It would be difficult to make a case that the budget would have looked significantly different without the procedural changes in Congress. Yet this is not a critical indictment of the reforms. It simply means that although budget priorities are more clearly expressed by Congress, the preferences of members have not changed radically since before 1975. The major issues in the budget reform movement were, in fact, as much procedural as they were policy issues. Process for process's sake? Perhaps in this case it is more than a hollow exercise. In half a decade, Congress has institutionalized a set of procedures which increase their decision-making capability and their power in national politics. A radical departure from the past decisions is not necessary to demonstrate this shift.

The complex decisions on authorizations, appropriations, entitlements, and taxes are better integrated than before. The process is inherently more "responsible" because the parts must be fit into a whole. As we have seen, this discipline has not been easy, nor has it been complete. The establishment of the process probably will have more important policy implications in the coming decades than it did in the first five years.

There are a number of specific examples of savings in expenditures due to the budget process, but early assessments and the members themselves tend to overemphasize them. The targets established in the first resolutions made cuts in committee estimates but they have not generally been severe comparable to OMB cuts of agency requests, for example.[23] As pressures build to cut spending and balance the budget, the means to accomplish these goals in the 1980s are in place. Conversely, an activist majority in Congress could once again expand the federal sector or establish other new policy directions. The budget process is important not for its own sake, or for the policy changes it has already made, but for the changes it might facilitate in the future.

A number of problems remain. Specific weaknesses such as waivers and failure to integrate or influence revenue decisions have been noted. But a more significant problem lies in the Congress itself, one that is often missed by participants or close observers who have become enamored with the process. The basic characteristics of a representative body that made Congress irresponsible in the first place are still present—the penchant for pork and economizing only with someone else's project or program. The budget process actually may have increased spending advocacy in Congress. Budget reform has made Congress schizophrenic, struggling with its concomitant desires to spend and to save. But the problem is more explicit now, and members are more aware of the inconsistencies that face them.

NOTES

1. Joel Havemann, *Congress and the Budget* (Bloomington: Indiana University Press, 1978), pp. 157-158.

2. Compiled from records of waivers requested, and reasons, U.S. Senate Budget Committee.

3. Havemann, *Congress and the Budget*, p. 167.

4. U.S. House of Representatives, Budget Committee Hearings, "Oversight of the Congressional Budget Process," 95th Congress, 1st sess., October 5-6, 1977. Letter from Representative Elford Cederberg (R-Mich.) to Chairman Giaimo.

5. Allen Schick, *The Impoundment Control Act of 1974: Legislative History and Implementation* (Washington: Congressional Research Service, 1976), p. 10.

6. Havemann, *Congress and the Budget*, pp. 179-180.

7. Elmer Staats, Letter to Speaker of House, December 4, 1974, reported in Ibid., p. 180.

8. Louis Fisher, *Presidential Spending Power* (Princeton, N.J.: Princeton University Press, 1976), p. 201.

9. See Havemann, *Congress and the Budget*, pp. 183-184, for a more detailed history of this case.

10. Ibid., p. 107.

11. U.S. House of Representatives, House Budget Committee, "Congressional Budget Office Oversight," Hearings, 95th Congress, 1st sess., June 2, 1977. p. 7.

12. Ibid., p. 4.

13. House Commission on Information and Facilities, "Congressional Budget Office: A Study of Its Organizational Effectiveness," 95th Congress, 1st sess., January 4, 1977, #95-20.

14. Havemann, *Congress and the Budget*, pp. 117-122.

15. James A. Thurber, "Congressional Budget Reform and New Demands for Policy Analysis," *Policy Analysis* 2, no. 4 (Spring 1976): 197-214.

16. See recommendations of House Commission on Information and Facilities and CBO responses, in "Congressional Budget Office Oversight," pp. 27-29.

17. Statement by Representative John Conyers, "Oversight of the Congressional Budget Process," pp. 128-130.

18. Ibid., p. 144.

19. "Recommendations for Improving Congressional Control Over Budgetary Outlay and Receipt Totals," Report on the Joint Study Committee on Budget Control, April 18, 1973, 93rd Cong., 1st sess., p. 7.

20. Public Law 93-344, Section 102(2) (C). See Appendix.

21. Quoted in Joel Havemann, *National Journal* (November 5, 1977), p. 1733.

22. Comments of Representative William Lehman (D-Fla.), "Oversight of the Congressional Budget Process," p. 145.

23. Lance T. LeLoup and William Moreland, "Agency Strategies and Executive Review: The Hidden Politics of Budgeting," *Public Administration Review* 38, no. 3 (May-June, 1978): 232-239.

8

Congress, the President, and the Power of the Purse

*He who has his thumb on the
purse, has the power.*
—Otto Von Bismarck

Developments in the twentieth century had left the Congress relatively incapable of exerting significant influence on macroeconomic issues, or taking an overview of its own spending habits. The Budget and Impoundment Control Act of 1974, which altered the executive-legislative power balance, coincided with several other significant changes in national politics. The Budget Act, the War Powers Act, and the impeachment hearings of Richard Nixon will cast a long shadow on the history of presidential-congressional relations. These concurrent actions by the Congress were no historical accident. Although reacting to different problems, the Nixon presidency was a major catalyst for all three (and other lesser actions undertaken by Congress to strengthen its position vis-à-vis the president). A budget act might have been enacted in the 1970s without Nixon since the deficiencies were apparent before he took office. But certainly his impoundments helped to speed the corrective action by Congress.

The 1970s witnessed a shift in both the perceptions and the power of the presidency. The "imperial,"[1] "textbook,"[2] "isolated"[3] presidency has been carved down to size in public appraisals, in scholarly and journalistic accounts, and, to some extent, by congressional action. In the 1980s, the resurgence of the post-Watergate era diminished, the spectre of a monolithic presidential establishment emasculating Congress has faded. Yet, one must be wary in assessing the shifts in presidential-congressional power. Hugh Heclo, noting the ebb and flow of popular and scholarly opinion, claims that such assessments tend to be "trenchant interpretations of current events."[4] Noting these words of caution, let us examine the record since 1975.

CONGRESSIONAL CHANGES IN PRESIDENTIAL REQUESTS

To what degree is Congress less dependent on presidential requests as its guide than it was before 1975? Budget reformers did not want to formulate a congressional budget without the president's requests, but wished to be able to set alternative policy directions if they disagreed with the president.

Table 8-1 shows comparisons of the presidents' requests and congressional action through the two concurrent resolutions. The final column indicates the percentage change in the presidents' requests approved in the second concurrent resolution. This provides some indication of the relative independence of congressional estimates from the presidents' budget. There are several problems with this measure, however. It must be recognized that some of the change from the presidents' figures to the congressional figures reflect factors other than policy differences: changing economic trends, underspending, and the presidents' own July revisions (not shown). Nonetheless, some conclusions can be drawn.

Table 8-1.
**COMPARISONS OF PRESIDENTIAL REQUESTS WITH
CONGRESSIONAL RESOLUTIONS, 1976-1979 ($ in billions)**

Fiscal Year	President and Request		Congressional Action First Resolution	Second Resolution	% Change between President's Request and Second Resolution	
1976						
Outlays	$349.4		367.0	374.9	+ 7.1%	
Revenue	297.5		298.2	300.8	+ 1.0%	
Deficit	51.9		68.8	74.1	+46.0%	
1977						
Outlays	394.2		413.3	413.1*	+ 4.8%	
Revenue	351.3		362.5	362.5	+ 3.4%	
Deficit	43.0		50.8	50.6	+17.6%	
1978[†]	Ford	Carter			Ford	Carter
Outlays	440.0	459.4	460.9	458.3	+ 4.7%	+ .3%
Revenue	393.0	401.6	396.3	397.0	+ 1.0%	−1.1%
Deficit	47.0	57.7	64.7	61.2	+30.2%	+6.0%
1979						
Outlays	500.2		498.8	487.5	− 2.6%	
Revenue	439.6		447.9	448.7	+ 2.3%	
Deficit	60.6		50.9	38.8	−37.0%	

Sources: Budget of the United States, Budget Resolutions.

*Excludes the third Resolution, and the revised resolution, after Carter's inauguration.
[†]Ford submitted Fiscal Year 1978 Budget in January; Carter submitted revisions in March 1977.

President Ford discovered in 1975 that Congress was willing and able to make changes in the executive budget. The 7.1 percent increase in outlays over the president's requests represented the largest congressional alteration in the first five years. The next year, fiscal 1977, Congress increased Ford's outlay figure by almost 5 percent. Given the stability of the budget from year to year, these represent significant increases. Ford was accused of submitting unrealistically low estimates to Congress as a political move. But the major reasons for the differences were policy related—Congress wanted a more stimulative fiscal policy and was concerned about the 8 percent unemployment rate.

Table 8-1 shows that Congress has approved budget totals much closer to President Carter's requests than to President Ford's. In 1977, Ford submitted a lame duck budget several days before Carter's inauguration. In March, Carter sent revised requests to Congress, and the House and Senate agreed on totals similar to the requests in September. In fiscal 1979, the final totals approved by Congress were 2.6 percent below the $500 billion requested by Carter in January. This difference in outlays was primarily a function of underspending and revised estimates for uncontrollables, not a leaner fiscal policy. Six months later, inflation had raised the outlay total for fiscal 1979 above Carter's initial request.

The increase in revenues by Congress in fiscal 1979, however, did reflect a policy difference with the president. Increasingly concerned with inflation, Congress rejected much of the president's tax cut proposals. In general, congressional totals for receipts have been closer to the presidents' figures than outlays. Most often, the differences reflect varying economic assumptions as much as policy disputes. Even with President Ford in 1975, Congress virtually accepted his projected tax revenues.

Figures for the deficit reflect the greatest variation with the presidents' proposals, but this, too, is misleading. To date, the deficit has continued to be a remainder after revenue and expenditure totals have been established. Although the deficit is highly controversial, the major policy disputes have involved spending, and to a lesser extent, taxes. It would be possible to use tax cuts or surcharges to achieve a desired deficit, but this has not occurred.

The relationship between the president and the Congress needs to be explored beyond the aggregate budget totals, but those figures represent the most obvious manifestations of budget disputes. Within the functional subtotals, agency, and program requests, relations between the president and Congress remain largely unchanged. Individual requests may be highly controversial. Expensive spending programs proposed by the president may be accepted or rejected, but now must have a ''place'' in the concurrent resolution.

The Congress is less dependent on the president in budgeting than before 1975. Presidents are restricted in their ability to impound funds.

Congress now considers fiscal policy with their own economists and experts to advise them. House Budget Committee Chairman Brock Adams, after one of the first budget resolutions was passed, remarked that "Perhaps the most important aspect of the resolution is the fact that it contains the budget of Congress and not that of the President."[5] This sentiment was widespread among congressmen (even some who voted against the resolutions). But how accurate is that conclusion?

THE BALANCE OF FISCAL POWER

Despite the changes in the aggregate totals requested by the president, congressional action on functional and program level requests is not very different from that under the old system. Defense issues, for example, are still fought in the Armed Services Committees, Defense Appropriations Subcommittees, and on the House and Senate floor. The decision of Congress to accept Carter's cancellation of the B-1 bomber and proceed with the M-X missile system resembles, in process, the decision to accept Nixon's recommendation on the ABM system a decade before. What is different is the linking of the B-1 and M-X decisions to other budget decisions, and the need to accommodate decisions on parts with decisions on the whole budget.

Can Congress make fiscal policy? With the economic advice of the Joint Economic Committee (JEC) now supplemented with Budget Committee staffs and CBO, they have a capability that did not exist before. Yet the president still remains dominant in this arena with OMB, Treasury, the Council of Economic Advisors *acting*, and Congress *reacting*. The president's budget remains a key referent for Congressional deliberations, even in the Senate where markup is based on current policy estimates. Budget reform has made it possible for Congress to challenge and alter presidential fiscal policy, but it has not diminished the president's role of initiator.

A desire for congressional "independence" from the president, in a literal sense, is not a desirable goal for the nation. We are stuck with the Madisonian system of institutional conflict for all its advantages and shortcomings. We are not served well when the conflict between institutions becomes so great that rivalry and jealousy outstrip the recognition of mutual purpose, as occurred in the 1960s and 1970s. Perhaps the antipathy towards the president in 1974 and its aftereffects helped create momentum to successfully launch budget reforms in Congress. But if the reform is to be useful, it demands integration, not independence.

A confounding factor in assessing the balance of budgetary power is the considerable margin of error found even in annual budget planning. Projections of revenues, entitlement expenditures, economic trends as well as underspending and agency discretion in budget execution make it impossible for macrobudgeting to be precise. The margin of error may be as high as 2-3 percent, $12 to $18 billion in a $600 billion budget. As one considers multiyear budgeting, the imprecision increases geometrically. Congressional alteration of presidential totals is rarely as great as the error in estimating outlays.

Despite the lack of precision in national budgeting, the question of the relative role of Congress and the president remains important. In the long run, the focus of budget planning should remain within the executive branch; it needs to come from the president. The executive branch is still more capable of formulating the budget and setting the economic agenda. Despite the traditional notions of executive advocacy and legislative guardianship, the president and OMB remain the most effective economizers in government. Congressional budget reform has not notably altered the degree of guardianship exercised by Congress as a whole. The legislative branch retains a strong parochial orientation; budget reform has not diminished the attractiveness of public works projects, defense installations or aid to impacted areas. The budget debate in Congress frequently includes relative shares analysis, with senators and representatives worrying about getting their proportion of the federal pie. Budget reform has not altered the basic nature of Congress as a "district oriented" institution.

Congressional budget reform should not be seen as a vehicle to diminish presidential power (except in its capricious exercise, such as Nixon's impoundments), but rather as a means for strengthening the ability of Congress to perform its role within the larger budget system. To a great extent, it has done this. If we purge ourselves of the belief that conflict should be the dominant mode of executive-legislative interactions in budgeting, it is easier to recognize the roles should be different. It also allows more reasonable judgments on further changes that can improve the entire process, not weaken one participant vis-à-vis the other.

The primary role of the Congress should be to scrutinize and oversee executive requests, and cooperate in establishing future policy directions through the budget. It should not be to supplant or compete against the executive budget. Has budget reform gone too far, further fragmenting the national policy process? No. A strong, responsible set of procedures to deal with the executive budget were sorely needed. Some limitations on executive impoundments were called for, as was better congressional information. But the future reforms of congressional budgeting should take a different direction, one aimed at improving oversight, program review, and longer term decision making. The increased budgetary capability in Congress stands as a protection against arbitrary or irresponsible presidential proposals, but rarely will it serve this purpose. In the vast majority of times, Congress should be working to improve the quality and effectiveness of national policies.

The future of presidential-congressional relations in budgeting depends on many trends and factors that no one can anticipate. But in the near future, additional reforms that affect their relationship and overall budgeting performance may be implemented.

IMPROVING BUDGET PLANNING

An area of weakness in national budgeting is the limitation to annual budget planning. Budget reform reconstituted the annual budget process in Congress, but the budget is made up primarily of multiyear decisions which commit funds to be spent for many years into the future. The controllable portion of the budget is about 25 percent, but the actual annual discretion is only about 5 percent above or below current policy.[6] Despite the interest, concern, and conflict over annual budgets, most budgetary decisions are non-annual.

The Budget Act did not significantly alter the annual focus of decision making, but it did take two important steps towards more conscious consideration of multiyear spending. The CBO five-year projections and bill costing both are preliminary steps to more explicit multiyear budgeting.

Five years' experience with a centralized budgeting system should have taught Congress that the actions it takes today will impinge on its decisions tomorrow. Implicitly, this is already a multiyear system, but without any mechanism for coordination or explicit choices. The fact remains that although congressional action affects the future, there is no vehicle within the current process to specify targets beyond the next twelve-month period. The budget experiences of the last half of the 1970s also should have made it clear that many desired goals are not achieved in a single year.

One recommendation is that the president and Congress adopt advanced targeting as a form of multiyear budgeting.[7] The five-year CBO projections, according to its advocates, provide the necessary framework for advance targeting in Congress. Instead of approving targets just for the next fiscal year, Congress would approve by resolution, targets for spending, and revenues for the next 2-10 years.

While not a certainty, it seems a probability that, had the Congress ten years ago begun each year to state advance targets for itself, for a five- or even a two-year period, the order in which things occurred, and the way in which federal resources were raised and allocated, might very well have been different from the actual events. It is common to assert that this country cannot now afford national health insurance even if there were agreement on the form it should take. The sting of this truth, assuming it to be a truth, would be less if we could tell ourselves that our present dilemma is at least the result of explicit choice making in the past, instead of the accidental product of ten thousand past decisions, each made without much reference to their impact on this year or this decade.[8]

There are several drawbacks to this plan. One is the additional area of controversy that will be added to the budget process. Unless advance targets are approved in separate resolutions from the current resolutions, the process might break down. The level of uncertainty and the margin of error rise geometrically as one projects farther in the future. If economists cannot yet make forecasts with precision six to twelve months in the future, there are sure to be widely varying projections for longer periods. On the other hand, the recognition of the inherent imprecision, and the ability of Congress to revise advance targets every year might be sufficient to manage conflict in the future.

Such an exercise in multiyear budget planning would be more effective if it was first adopted in the executive budget. President Ford's 1978 budget included projected targets for the next fiscal year.[9] The Carter administration has shown some inclination to move in this direction in the fiscal 1981 budget, but major policy initiatives in 1978 such as higher education student aid and national urban policy revealed no evidence of multiyear planning.[10] The passage of the Humphrey-Hawkins Full Employment Bill, even in its watered-down state, placed greater multiyear planning requirements on the president. The Economic Report of the president must now set out a five-year plan for GNP to reach a full employment level.[11] Innovations in multiyear budgeting would be more useful if originated by the president, with Congress responding in terms of advance targets. The Senate in 1979 adopted the Long amendment which requires the president and Congress to submit a balanced budget alternative for the next two fiscal years. The Senate included these projections with their first resolution on the 1980 budget, but the House did not.

Advance targeting would be a progressive step. Even if Congress alters its original goals beyond recognition, advance targeting fosters the idea that budget choices have multiyear implications, and clarifies trade offs between fiscal and allocative goals. At worst, it could provide another forum for partisan bickering. At best, it could mark a significant change in the attitudes and provide a more rational framework for budget decision making.

CONCLUSION

As one observer has noted, "perfect control is an imperfect goal."[12] Congress has relinquished much of its discretion over taxing and spending to the executive, but has given up control for a reason.

Congress has not sought absolute budget control because it is impossible to attain and because such control would have unwanted side effects. Congress has decided to give workers some security about their future by providing Social Security benefits through permanent appropriations. It has decided to assure prompt payment of interest charges by permanently appropriating necessary funds. Congress had decided to give State and Local units of government some advance notice of future assistance by establishing a multiyear revenue-sharing program. In these and other instances, Congress has willingly accepted a loss of budget control in order to pursue other budget values: efficiency, stability, and financial certainty. [13]

Within this context, there remain actions that Congress could take to shore up its control of the budget. Congress could bring off-budget items into the regular budget. Congress could mandate changes to increase control over guaranteed loans, government sponsored corporations, borrowing, and contract authority.

But Congress must consider more than control and recognize the limits of its ability to control spending while promoting efficient policies and long-term planning. Moving in this direction, Congress will find that it has greater flexibility over future budgets. It will help reveal the relationship between future control and current discretion. Improvements in the program review process is also necessary whether through sunset laws or regularized reauthorizations.

Looking back only a decade, Congress has regained a share of the power of the purse. The process has been a success because it has given Congress the ability to make more responsible decisions on the national budget. Although the policy effects have not yet been dramatic, they have been important. Yet Congress must avoid self-satisfaction with the budget process; many problem areas remain. With the experience of the 1970s, however, we have seen that Congress can fulfill its constitutional responsibilities. Without replacing the executive in budgeting, Congress can play the significant role that once appeared relinquished.

NOTES

1. Arthur Schlesinger, *The Imperial Presidency* (Boston: Houghton Mifflin, 1973).

2. Thomas Cronin, "Superman, Our Textbook President," *Washington Monthly 2* (October, 1970).

3. George Reedy, *The Twilight of the Presidency* (New York: World Publishing Company, 1970).

4. Hugh Heclo, *Studying the Presidency: A Report to the Ford Foundation* (Naugatuck, Conn.: Ford Foundation, 1977).

5. *Congressional Quarterly Weekly Reports*, Sept. 11, 1976, p. 2455.

6. Lance T. LeLoup, "Discretion in National Budgeting: Controlling the Controllables," *Policy Analysis 4* (Fall 1978): 455-476.

7. Congressional Budget Office, *Advance Budgeting: A Report to Congress*, February 24, 1977.

8. Ibid., p. 3.

9. Ibid.

10. Robert Hartman, "Multiyear Budget Planning," in Joseph Pechman, ed., *Setting National Priorities: The 1979 Budget* (Washington: Brookings Institution, 1978), Appendix B, p. 309.

11. Ibid.

12. Allen Schick, "Congressional Control of Expenditures," Budget Committee, U.S. House of Representatives, January 1977, p. 126.

13. Ibid.

Appendix
Public Law 93-344

Public Law 93-344
93rd Congress, H. R. 7130
July 12, 1974

An Act

88 STAT. 297

To establish a new congressional budget process ; to establish Committees on the Budget in each House ; to establish a Congressional Budget Office ; to establish a procedure providing congressional control over the impoundment of funds by the executive branch ; and for other purposes.

Be it enacted by the Senate and House of Representatives of the United States of America in Congress assembled,

SHORT TITLES; TABLE OF CONTENTS

SECTION 1. (a) SHORT TITLES.—This Act may be cited as the "Congressional Budget and Impoundment Control Act of 1974". Titles I through IX may be cited as the "Congressional Budget Act of 1974", and title X may be cited as the "Impoundment Control Act of 1974".

(b) TABLE OF CONTENTS.—

Congressional Budget and Impoundment Control Act of 1974.
31 USC 1301 note.

38-109 O

Pub. Law 93-344   July 12, 1974

DECLARATION OF PURPOSES

31 USC 1301.   SEC. 2. The Congress declares that it is essential—

(1) to assure effective congressional control over the budgetary process;

(2) to provide for the congressional determination each year of the appropriate level of Federal revenues and expenditures;

(3) to provide a system of impoundment control;

(4) to establish national budget priorities; and

(5) to provide for the furnishing of information by the executive branch in a manner that will assist the Congress in discharging its duties.

DEFINITIONS

SEC. 3. (a) IN GENERAL.—For purposes of this Act—   31 USC 1302.
    (1) The terms "budget outlays" and "outlays" mean, with respect to any fiscal year, expenditures and net lending of funds under budget authority during such year.
    (2) The term "budget authority" means authority provided by law to enter into obligations which will result in immediate or future outlays involving Government funds, except that such term does not include authority to insure or guarantee the repayment of indebtedness incurred by another person or government.
    (3) The term "tax expenditures" means those revenue losses attributable to provisions of the Federal tax laws which allow a special exclusion, exemption, or deduction from gross income or which provide a special credit, a preferential rate of tax, or a deferral of tax liability; and the term "tax expenditures budget" means an enumeration of such tax expenditures.
    (4) The term "concurrent resolution on the budget" means—
        (A) a concurrent resolution setting forth the congressional budget for the United States Government for a fiscal year as provided in section 301;
        (B) a concurrent resolution reaffirming or revising the congressional budget for the United States Government for a fiscal year as provided in section 310; and
        (C) any other concurrent resolution revising the congressional budget for the United States Government for a fiscal year as described in section 304.
    (5) The term "appropriation Act" means an Act referred to in section 105 of title 1, United States Code.   Post, p. 322.
(b) JOINT COMMITTEE ON ATOMIC ENERGY.—For purposes of titles II, III, and IV of this Act, the Members of the House of Representatives who are members of the Joint Committee on Atomic Energy shall be treated as a standing committee of the House, and the Members of the Senate who are members of the Joint Committee shall be treated as a standing committee of the Senate.

TITLE I—ESTABLISHMENT OF HOUSE AND SENATE BUDGET COMMITTEES

Congressional Budget Act of 1974.

BUDGET COMMITTEE OF THE HOUSE OF REPRESENTATIVES

SEC. 101. (a) Clause 1 of Rule X of the Rules of the House of Representatives is amended by redesignating paragraphs (e) through (u) as paragraphs (f) through (v), respectively, and by inserting after paragraph (d) the following new paragraph:
"(e) Committee on the Budget, to consist of twenty-three Members   Membership.
as follows:
    "(1) five Members who are members of the Committee on Appropriations;
    "(2) five Members who are members of the Committee on Ways and Means;
    "(3) eleven Members who are members of other standing committees;
    "(4) one Member from the leadership of the majority party; and

174

Pub. Law 93-344   July 12, 1974

88 STAT. 300

Term.

Seniority rule,
exception.

Committee
sessions.

Subpenas.

Duties.

"(5) one Member from the leadership of the minority party. No Member shall serve as a member of the Committee on the Budget during more than two Congresses in any period of five successive Congresses beginning after 1974 (disregarding for this purpose any service performed as a member of such committee for less than a full session in any Congress). All selections of Members to serve on the committee shall be made without regard to seniority."

(b) Rule X of the Rules of the House of Representatives is amended by adding at the end thereof the following new clause:

"6. For carrying out the purposes set forth in clause 5 of Rule XI, the Committee on the Budget or any subcommittee thereof is authorized to sit and act at such times and places within the United States, whether the House is in session, has recessed, or has adjourned, to hold such hearings, to require the attendance of such witnesses and the production of such books or papers or documents or vouchers by subpena or otherwise, and to take such testimony and records, as it deems necessary. Subpenas may be issued over the signature of the chairman of the committee or of any member of the committee designated by him; and may be served by any person designated by such chairman or member. The chairman of the committee, or any member thereof, may administer oaths to witnesses."

(c) Rule XI of the Rules of the House of Representatives is amended by redesignating clauses 5 through 33 as clauses 6 through 34, respectively, and by inserting after clause 4 the following new clause:

"5. Committee on the Budget

"(a) All concurrent resolutions on the budget (as defined in section 3(a)(4) of the Congressional Budget Act of 1974) and other matters required to be referred to the committee under titles III and IV of that Act.

"(b) The committee shall have the duty—

"(1) to report the matters required to be reported by it under titles III and IV of the Congressional Budget Act of 1974;

"(2) to make continuing studies of the effect on budget outlays of relevant existing and proposed legislation and to report the results of such studies to the House on a recurring basis;

"(3) to request and evaluate continuing studies of tax expenditures, to devise methods of coordinating tax expenditures, policies, and programs with direct budget outlays, and to report the results of such studies to the House on a recurring basis; and

"(4) to review, on a continuing basis, the conduct by the Congressional Budget Office of its functions and duties."

BUDGET COMMITTEE OF THE SENATE

Sec. 102. (a) Paragraph 1 of rule XXV of the Standing Rules of the Senate is amended by adding at the end thereof the following new subparagraph:

"(r)(1) Committee on the Budget, to which committee shall be referred all concurrent resolutions on the budget (as defined in section 3(a)(4) of the Congressional Budget Act of 1974) and all other matters required to be referred to that committee under titles III and IV of that Act, and messages, petitions, memorials, and other matters relating thereto.

July 12, 1974   Pub. Law 93-344

88 STAT. 301
Duties.

"(2) Such committee shall have the duty—

"(A) to report the matters required to be reported by it under titles III and IV of the Congressional Budget Act of 1974;

"(B) to make continuing studies of the effect on budget outlays of relevant existing and proposed legislation and to report the results of such studies to the Senate on a recurring basis;

"(C) to request and evaluate continuing studies of tax expenditures, to devise methods of coordinating tax expenditures, policies, and programs with direct budget outlays, and to report the results of such studies to the Senate on a recurring basis; and

"(D) to review, on a continuing basis, the conduct by the Congressional Budget Office of its functions and duties."

(b) The table contained in paragraph 2 of rule XXV of the Standing Rules of the Senate is amended by inserting after—

"Banking, Housing and Urban Affairs_____ _____ 15"

the following:

"Budget _____ 15".

(c) Paragraph 6 of rule XXV of the Standing Rules of the Senate is amended by adding at the end thereof the following new subparagraph:

"(h) For purposes of the first sentence of subparagraph (a), membership on the Committee on the Budget shall not be taken into account until that date occurring during the first session of the Ninety-fifth Congress, upon which the appointment of the majority and minority party members of the standing committees of the Senate is initially completed."

(d) Each meeting of the Committee on the Budget of the Senate, or any subcommittee thereof, including meetings to conduct hearings, shall be open to the public, except that a portion or portions of any such meeting may be closed to the public if the committee or subcommittee, as the case may be, determines by record vote of a majority of the members of the committee or subcommittee present that the matters to be discussed or the testimony to be taken at such portion or portions—

     Open and closed meetings.
     2 USC 190a-3.

(1) will disclose matters necessary to be kept secret in the interests of national defense or the confidential conduct of the foreign relations of the United States;

(2) will relate solely to matters of committee staff personnel or internal staff management or procedure;

(3) will tend to charge an individual with crime or misconduct, to disgrace or injure the professional standing of an individual, or otherwise to expose an individual to public contempt or obloquy, or will represent a clearly unwarranted invasion of the privacy of an individual;

(4) will disclose the identity of any informer or law enforcement agent or will disclose any information relating to the investigation or prosecution of a criminal offense that is required to be kept secret in the interests of effective law enforcement; or

(5) will disclose information relating to the trade secrets or financial or commercial information pertaining specifically to a given person if—

Pub. Law 93-344   July 12, 1974

88 STAT. 302

(A) an Act of Congress requires the information to be kept confidential by Government officers and employees; or

(B) the information has been obtained by the Government on a confidential basis, other than through an application by such person for a specific Government financial or other benefit, and is required to be kept secret in order to prevent undue injury to the competitive position of such person.

(e) Paragraph 7(b) of rule XXV of the Standing Rules of the Senate and section 133A(b) of the Legislative Reorganization Act of 1946 shall not apply to the Committee on the Budget of the Senate.

84 Stat. 1151,
1153.
2 USC 190a-1.

TITLE II—CONGRESSIONAL BUDGET OFFICE

ESTABLISHMENT OF OFFICE

2 USC 601.

SEC. 201. (a) IN GENERAL.—

(1) There is established an office of the Congress to be known as the Congressional Budget Office (hereinafter in this title referred to as the "Office"). The Office shall be headed by a Director; and there shall be a Deputy Director who shall perform such duties as may be assigned to him by the Director and, during the absence or incapacity of the Director or during a vacancy in that office, shall act as Director.

Appointment.

(2) The Director shall be appointed by the Speaker of the House of Representatives and the President pro tempore of the Senate after considering recommendations received from the Committees on the Budget of the House and the Senate, without regard to political affiliation and solely on the basis of his fitness to perform his duties. The Deputy Director shall be appointed by the Director.

Term.

(3) The term of office of the Director first appointed shall expire at noon on January 3, 1979, and the terms of office of Directors subsequently appointed shall expire at noon on January 3 of each fourth year thereafter. Any individual appointed as Director to fill a vacancy prior to the expiration of a term shall serve only for the unexpired portion of that term. An individual serving as Director at the expiration of a term may continue to serve until his successor is appointed. Any Deputy Director shall serve until the expiration of the term of office of the Director who appointed him (and until his successor is appointed), unless sooner removed by the Director.

Removal.

(4) The Director may be removed by either House by resolution.

Compensation.

(5) The Director shall receive compensation at a per annum gross rate equal to the rate of basic pay, as in effect from time to time, for level III of the Executive Schedule in section 5314

83 Stat. 863.

of title 5, United States Code. The Deputy Director shall receive compensation at a per annum gross rate equal to the rate of basic pay, as so in effect, for level IV of the Executive Schedule in section 5315 of such title.

Appointment and
compensation.

(b) PERSONNEL.—The Director shall appoint and fix the compensation of such personnel as may be necessary to carry out the duties and functions of the Office. All personnel of the Office shall be appointed without regard to political affiliation and solely on the basis of their fitness to perform their duties. The Director may prescribe the duties and responsibilities of the personnel of the Office, and delegate to them authority to perform any of the duties, powers, and functions imposed

July 12, 1974

Pub. Law 93-344

88 STAT. 303

on the Office or on the Director. For purposes of pay (other than pay of the Director and Deputy Director) and employment benefits, rights, and privileges, all personnel of the Office shall be treated as if they were employees of the House of Representatives.

(c) EXPERTS AND CONSULTANTS.—In carrying out the duties and functions of the Office, the Director may procure the temporary (not to exceed one year) or intermittent services of experts or consultants or organizations thereof by contract as independent contractors, or, in the case of individual experts or consultants, by employment at rates of pay not in excess of the daily equivalent of the highest rate of basic pay payable under the General Schedule of section 5332 of title 5, United States Code.

(d) RELATIONSHIP TO EXECUTIVE BRANCH.—The Director is authorized to secure information, data, estimates, and statistics directly from the various departments, agencies, and establishments of the executive branch of Government and the regulatory agencies and commissions of the Government. All such departments, agencies, establishments, and regulatory agencies and commissions shall furnish the Director any available material which he determines to be necessary in the performance of his duties and functions (other than material the disclosure of which would be a violation of law). The Director is also authorized, upon agreement with the head of any such department, agency, establishment, or regulatory agency or commission, to utilize its services, facilities, and personnel with or without reimbursement; and the head of each such department, agency, establishment, or regulatory agency or commission is authorized to provide the Office such services, facilities, and personnel.

(e) RELATIONSHIP TO OTHER AGENCIES OF CONGRESS.—In carrying out the duties and functions of the Office, and for the purpose of coordinating the operations of the Office with those of other congressional agencies with a view to utilizing most effectively the information, services, and capabilities of all such agencies in carrying out the various responsibilities assigned to each, the Director is authorized to obtain information, data, estimates, and statistics developed by the General Accounting Office, the Library of Congress, and the Office of Technology Assessment, and (upon agreement with them) to utilize their services, facilities, and personnel with or without reimbursement. The Comptroller General, the Librarian of Congress, and the Technology Assessment Board are authorized to provide the Office with the information, data, estimates, and statistics, and the services, facilities, and personnel, referred to in the preceding sentence.

(f) APPROPRIATIONS.—There are authorized to be appropriated to the Office for each fiscal year such sums as may be necessary to enable it to carry out its duties and functions. Until sums are first appropriated pursuant to the preceding sentence, but for a period not exceeding 12 months following the effective date of this subsection, the expenses of the Office shall be paid from the contingent fund of the Senate, in accordance with the paragraph relating to the contingent fund of the Senate under the heading "UNDER LEGISLATIVE" in the Act of October 1, 1888 (28 Stat. 546; 2 U.S.C. 68), and upon vouchers approved by the Director.

5 USC 5332
note.
Data, availability.

GAO, Library of Congress, Office of Technology Assessment, use of facilities.

178

DUTIES AND FUNCTIONS

2 USC 602.

SEC. 202. (a) ASSISTANCE TO BUDGET COMMITTEES.—It shall be the duty and function of the Office to provide to the Committees on the Budget of both Houses information which will assist such committees in the discharge of all matters within their jurisdictions, including (1) information with respect to the budget, appropriation bills, and other bills authorizing or providing budget authority or tax expenditures, (2) information with respect to revenues, receipts, estimated future revenues and receipts, and changing revenue conditions, and (3) such related information as such Committees may request.

(b) ASSISTANCE TO COMMITTEES ON APPROPRIATIONS, WAYS AND MEANS, AND FINANCE.—At the request of the Committee on Appropriations of either House, the Committee on Ways and Means of the House of Representatives, or the Committee on Finance of the Senate, the Office shall provide to such Committee any information which will assist it in the discharge of matters within its jurisdiction, including information described in clauses (1) and (2) of subsection (a) and such related information as the Committee may request.

(c) ASSISTANCE TO OTHER COMMITTEES AND MEMBERS.—

(1) At the request of any other committee of the House of Representatives or the Senate or any joint committee of the Congress, the Office shall provide to such committee or joint committee any information compiled in carrying out clauses (1) and (2) of subsection (a), and, to the extent practicable, such additional information related to the foregoing as may be requested.

(2) At the request of any Member of the House or Senate, the Office shall provide to such Member any information compiled in carrying out clauses (1) and (2) of subsection (a), and, to the extent available, such additional information related to the foregoing as may be requested.

(d) ASSIGNMENT OF OFFICE PERSONNEL TO COMMITTEES AND JOINT COMMITTEES.—At the request of the Committee on the Budget of either House, personnel of the Office shall be assigned, on a temporary basis, to assist such committee. At the request of any other committee of either House or any joint committee of the Congress, personnel of the Office may be assigned, on a temporary basis, to assist such committee or joint committee with respect to matters directly related to the applicable provisions of subsection (b) or (c).

(e) TRANSFER OF FUNCTIONS OF JOINT COMMITTEE ON REDUCTION OF FEDERAL EXPENDITURES.—

(1) The duties, functions, and personnel of the Joint Committee on Reduction of Federal Expenditures are transferred to the Office, and the Joint Committee is abolished.

Repeal.
79 Stat. 1026.
31 USC 571.
Contents.

(2) Section 601 of the Revenue Act of 1941 (55 Stat. 726) is repealed.

(f) REPORTS TO BUDGET COMMITTEES.—

(1) On or before April 1 of each year, the Director shall submit to the Committees on the Budget of the House of Representatives and the Senate a report, for the fiscal year commencing on October 1 of that year, with respect to fiscal policy, including (A) alternative levels of total revenues, total new budget authority, and total outlays (including related surpluses and deficits), and (B) the levels of tax expenditures under existing law, taking into account projected economic factors and any changes in such levels based on proposals in the budget submitted by the President for such fiscal year. Such report shall also include a discussion of national budget priorities, including alternative ways of allocating

179

July 12, 1974   Pub. Law 93-344
88 STAT. 305

budget authority and budget outlays for such fiscal year among
major programs or functional categories, taking into account
how such alternative allocations will meet major national needs
and affect balanced growth and development of the United States.

(2) The Director shall from time to time submit to the Committees on the Budget of the House of Representatives and the
Senate such further reports (including reports revising the
report required by paragraph (1)) as may be necessary or appropriate to provide such Committees with information, data, and
analyses for the performance of their duties and functions.

*Reports, sub-
mittal to
Budget com-
mittees.*

(g) USE OF COMPUTERS AND OTHER TECHNIQUES.—The Director
may equip the Office with up-to-date computer capability (upon
approval of the Committee on House Administration of the House of
Representatives and the Committee on Rules and Administration of
the Senate), obtain the services of experts and consultants in computer
technology, and develop techniques for the evaluation of budgetary
requirements.

*Experts and
consultants.*

PUBLIC ACCESS TO BUDGET DATA

SEC. 203. (a) RIGHT TO COPY.—Except as provided in subsections
(c) and (d), the Director shall make all information, data, estimates,
and statistics obtained under sections 201(d) and 201(e) available for
public copying during normal business hours, subject to reasonable
rules and regulations, and shall to the extent practicable, at the request
of any person, furnish a copy of any such information, data, estimates,
or statistics upon payment by such person of the cost of making and
furnishing such copy.

2 USC 603.

(b) INDEX.—The Director shall develop and maintain filing, coding,
and indexing systems that identify the information, data, estimates,
and statistics to which subsection (a) applies and shall make such
systems available for public use during normal business hours.

(c) EXCEPTIONS.—Subsection (a) shall not apply to information,
data, estimates, and statistics—

    (1) which are specifically exempted from disclosure by law; or
    (2) which the Director determines will disclose—

        (A) matters necessary to be kept secret in the interests of
national defense or the confidential conduct of the foreign
relations of the United States;

        (B) information relating to trade secrets or financial or
commercial information pertaining specifically to a given
person if the information has been obtained by the Government on a confidential basis, other than through an application by such person for a specific financial or other benefit,
and is required to be kept secret in order to prevent undue
injury to the competitive position of such person; or

        (C) personnel or medical data or similar data the dis-
closure of which would constitute a clearly unwarranted
invasion of personal privacy;

    unless the portions containing such matters, information, or data
have been excised.

(d) INFORMATION OBTAINED FOR COMMITTEES AND MEMBERS.—Subsection (a) shall apply to any information, data, estimates, and statistics obtained at the request of any committee, joint committee, or
Member unless such committee, joint committee, or Member has
instructed the Director not to make such information, data, estimates,
or statistics available for public copying.

180

Pub. Law 93-344   July 12, 1974

TITLE III—CONGRESSIONAL BUDGET PROCESS

TIMETABLE

31 USC 1321.

SEC. 300. The timetable with respect to the congressional budget process for any fiscal year is as follows:

On or before:	Action to be completed:
November 10	President submits current services budget.
15th day after Congress meets	President submits his budget.
March 15	Committees and joint committees submit reports to Budget Committees.
April 1	Congressional Budget Office submits report to Budget Committees.
April 15	Budget Committees report first concurrent resolution on the budget to their Houses.
May 15	Committees report bills and resolutions authorizing new budget authority.
May 15	Congress completes action on first concurrent resolution on the budget.
7th day after Labor Day	Congress completes action on bills and resolutions providing new budget authority and new spending authority.
September 15	Congress completes action on second required concurrent resolution on the budget.
September 25	Congress completes action on reconciliation bill or resolution, or both, implementing second required concurrent resolution.
October 1	Fiscal year begins.

ADOPTION OF FIRST CONCURRENT RESOLUTION

31 USC 1322.

Contents.

SEC. 301. (a) ACTION TO BE COMPLETED BY MAY 15.—On or before May 15 of each year, the Congress shall complete action on the first concurrent resolution on the budget for the fiscal year beginning on October 1 of such year. The concurrent resolution shall set forth—

(1) the appropriate level of total budget outlays and of total new budget authority;

(2) an estimate of budget outlays and an appropriate level of new budget authority for each major functional category, for contingencies, and for undistributed intragovernmental transactions, based on allocations of the appropriate level of total budget outlays and of total new budget authority;

(3) the amount, if any, of the surplus or the deficit in the budget which is appropriate in light of economic conditions and all other relevant factors;

(4) the recommended level of Federal revenues and the amount, if any, by which the aggregate level of Federal revenues should be increased or decreased by bills and resolutions to be reported by the appropriate committees;

(5) the appropriate level of the public debt, and the amount, if any, by which the statutory limit on the public debt should be increased or decreased by bills and resolutions to be reported by the appropriate committees; and

(6) such other matters relating to the budget as may be appropriate to carry out the purposes of this Act.

(b) ADDITIONAL MATTERS IN CONCURRENT RESOLUTION.—The first concurrent resolution on the budget may also require—

181

(1) a procedure under which all or certain bills and resolutions providing new budget authority or providing new spending authority described in section 401(c)(2)(C) for such fiscal year shall not be enrolled until the concurrent resolution required to be reported under section 310(a) has been agreed to, and, if a reconciliation bill or reconciliation resolution, or both, are required to be reported under section 310(c), until Congress has completed action on that bill or resolution, or both; and

(2) any other procedure which is considered appropriate to carry out the purposes of this Act.

Not later than the close of the Ninety-fifth Congress, the Committee on the Budget of each House shall report to its House on the implementation of procedures described in this subsection.

Report to Congress.

(c) VIEWS AND ESTIMATES OF OTHER COMMITTEES.—On or before March 15 of each year, each standing committee of the House of Representatives shall submit to the Committee on the Budget of the House, each standing committee of the Senate shall submit to the Committee on the Budget of the Senate, and the Joint Economic Committee and Joint Committee on Internal Revenue Taxation shall submit to the Committees on the Budget of both Houses—

Submittal to congressional committees.

(1) its views and estimates with respect to all matters set forth in subsection (a) which relate to matters within the respective jurisdiction or functions of such committee or joint committee; and

(2) except in the case of such joint committees, the estimate of the total amounts of new budget authority, and budget outlays resulting therefrom, to be provided or authorized in all bills and resolutions within the jurisdiction of such committee which such committee intends to be effective during the fiscal year beginning on October 1 of such year.

The Joint Economic Committee shall also submit to the Committees on the Budget of both Houses, its recommendations as to the fiscal policy appropriate to the goals of the Employment Act of 1946. Any other committee of the House or Senate may submit to the Committee on the Budget of its House, and any other joint committee of the Congress may submit to the Committees on the Budget of both Houses, its views and estimates with respect to all matters set forth in subsection (a) which relate to matters within its jurisdiction or functions.

60 Stat. 23.
15 USC 1021 note.

(d) HEARINGS AND REPORT.—In developing the first concurrent resolution on the budget referred to in subsection (a) for each fiscal year, the Committee on the Budget of each House shall hold hearings and shall receive testimony from Members of Congress and such appropriate representatives of Federal departments and agencies, the general public, and national organizations as the committee deems desirable. On or before April 15 of each year, the Committee on the Budget of each House shall report to its House the first concurrent resolution on the budget referred to in subsection (a) for the fiscal year beginning on October 1 of such year. The report accompanying such concurrent resolution shall include, but not be limited to—

Concurrent resolution, development.

Report to Congress.

Contents.

(1) a comparison of revenues estimated by the committee with those estimated in the budget submitted by the President;

(2) a comparison of the appropriate levels of total budget outlays and total new budget authority, as set forth in such concurrent resolution, with total budget outlays estimated and total new budget authority requested in the budget submitted by the President;

(3) with respect to each major functional category, an estimate of budget outlays and an appropriate level of new budget authority for all proposed programs and for all existing programs (including renewals thereof), with the estimate and level for existing programs being divided between permanent authority and funds provided in appropriation Acts, and each such division being subdivided between controllable amounts and all other amounts;

(4) an allocation of the level of Federal revenues recommended in the concurrent resolution among the major sources of such revenues;

(5) the economic assumptions and objectives which underlie each of the matters set forth in such concurrent resolution and alternative economic assumptions and objectives which the committee considered;

(6) projections, not limited to the following, for the period of five fiscal years beginning with such fiscal year of the estimated levels of total budget outlays, total new budget outlays, total new budget authority, the estimated revenues to be received, and the estimated surplus or deficit, if any, for each fiscal year in such period, and the estimated levels of tax expenditures (the tax expenditures budget) by major functional categories;

(7) a statement of any significant changes in the proposed levels of Federal assistance to State and local governments; and

(8) information, data, and comparisons indicating the manner in which, and the basis on which, the committee determined each of the matters set forth in the concurrent resolution, and the relationship of such matters to other budget categories.

MATTERS TO BE INCLUDED IN JOINT STATEMENT OF MANAGERS;
REPORTS BY COMMITTEES

31 USC 1323.

SEC. 302. (a) ALLOCATION OF TOTALS.—The joint explanatory statement accompanying a conference report on a concurrent resolution on the budget shall include an estimated allocation, based upon such concurrent resolution as recommended in such conference report, of the appropriate levels of total budget outlays and total new budget authority among each committee of the House of Representatives and the Senate which has jurisdiction over bills and resolutions providing such new budget authority.

Subdivisions.

(b) REPORTS BY COMMITTEES.—As soon as practicable after a concurrent resolution on the budget is agreed to—

(1) the Committee on Appropriations of each House shall, after consulting with the Committee on Appropriations of the other House, (A) subdivide among its subcommittees the allocation of budget outlays and new budget authority allocated to it in the joint explanatory statement accompanying the conference report on such concurrent resolution, and (B) further subdivide the amount with respect to each such subcommittee between controllable amounts and all other amounts; and

(2) every other committee of the House and Senate to which an allocation was made in such joint explanatory statement shall, after consulting with the committee or committees of the other House to which all or part of its allocation was made, (A) subdivide such allocation among its subcommittees or among programs over which it has jurisdiction, and (B) further subdivide the amount with respect to each subcommittee or program between controllable amounts and all other amounts.

July 12, 1974   Pub. Law 93-344

88 STAT. 309

Each such committee shall promptly report to its House the subdivisions made by it pursuant to this subsection. Congressional committees' report of subdivisions.

(c) SUBSEQUENT CONCURRENT RESOLUTIONS.—In the case of a concurrent resolution on the budget referred to in section 304 or 310, the allocation under subsection (a) and the subdivisions under subsection (b) shall be required only to the extent necessary to take into account revisions made in the most recently agreed to concurrent resolution on the budget.

FIRST CONCURRENT RESOLUTION ON THE BUDGET MUST BE ADOPTED BEFORE LEGISLATION PROVIDING NEW BUDGET AUTHORITY, NEW SPENDING AUTHORITY, OR CHANGES IN REVENUES OR PUBLIC DEBT LIMIT IS CONSIDERED

SEC. 303. (a) IN GENERAL.—It shall not be in order in either the House of Representatives or the Senate to consider any bill or resolution (or amendment thereto) which provides— 31 USC 1324.

(1) new budget authority for a fiscal year;

(2) an increase or decrease in revenues to become effective during a fiscal year;

(3) an increase or decrease in the public debt limit to become effective during a fiscal year; or

(4) new spending authority described in section 401(c)(2)(C) to become effective during a fiscal year;

until the first concurrent resolution on the budget for such year has been agreed to pursuant to section 301.

(b) EXCEPTIONS.—Subsection (a) does not apply to any bill or resolution—

(1) providing new budget authority which first becomes available in a fiscal year following the fiscal year to which the concurrent resolution applies; or

(2) increasing or decreasing revenues which first become effective in a fiscal year following the fiscal year to which the concurrent resolution applies.

(c) WAIVER IN THE SENATE.—

(1) The committee of the Senate which reports any bill or resolution to which subsection (a) applies may at or after the time it reports such bill or resolution, report a resolution to the Senate (A) providing for the waiver of subsection (a) with respect to such bill or resolution, and (B) stating the reasons why the waiver is necessary. The resolution shall then be referred to the Committee on the Budget of the Senate. That committee shall report the resolution to the Senate within 10 days after the resolution is referred to it (not counting any day on which the Senate is not in session) beginning with the day following the day on which it is so referred, accompanied by that committee's recommendations and reasons for such recommendations with respect to the resolution. If the committee does not report the resolution within such 10-day period, it shall automatically be discharged from further consideration of the resolution and the resolution shall be placed on the calendar. Resolution referral. Report to Senate.

(2) During the consideration of any such resolution, debate shall be limited to one hour, to be equally divided between, and controlled by, the majority leader and minority leader or their designees, and the time on any debatable motion or appeal shall be limited to twenty minutes, to be equally divided between, and controlled by, the mover and the manager of the resolution. In the event the manager of the resolution is in favor of any such motion Debate, time limitation.

184

or appeal, the time in opposition thereto shall be controlled by the
minority leader or his designee. Such leaders, or either of them,
may, from the time under their control on the passage of such
resolution, allot additional time to any Senator during the consideration of any debatable motion or appeal. No amendment to
the resolution is in order.

(3) If, after the Committee on the Budget has reported (or
been discharged from further consideration of) the resolution,
the Senate agrees to the resolution, then subsection (a) of this
section shall not apply with respect to the bill or resolution to
which the resolution so agreed to applies.

PERMISSIBLE REVISIONS OF CONCURRENT RESOLUTIONS OF THE BUDGET

31 USC 1325.

SEC. 304. At any time after the first concurrent resolution on the
budget for a fiscal year has been agreed to pursuant to section 301, and
before the end of such fiscal year, the two Houses may adopt a concurrent resolution on the budget which revises the concurrent resolution on the budget for such fiscal year most recently agreed to.

PROVISIONS RELATING TO THE CONSIDERATION OF CONCURRENT RESOLUTIONS ON THE BUDGET

31 USC 1326.

SEC. 305. (a) PROCEDURE IN HOUSE OF REPRESENTATIVES AFTER
REPORT OF COMMITTEE; DEBATE.—

(1) When the Committee on the Budget of the House has
reported any concurrent resolution on the budget, it is in order
at any time after the tenth day (excluding Saturdays, Sundays,
and legal holidays) following the day on which the report upon
such resolution has been available to Members of the House (even
though a previous motion to the same effect has been disagreed
to) to move to proceed to the consideration of the concurrent resolution. The motion is highly privileged and is not debatable. An
amendment to the motion is not in order, and it is not in order to
move to reconsider the vote by which the motion is agreed to or
disagreed to.

Debate, time limitation.

(2) General debate on any concurrent resolution on the budget
in the House of Representatives shall be limited to not more than
10 hours, which shall be divided equally between the majority and
minority parties. A motion further to limit debate is not debatable. A motion to recommit the concurrent resolution is not in
order, and it is not in order to move to reconsider the vote by
which the concurrent resolution is agreed to or disagreed to.

(3) Consideration of any concurrent resolution on the budget
by the House of Representatives shall be in the Committee of the
Whole, and the resolution shall be read for amendment under the
five-minute rule in accordance with the applicable provisions of
rule XXIII of the Rules of the House of Representatives. After
the Committee rises and reports the resolution back to the House,
the previous question shall be considered as ordered on the resolution and any amendments thereto to final passage without intervening motion; except that it shall be in order at any time prior
to final passage (notwithstanding any other rule or provision of
law) to adopt an amendment (or a series of amendments) changing any figure or figures in the resolution as so reported to the
extent necessary to achieve mathematical consistency.

July 12, 1974   Pub. Law 93-344

88 STAT. 311

(4) Debate in the House of Representatives on the conference report or any concurrent resolution on the budget shall be limited to not more than 5 hours, which shall be divided equally between the majority and minority parties. A motion further to limit debate is not debatable. A motion to recommit the conference report is not in order, and it is not in order to move to reconsider the vote by which the conference report is agreed to or disagreed to. Debate, time limitation.

(5) Motions to postpone, made with respect to the consideration of any concurrent resolution on the budget, and motions to proceed to the consideration of other business, shall be decided without debate.

(6) Appeals from the decisions of the Chair relating to the application of the Rules of the House of Representatives to the procedure relating to any concurrent resolution on the budget shall be decided without debate.

(b) PROCEDURE IN SENATE AFTER REPORT OF COMMITTEE; DEBATE; AMENDMENTS.—

(1) Debate in the Senate on any concurrent resolution on the budget, and all amendments thereto and debatable motions and appeals in connection therewith, shall be limited to not more than 50 hours, except that, with respect to the second required concurrent resolution referred to in section 310(a), all such debate shall be limited to not more than 15 hours. The time shall be equally divided between, and controlled by, the majority leader and the minority leader or their designees. Debate, time limitation.

(2) Debate in the Senate on any amendment to a concurrent resolution on the budget shall be limited to 2 hours, to be equally divided between, and controlled by, the mover and the manager of the concurrent resolution, and debate on any amendment to an amendment, debatable motion, or appeal shall be limited to 1 hour, to be equally divided between, and controlled by, the mover and the manager of the concurrent resolution, except that in the event the manager of the concurrent resolution is in favor of any such amendment, motion, or appeal, the time in opposition thereto shall be controlled by the minority leader or his designee. No amendment that is not germane to the provisions of such concurrent resolution shall be received. Such leaders, or either of them, may, from the time under their control on the passage of the concurrent resolution, allot additional time to any Senator during the consideration of any amendment, debatable motion, or appeal.

(3) A motion to further limit debate is not debatable. A motion to recommit (except a motion to recommit with instructions to report back within a specified number of days, not to exceed 3, not counting any day on which the Senate is not in session) is not in order. Debate on any such motion to recommit shall be limited to 1 hour, to be equally divided between, and controlled by, the mover and the manager of the concurrent resolution.

(4) Notwithstanding any other rule, an amendment, or series of amendments, to a concurrent resolution on the budget proposed in the Senate shall always be in order if such amendment or series of amendments proposes to change any figure or figures then contained in such concurrent resolution so as to make such concurrent resolution mathematically consistent or so as to maintain such consistency.

Pub. Law 93-344   July 12, 1974

(c) ACTION ON CONFERENCE REPORTS IN THE SENATE.—

(1) The conference report on any concurrent resolution on the budget shall be in order in the Senate at any time after the third day (excluding Saturdays, Sundays, and legal holidays) following the day on which such a conference report is reported and is available to Members of the Senate. A motion to proceed to the consideration of the conference report may be made even though a previous motion to the same effect has been disagreed to.

Debate, time limitation.

(2) During the consideration in the Senate of the conference report on any concurrent resolution on the budget, debate shall be limited to 10 hours, to be equally divided between, and controlled by, the majority leader and minority leader or their designees. Debate on any debatable motion or appeal related to the conference report shall be limited to 1 hour, to be equally divided between, and controlled by, the mover and the manager of the conference report.

(3) Should the conference report be defeated, debate on any request for a new conference and the appointment of conferees shall be limited to 1 hour, to be equally divided between, and controlled by, the manager of the conference report and the minority leader or his designee, and should any motion be made to instruct the conferees before the conferees are named, debate on such motion shall be limited to one-half hour, to be equally divided between, and controlled by, the mover and the manager of the conference report. Debate on any amendment to any such instructions shall be limited to 20 minutes, to be equally divided between and controlled by the mover and the manager of the conference report. In all cases when the manager of the conference report is in favor of any motion, appeal, or amendment, the time in opposition shall be under the control of the minority leader or his designee.

(4) In any case in which there are amendments in disagreement, time on each amendment shall be limited to 30 minutes, to be equally divided between, and controlled by, the manager of the conference report and the minority leader or his designee. No amendment that is not germane to the provisions of such amendments shall be received.

Conference report, submittal to Congress.

(d) REQUIRED ACTION BY CONFERENCE COMMITTEE.—If, at the end of 7 days (excluding Saturdays, Sundays, and legal holidays) after the conferees of both Houses have been appointed to a committee of conference on a concurrent resolution on the budget, the conferees are unable to reach agreement with respect to all matters in disagreement between the two Houses, then the conferees shall submit to their respective Houses, on the first day thereafter on which their House is in session—

(1) a conference report recommending those matters on which they have agreed and reporting in disagreement those matters on which they have not agreed; or

(2) a conference report in disagreement, if the matter in disagreement is an amendment which strikes out the entire text of the concurrent resolution and inserts a substitute text.

(e) CONCURRENT RESOLUTION MUST BE CONSISTENT IN THE SENATE.—It shall not be in order in the Senate to vote on the question of agreeing to—

(1) a concurrent resolution on the budget unless the figures then contained in such resolution are mathematically consistent; or

(2) a conference report on a concurrent resolution on the budget unless the figures contained in such resolution, as recommended in such conference report, are mathematically consistent.

LEGISLATION DEALING WITH CONGRESSIONAL BUDGET MUST BE HANDLED
BY BUDGET COMMITTEES

SEC. 306. No bill or resolution, and no amendment to any bill or   31 USC 1327.
resolution, dealing with any matter which is within the jurisdiction
of the Committee on the Budget of either House shall be considered
in that House unless it is a bill or resolution which has been reported
by the Committee on the Budget of that House (or from the consideration of which such committee has been discharged) or unless it is an
amendment to such a bill or resolution.

HOUSE COMMITTEE ACTION ON ALL APPROPRIATION BILLS TO BE COMPLETED
BEFORE FIRST APPROPRIATION BILL IS REPORTED

SEC. 307. Prior to reporting the first regular appropriation bill for   31 USC 1328.
each fiscal year, the Committee on Appropriations of the House of
Representatives shall, to the extent practicable, complete subcommittee markup and full committee action on all regular appropriation
bills for that year and submit to the House a summary report compar-   Summary report,
ing the committee's recommendations with the appropriate levels of   submittal to
budget outlays and new budget authority as set forth in the most   House.
recently agreed to concurrent resolution on the budget for that year.

REPORTS, SUMMARIES, AND PROJECTIONS OF CONGRESSIONAL BUDGET
ACTIONS

SEC. 308. (a) REPORTS ON LEGISLATION PROVIDING NEW BUDGET   31 USC 1329.
AUTHORITY OR TAX EXPENDITURES.—Whenever a committee of either
House reports a bill or resolution to its House providing new budget
authority (other than continuing appropriations) or new or increased
tax expenditures for a fiscal year, the report accompanying that bill   Contents.
or resolution shall contain a statement, prepared after consultation
with the Director of the Congressional Budget Office, detailing—
    (1) in the case of a bill or resolution providing new budget
authority—
        (A) how the new budget authority provided in that bill
    or resolution compares with the new budget authority set
    forth in the most recently agreed to concurrent resolution
    on the budget for such fiscal year and the reports submitted
    under section 302;
        (B) a projection for the period of 5 fiscal years begin-
    ning with such fiscal year of budget outlays, associated with
    the budget authority provided in that bill or resolution, in
    each fiscal year in such period; and
        (C) the new budget authority, and budget outlays result-
    ing therefrom, provided by that bill or resolution for finan-
    cial assistance to State and local governments; and
    (2) in the case of a bill or resolution providing new or increased
tax expenditures—
        (A) how the new or increased tax expenditures provided in
    that bill or resolution will affect the levels of tax expenditures
    under existing law as set forth in the report accompanying
    the first concurrent resolution on the budget for such fiscal
    year, or, if a report accompanying a subsequently agreed to
    concurrent resolution for such year sets forth such levels,
    then as set forth in that report; and
        (B) a projection for the period of 5 fiscal years beginning
    with such fiscal year of the tax expenditures which will result
    from that bill or resolution in each fiscal year in such period.

188

88 STAT. 314

No projection shall be required for a fiscal year under paragraph (1)
(B) or (2)(B) if the committee determines that a projection for that
fiscal year is impracticable and states in its report the reason for such
impracticability.

(b) UP-TO-DATE TABULATION OF CONGRESSIONAL BUDGET ACTIONS.—
Periodic reports. The Director of the Congressional Budget Office shall issue periodic
reports detailing and tabulating the progress of congressional action
on bills and resolutions providing new budget authority and changing
Contents. revenues and the public debt limit for a fiscal year. Such reports shall
include, but are not limited to—

(1) an up-to-date tabulation comparing the new budget authority for such fiscal year in bills and resolutions on which Congress
has completed action and estimated outlays, associated with such
new budget authority, during such fiscal year to the new budget
authority and estimated outlays set forth in the most recently
agreed to concurrent resolution on the budget for such fiscal year
and the reports submitted under section 302;

(2) an up-to-date status report on all bills and resolutions providing new budget authority and changing revenues and the
public debt limit for such fiscal year in both Houses;

(3) an up-to-date comparison of the appropriate level of revenues contained in the most recently agreed to concurrent resolution on the budget for such fiscal year with the latest estimate of
revenues for such year (including new revenues anticipated
during such year under bills and resolutions on which the Congress has completed action); and

(4) an up-to-date comparison of the appropriate level of the
public debt contained in the most recently agreed to concurrent
resolution on the budget for such fiscal year with the latest estimate of the public debt during such fiscal year.

Report. (c) FIVE-YEAR PROJECTION OF CONGRESSIONAL BUDGET ACTION.—As
soon as practicable after the beginning of each fiscal year, the Director
of the Congressional Budget Office shall issue a report projecting for
the period of 5 fiscal years beginning with such fiscal year—

(1) total new budget authority and total budget outlays for
each fiscal year in such period;

(2) revenues to be received and the major sources thereof, and
the surplus or deficit, if any, for each fiscal year in such period;
and

(3) tax expenditures for each fiscal year in such period.

COMPLETION OF ACTION ON BILLS PROVIDING NEW BUDGET AUTHORITY
AND CERTAIN NEW SPENDING AUTHORITY

31 USC 1330. SEC. 309. Except as otherwise provided pursuant to this title, not
later than the seventh day after Labor Day of each year, the Congress
shall complete action on all bills and resolutions—

(1) providing new budget authority for the fiscal year beginning on October 1 of such year, other than supplemental, deficiency, and continuing appropriation bills and resolutions, and
other than the reconciliation bill for such year, if required to be
reported under section 310(c); and

(2) providing new spending authority described in section 401
(c)(2)(C) which is to become effective during such fiscal year.

Paragraph (1) shall not apply to any bill or resolution if legislation
authorizing the enactment of new budget authority to be provided in
such bill or resolution has not been timely enacted.

Pub. Law 93-344
                                                      88 STAT. 315

**SECOND REQUIRED CONCURRENT RESOLUTION AND RECONCILIATION
PROCESS**

SEC. 310. (a) REPORTING OF CONCURRENT RESOLUTION.—The Com- 31 USC 1331.
mittee on the Budget of each House shall report to its House a concurrent resolution on the budget which reaffirms or revises the
concurrent resolution on the budget most recently agreed to with
respect to the fiscal year beginning on October 1 of such year. Any such
concurrent resolution on the budget shall also, to the extent necessary—
    (1) specify the total amount by which—
        (A) new budget authority for such fiscal year;
        (B) budget authority initially provided for prior fiscal
    years; and
        (C) new spending authority described in section 401 (c) (2)
        (C) which is to become effective during such fiscal year,
    contained in laws, bills, and resolutions within the jurisdiction
    of a committee, is to be changed and direct that committee to
    determine and recommend changes to accomplish a change of
    such total amount;
    (2) specify the total amount by which revenues are to be
    changed and direct that the committees having jurisdiction to
    determine and recommend changes in the revenue laws, bills, and
    resolutions to accomplish a change of such total amount;
    (3) specify the amount by which the statutory limit on the
    public debt is to be changed and direct the committees having
    jurisdiction to recommend such change; or
    (4) specify and direct any combination of the matters described
    in paragraphs (1), (2), and (3).
Any such concurrent resolution may be reported, and the report Filing.
accompanying it may be filed, in either House notwithstanding that
that House is not in session on the day on which such concurrent
resolution is reported.
    (b) COMPLETION OF ACTION ON CONCURRENT RESOLUTION.—Not later
than September 15 of each year, the Congress shall complete action
on the concurrent resolution on the budget referred to in subsection
(a).
    (c) RECONCILIATION PROCESS.—If a concurrent resolution is agreed
to in accordance with subsection (a) containing directions to one or
more committees to determine and recommend changes in laws, bills,
or resolutions, and—
    (1) only one committee of the House or the Senate is directed to
    determine and recommend changes, that committee shall promptly
    make such determination and recommendations and report to its
    House a reconciliation bill or reconciliation resolution, or both,
    containing such recommendations; or
    (2) more than one committee of the House or the Senate is
    directed to determine and recommend changes, each such com-
    mittee so directed shall promptly make such determination and
    recommendations, whether such changes are to be contained in a
    reconciliation bill or reconciliation resolution, and submit such
    recommendations to the Committee on the Budget of its House,
    which upon receiving all such recommendations, shall report to
    its House a reconciliation bill or reconciliation resolution, or both,
    carrying out all such recommendations without any substantive
    revision.

Pub. Law 93-344   July 12, 1974

88 STAT. 316

Reconciliation   For purposes of this subsection, a reconciliation resolution is a con-
resolution.   current resolution directing the Clerk of the House of Representatives
                  or the Secretary of the Senate, as the case may be, to make specified
                  changes in bills and resolutions which have not been enrolled.
                      (d) COMPLETION OF RECONCILIATION PROCESS.—Congress shall com-
                  plete action on any reconciliation bill or reconciliation resolution
                  reported under subsection (c) not later than September 25 of each
                  year.
                      (e) PROCEDURE IN THE SENATE.—
                          (1) Except as provided in paragraph (2), the provisions of
                      section 305 for the consideration in the Senate of concurrent reso-
                      lutions on the budget and conference reports thereon shall also
                      apply to the consideration in the Senate of reconciliation bills and
                      reconciliation resolutions reported under subsection (c) and con-
                      ference reports thereon.
Debate, time   (2) Debate in the Senate on any reconciliation bill or resolu-
limitation.   tion reported under subsection (c), and all amendments thereto
                      and debatable motions and appeals in connection therewith, shall
                      be limited to not more than 20 hours.
                      (f) CONGRESS MAY NOT ADJOURN UNTIL ACTION IS COMPLETED.—It
                  shall not be in order in either the House of Representatives or the
                  Senate to consider any resolution providing for the adjournment sine
                  die of either House unless action has been completed on the concurrent
                  resolution on the budget required to be reported under subsection (a)
                  for the fiscal year beginning on October 1 of such year, and, if a
                  reconciliation bill or resolution, or both, is required to be reported
                  under subsection (c) for such fiscal year, unless the Congress has com-
                  pleted action on that bill or resolution, or both.

          NEW BUDGET AUTHORITY, NEW SPENDING AUTHORITY AND REVENUE
                    LEGISLATION MUST BE WITHIN APPROPRIATE LEVELS

31 USC 1332.   SEC. 311. (a) LEGISLATION SUBJECT TO POINT OF ORDER.—After the
                  Congress has completed action on the concurrent resolution on the
                  budget required to be reported under section 310(a) for a fiscal year,
                  and, if a reconciliation bill or resolution, or both, for such fiscal year
                  are required to be reported under section 310(c), after that bill has
                  been enacted into law or that resolution has been agreed to, it shall
                  not be in order in either the House of Representatives or the Senate to
                  consider any bill, resolution, or amendment providing additional new
                  budget authority for such fiscal year, providing new spending author-
                  ity described in section 401(c)(2)(C) to become effective during such
                  fiscal year, or reducing revenues for such fiscal year, or any confer-
                  ence report on any such bill or resolution, if—
                          (1) the enactment of such bill or resolution as reported;
                          (2) the adoption and enactment of such amendment; or
                          (3) the enactment of such bill or resolution in the form recom-
                      mended in such conference report;
                  would cause the appropriate level of total new budget authority or
                  total budget outlays set forth in the most recently agreed to concur-
                  rent resolution on the budget for such fiscal year to be exceeded, or
                  would cause revenues to be less than the appropriate level of revenues
                  set forth in such concurrent resolution.
                      (b) DETERMINATION OF OUTLAYS AND REVENUES.—For purposes of
                  subsection (a), the budget outlays to be made during a fiscal year and
                  revenues to be received during a fiscal year shall be determined on the
                  basis of estimates made by the Committee on the Budget of the House
                  of Representatives or the Senate, as the case may be.

July 12, 1974   Pub. Law 93-344
88 STAT. 317

TITLE IV—ADDITIONAL PROVISIONS TO IMPROVE FISCAL PROCEDURES

BILLS PROVIDING NEW SPENDING AUTHORITY

SEC. 401. (a) LEGISLATION PROVIDING CONTRACT OR BORROWING 31 USC 1351.
AUTHORITY.—It shall not be in order in either the House of Representatives or the Senate to consider any bill or resolution which provides new spending authority described in subsection (c)(2)(A) or (B) (or any amendment which provides such new spending authority), unless that bill, resolution, or amendment also provides that such new spending authority is to be effective for any fiscal year only to such extent or in such amounts as are provided in appropriation Acts.

(b) LEGISLATION PROVIDING ENTITLEMENT AUTHORITY.—

(1) It shall not be in order in either the House of Representatives or the Senate to consider any bill or resolution which provides new spending authority described in subsection (c)(2)(C) (or any amendment which provides such new spending authority) which is to become effective before the first day of the fiscal year which begins during the calendar year in which such bill or resolution is reported.

(2) If any committee of the House of Representatives or the Senate reports any bill or resolution which provides new spending authority described in subsection (c)(2)(C) which is to become effective during a fiscal year and the amount of new budget authority which will be required for such fiscal year if such bill or resolution is enacted as so reported exceeds the appropriate allocation of new budget authority reported under section 302(b) in connection with the most recently agreed to concurrent resolution on the budget for such fiscal year, such bill or resolution shall then be referred to the Committee on Appropriations of that House with instructions to report it, with the committee's recommendations, within 15 calendar days (not counting any day on which that House is not in session) beginning with the day following the day on which it is so referred. If the Committee on Appropriations of either House fails to report a bill or resolution referred to it under this paragraph within such 15-day period, the committee shall automatically be discharged from further consideration of such bill or resolution and such bill or resolution shall be placed on the appropriate calendar. *Referral to Appropriations Committee.* *Discharge from consideration.* *Placement on calendar.*

(3) The Committee on Appropriations of each House shall have jurisdiction to report any bill or resolution referred to it under paragraph (2) with an amendment which limits the total amount of new spending authority provided in such bill or resolution. *Committee jurisdiction.*

(c) DEFINITIONS.—

(1) For purposes of this section, the term "new spending authority" means spending authority not provided by law on the effective date of this section, including any increase in or addition to spending authority provided by law on such date.

(2) For purposes of paragraph (1), the term "spending authority" means authority (whether temporary or permanent)—

(A) to enter into contracts under which the United States is obligated to make outlays, the budget authority for which is not provided in advance by appropriation Acts;

(B) to incur indebtedness (other than indebtedness incurred under the Second Liberty Bond Act) for the repayment of which the United States is liable, the budget authority for which is not provided in advance by appropriation Acts; and *40 Stat. 288.* *31 USC 774.*

(C) to make payments (including loans and grants), the budget authority for which is not provided for in advance by appropriation Acts, to any person or government if, under the provisions of the law containing such authority, the United States is obligated to make such payments to persons or governments who meet the requirements established by such law.

Such term does not include authority to insure or guarantee the repayment of indebtedness incurred by another person or government.

(d) EXCEPTIONS.—

(1) Subsections (a) and (b) shall not apply to new spending authority if the budget authority for outlays which will result from such new spending authority is derived—

49 Stat. 620.
42 USC 1305.

(A) from a trust fund established by the Social Security Act (as in effect on the date of the enactment of this Act); or

(B) from any other trust fund, 90 percent or more of the receipts of which consist or will consist of amounts (transferred from the general fund of the Treasury) equivalent to amounts of taxes (related to the purposes for which such outlays are or will be made) received in the Treasury under specified provisions of the Internal Revenue Code of 1954.

68A Stat. 3.
26 USC 1 et seq.

(2) Subsections (a) and (b) shall not apply to new spending authority which is an amendment to or extension of the State and Local Fiscal Assistance Act of 1972, or a continuation of the program of fiscal assistance to State and local governments provided by that Act, to the extent so provided in the bill or resolution providing such authority.

86 Stat. 919.
31 USC 1221 note.

(3) Subsections (a) and (b) shall not apply to new spending authority to the extent that—

(A) the outlays resulting therefrom are made by an organization which is (i) a mixed-ownership Government corporation (as defined in section 201 of the Government Corporation Control Act), or (ii) a wholly owned Government corporation (as defined in section 101 of such Act) which is specifically exempted by law from compliance with any or all of the provisions of that Act; or

59 Stat. 600;
87 Stat. 1005.
31 USC 856.
59 Stat. 597;
86 Stat. 1274.
31 USC 846.

(B) the outlays resulting therefrom consist exclusively of the proceeds of gifts or bequests made to the United States for a specific purpose.

REPORTING OF AUTHORIZING LEGISLATION

31 USC 1352.

SEC. 402. (a) REQUIRED REPORTING DATE.—Except as otherwise provided in this section, it shall not be in order in either the House of Representatives or the Senate to consider any bill or resolution which, directly or indirectly, authorizes the enactment of new budget authority for a fiscal year, unless that bill or resolution is reported in the House or the Senate, as the case may be, on or before May 15 preceding the beginning of such fiscal year.

(b) EMERGENCY WAIVER IN THE HOUSE.—If the Committee on Rules of the House of Representatives determines that emergency conditions require a waiver of subsection (a) with respect to any bill or resolution, such committee may report, and the House may consider and adopt, a resolution waiving the application of subsection (a) in the case of such bill or resolution.

(c) WAIVER IN THE SENATE.—

(1) The committee of the Senate which reports any bill or resolution may, at or after the time it reports such bill or resolution, report a resolution to the Senate (A) providing for the waiver of subsection (a) with respect to such bill or resolution, and (B) stating the reasons why the waiver is necessary. The resolution shall then be referred to the Committee on the Budget of the Senate. That committee shall report the resolution to the Senate, within 10 days after the resolution is referred to it (not counting any day on which the Senate is not in session) beginning with the day following the day on which it is so referred accompanied by that committee's recommendations and reasons for such recommendations with respect to the resolution. If the committee does not report the resolution within such 10-day period, it shall automatically be discharged from further consideration of the resolution and the resolution shall be placed on the calendar. *Referral to Budget Committee. Report to Senate. Discharge from consideration. Placement on calendar.*

(2) During the consideration of any such resolution, debate shall be limited to one hour, to be equally divided between, and controlled by, the majority leader and the minority leader or their designees, and the time on any debatable motion or appeal shall be limited to 20 minutes, to be equally divided between, and controlled by, the mover and the manager of the resolution. In the event the manager of the resolution is in favor of any such motion or appeal, the time in opposition thereto sha'l be controlled by the minority leader or his designee. Such leaders, or either of them, may, from the time under their control on the passage of such resolution, allot additional time to any Senator during the consideration of any debatable motion or appeal. No amendment to the resolution is in order. *Debate, time limitation.*

(3) If, after the Committee on the Budget has reported (or been discharged from further consideration of) the resolution, the Senate agrees to the resolution, then subsection (a) of this section shall not apply with respect to that bill or resolution referred to in the resolution.

(d) CERTAIN BILLS AND RESOLUTIONS RECEIVED FROM OTHER HOUSE.—Notwithstanding the provisions of subsection (a), if under that subsection it is in order in the House of Representatives to consider a bill or resolution of the House, then it shall be in order to consider a companion or similar bill or resolution of the Senate; and if under that subsection it is in order in the Senate to consider a bill or resolution of the Senate, then it shall be in order to consider a companion or similar bill of the House of Representatives.

(e) EXCEPTIONS.—

(1) Subsection (a) shall not apply with respect to new spending authority described in section 401(c)(2)(C).

(2) Subsection (a) shall not apply with respect to new budget authority authorized in a bill or resolution for any provision of the Social Security Act if such bill or resolution also provides new spending authority described in section 401(c)(2)(C) which, under section 401(d)(1)(A), is excluded from the application of section 401(b).

(f) STUDY OF EXISTING SPENDING AUTHORITY AND PERMANENT APPROPRIATIONS.—The Committees on Appropriations of the House of Representatives and the Senate shall study on a continuing basis those provisions of law, in effect on the effective date of this section, which provide spending authority or permanent budget authority. Each committee shall, from time to time, report to its House its recommendations for terminating or modifying such provisions. *Report to Congress.*

194

ANALYSIS BY CONGRESSIONAL BUDGET OFFICE

31 USC 1353.

SEC. 403. The Director of the Congressional Budget Office shall, to the extent practicable, prepare for each bill or resolution of a public character reported by any committee of the House of Representatives or the Senate (except the Committee on Appropriations of each House), and submit to such committee—

Submittal to congressional committees.

(1) an estimate of the costs which would be incurred in carrying out such bill or resolution in the fiscal year in which it is to become effective and in each of the 4 fiscal years following such fiscal year, together with the basis for each such estimate; and

(2) a comparison of the estimate of costs described in paragraph (1) with any available estimate of costs made by such committee or by any Federal agency.

The estimate and comparison so submitted shall be included in the report accompanying such bill or resolution if timely submitted to such committee before such report is filed.

JURISDICTION OF APPROPRIATIONS COMMITTEES

SEC. 404. (a) AMENDMENT OF HOUSE RULES.—Clause 2 of rule XI of the Rules of the House of Representatives is amended by redesignating paragraph (b) as paragraph (e) and by inserting after paragraph (a) the following new paragraphs:

Post, p. 322.

"(b) Rescission of appropriations contained in appropriation Acts (referred to in section 105 of title 1, United States Code).

"(c) The amount of new spending authority described in section 401(c)(2) (A) and (B) of the Congressional Budget Act of 1974 which is to be effective for a fiscal year.

"(d) New spending authority described in section 401(c)(2)(C) of the Congressional Budget Act of 1974 provided in bills and resolutions referred to the committee under section 401(b)(2) of that Act (but subject to the provisions of section 401(b)(3) of that Act)."

(b) AMENDMENT OF SENATE RULES.—Subparagraph (c) of paragraph 1 of rule XXV of the Standing Rules of the Senate is amended to read as follows:

"(c) Committee on Appropriations, to which committee shall be referred all proposed legislation, messages, petitions, memorials, and other matters relating to the following subjects:

"1. Except as provided in subparagraph (r), appropriation of the revenue for the support of the Government.

"2. Rescission of appropriations contained in appropriation Acts (referred to in section 105 of title 1, United States Code).

"3. The amount of new spending authority described in section 401 (c)(2) (A) and (B) of the Congressional Budget Act of 1974 provided in bills and resolutions referred to the committee under section 401(b)(2) of that Act (but subject to the provisions of section 401 (b)(3) of that Act).

"4. New advance spending authority described in section 401(c) (2)(C) of the Congressional Budget Act of 1974 provided in bills and resolutions referred to the committee under section 401(b)(2) of that Act (but subject to the provisions of section 401(b)(3) of that Act)."

July 12, 1974   Pub. Law 93-344
88 STAT. 321

TITLE V—CHANGE OF FISCAL YEAR

FISCAL YEAR TO BEGIN OCTOBER 1

SEC. 501. Section 237 of the Revised Statutes (31 U.S.C. 1020) is amended to read as follows:

"SEC. 237. (a) The fiscal year of the Treasury of the United States, in all matters of accounts, receipts, expenditures, estimates, and appropriations—

"(1) shall, through June 30, 1976, commence on July 1 of each year and end on June 30 of the following year; and

"(2) shall, beginning on October 1, 1976, commence on October 1 of each year and end on September 30 of the following year.

"(b) All accounts of receipts and expenditures required by law to be published annually shall be prepared and published for each fiscal year as established by subsection (a)."

Accounts, annual publication.

TRANSITION TO NEW FISCAL YEAR

SEC. 502. (a) As soon as practicable, the President shall prepare and submit to the Congress—

(1) after consultation with the Committees on Appropriations of the House of Representatives and the Senate, budget estimates for the United States Government for the period commencing July 1, 1976, and ending on September 30, 1976, in such form and detail as he may determine; and

(2) proposed legislation he considers appropriate with respect to changes in law necessary to provide authorizations of appropriations for that period.

31 USC 1020 note.
Budget estimates and proposed legislation, submittal to Congress.

(b) The Director of the Office of Management and Budget shall provide by regulation, order, or otherwise for the orderly transition by all departments, agencies, and instrumentalities of the United States Government and the government of the District of Columbia from the use of the fiscal year in effect on the date of enactment of this Act to the use of the new fiscal year prescribed by section 237 (a)(2) of the Revised Statutes. The Director shall prepare and submit to the Congress such additional proposed legislation as he considers necessary to accomplish this objective.

Supra.

(c) The Director of the Office of Management and Budget and the Director of the Congressional Budget Office jointly shall conduct a study of the feasibility and advisability of submitting the Budget or portions thereof, and enacting new budget authority or portions thereof, for a fiscal year during the regular session of the Congress which begins in the year preceding the year in which such fiscal year begins. The Director of the Office of Management and Budget and the Director of the Congressional Budget Office each shall submit a report of the results of the study conducted by them, together with his own conclusions and recommendations, to the Congress not later than 2 years after the effective date of this subsection.

Study.

Reports, submittal to Congress.

ACCOUNTING PROCEDURES

SEC. 503. (a) Subsection (a)(1) of the first section of the Act entitled "An Act to simplify accounting, facilitate the payment of obligations, and for other purposes", approved July 25, 1956, as amended (31 U.S.C. 701), is amended to read as follows:

70 Stat. 647.

Pub. Law 93-344 July 12, 1974

"(1) The obligated balance shall be transferred, at the time specified in subsection (b)(1) of this section, to an appropriation account of the agency or subdivision thereof responsible for the liquidation of the obligation, in which account shall be merged the amounts so transferred from all appropriation accounts for the same general purposes; and".

Transfers.
70 Stat. 647.
31 USC 701.

(b) Subsection (b) of such section is amended to read as follows:
"(b)(1) Any obligated balance referred to in subsection (a)(1) of this section shall be transferred as follows:

"(A) for any fiscal year or years ending on or before June 30, 1976, on that June 30 which falls in the first month of June which occurs twenty-four months after the end of such fiscal year or years; and

"(B) for the period commencing on July 1, 1976, and ending on September 30, 1976, and for any fiscal year commencing on or after October 1, 1976, on September 30 of the second fiscal year following that period or the fiscal year or years, as the case may be, for which the appropriation is available for obligation.

Withdrawals.

"(2) The withdrawals required by subsection (a)(2) of this section shall be made—

"(A) for any fiscal year ending on or before June 30, 1976, not later than September 30 of the fiscal year immediately following the fiscal year in which the period of availability for obligation expires; and

"(B) for the period commencing on July 1, 1976, and ending on September 30, 1976, and for any fiscal year commencing on or after October 1, 1976, not later than November 15 following such period or fiscal year, as the case may be, in which the period of availability for obligation expires."

CONVERSION OF AUTHORIZATIONS OF APPROPRIATIONS

31 USC 1020a.

SEC. 504. Any law providing for an authorization of appropriations commencing on July 1 of a year shall, if that year is any year after 1975, be considered as meaning October 1 of that year. Any law providing for an authorization of appropriations ending on June 30 of a year shall, if that year is any year after 1976, be considered as meaning September 30 of that year. Any law providing for an authorization of appropriations for the fiscal year 1977 or any fiscal year thereafter shall be construed as referring to that fiscal year ending on September 30 of the calendar year having the same calendar year number as the fiscal year number.

REPEALS

SEC. 505. The following provisions of law are repealed:
(1) the ninth paragraph under the headings "Legislative Establishment", "Senate", of the Deficiency Appropriation Act, fiscal year 1934 (48 Stat. 1022; 2 U.S.C. 66); and
(2) the proviso to the second paragraph under the headings "House of Representatives", "Salaries, Mileage, and Expenses of Members", of the Legislative-Judiciary Appropriation Act, 1955 (68 Stat. 400; 2 U.S.C. 81).

TECHNICAL AMENDMENT

61 Stat. 634.

SEC. 506. (a) Section 105 of title 1, United States Code, is amended by striking out "June 30" and inserting in lieu thereof "September 30".

Effective date.
1 USC 105
note.

(b) The provisions of subsection (a) of this section shall be effective with respect to Acts making appropriations for the support of the Government for any fiscal year commencing on or after October 1, 1976.

July 12, 1974   Pub. Law 93-344

88 STAT. 323

TITLE VI—AMENDMENTS TO BUDGET AND ACCOUNTING ACT, 1921

MATTERS TO BE INCLUDED IN PRESIDENT'S BUDGET

SEC. 601. Section 201 of the Budget and Accounting Act, 1921 (31 U.S.C. 11), is amended by adding at the end thereof the following new subsections: 64 Stat. 832; 84 Stat. 1169.

"(d) The Budget transmitted pursuant to subsection (a) for each fiscal year shall set forth separately the items enumerated in section 301(a)(1)–(5) of the Congressional Budget Act of 1974.   *Ante,* p. 306.

"(e) The Budget transmitted pursuant to subsection (a) for each fiscal year shall set forth the levels of tax expenditures under existing law for such fiscal year (the tax expenditure budget), taking into account projected economic factors, and any changes in such existing levels based on proposals contained in such Budget. For purposes of this subsection, the terms 'tax expenditures' and 'tax expenditures budget' have the meanings given to them by section 3(a)(3) of the Congressional Budget Act of 1974.   *Ante,* p. 299.

"(f) The Budget transmitted pursuant to subsection (a) for each fiscal year shall contain—

"(1) a comparison, for the last completed fiscal year, of the total amount of outlays estimated in the Budget transmitted pursuant to subsection (a) for each major program involving uncontrollable or relatively uncontrollable outlays and the total amount of outlays made under each such major program during such fiscal year;

"(2) a comparison, for the last completed fiscal year, of the total amount of revenues estimated in the Budget transmitted pursuant to subsection (a) and the total amount of revenues received during such year, and, with respect to each major revenue source, the amount of revenues estimated in the Budget transmitted pursuant to subsection (a) and the amount of revenues received during such year; and

"(3) an analysis and explanation of the difference between each amount set forth pursuant to paragraphs (1) and (2) as the amount of outlays or revenues estimated in the Budget submitted under subsection (a) for such fiscal year and the corresponding amount set forth as the amount of outlays made or revenues received during such fiscal year.

"(g) The President shall transmit to the Congress, on or before April 10 and July 15 of each year, a statement of all amendments to or revisions in the budget authority requested, the estimated outlays, and the estimated receipts for the ensuing fiscal year set forth in the Budget transmitted pursuant to subsection (a) (including any previous amendments or revisions proposed on behalf of the executive branch) that he deems necessary and appropriate based on the most current information available. Such statement shall contain the effect of such amendments and revisions on the summary data submitted under subsection (a) and shall include such supporting detail as is practicable. The statement transmitted on or before July 15 of any year may be included in the supplemental summary required to be transmitted under subsection (b) during such year. The Budget transmitted to the Congress pursuant to subsection (a) for any fiscal year, or the supporting detail transmitted in connection therewith, shall include a statement of all such amendments and revisions with respect to the fiscal year in progress made before the date of transmission of such Budget.   Presidential statement, transmittal to Congress.

Pub. Law 93-344   July 12, 1974

"(h) The Budget transmitted pursuant to subsection (a) for each
fiscal year shall include information with respect to estimates of appropriations for the next succeeding fiscal year for grants, contracts, or
other payments under any program for which there is an authorization of appropriations for such succeeding fiscal year and such appropriations are authorized to be included in an appropriation Act for
the fiscal year preceding the fiscal year in which the appropriation is
to be available for obligation.

"(i) The Budget transmitted pursuant to subsection (a) for each
fiscal year, beginning with the fiscal year ending September 30, 1979,
shall contain a presentation of budget authority, proposed budget
authority, outlays, proposed outlays, and descriptive information in
terms of—

"(1) a detailed structure of national needs which shall be used
to reference all agency missions and programs;

"(2) agency missions; and

"(3) basic programs.

To the extent practicable, each agency shall furnish information in
support of its budget requests in accordance with its assigned missions
in terms of Federal functions and subfunctions, including mission
responsibilities of component organizations, and shall relate its
programs to agency missions."

MIDYEAR REVIEW

84 Stat. 1169.

SEC. 602. Section 201 of the Budget and Accounting Act, 1921 (31
U.S.C. 11), is amended by striking out "on or before June 1 of each
year, beginning with 1972" and inserting in lieu thereof "on or before
July 15 of each year".

FIVE-YEAR BUDGET PROJECTIONS

64 Stat. 832;
70 Stat. 782.

SEC. 603. Section 201(a) of the Budget and Accounting Act, 1921
(31 U.S.C. 11), is amended—

(1) by inserting after "ensuing fiscal year" in paragraph (5)
"and projections for the four fiscal years immediately following
the ensuing fiscal year";

(2) by striking out "such year" in paragraph (5) and inserting
in lieu thereof "such years"; and

(3) by inserting after "ensuing fiscal year" in paragraph (6)
"and projections for the four fiscal years immediately following
the ensuing fiscal year".

ALLOWANCES FOR SUPPLEMENTAL BUDGET AUTHORITY AND UNCONTROLLABLE OUTLAYS

SEC. 604. Section 201(a) of the Budget and Accounting Act, 1921
(31 U.S.C. 11), is further amended—

(1) by striking out "and" at the end of paragraph (11);

(2) by striking out the period at the end of paragraph (12)
and inserting in lieu thereof "; and"; and

(3) by adding at the end thereof the following new paragraph:

"(13) an allowance for additional estimated expenditures and
proposed appropriations for the ensuing fiscal year, and an allowance for unanticipated uncontrollable expenditures for the
ensuing fiscal year."

88 STAT. 325

BUDGET DATA BASED ON CONTINUATION OF EXISTING LEVEL OF SERVICES

SEC. 605. (a) On or before November 10 of each year (beginning with 1975), the President shall submit to the Senate and the House of Representatives the estimated outlays and proposed budget authority which would be included in the Budget to be submitted pursuant to section 201 of the Budget and Accounting Act, 1921, for the ensuing fiscal year if all programs and activities were carried on during such ensuing fiscal year at the same level as the fiscal year in progress and without policy changes in such programs and activities. The estimated outlays and proposed budget authority submitted pursuant to this section shall be shown by function and subfunctions (in accordance with the classifications in the budget summary table entitled "Budget Authority and Outlays by Function and Agency"), by major programs within each such function, and by agency. Accompanying these estimates shall be the economic and programmatic assumptions underlying the estimated outlays and proposed budget authority, such as the rate of inflation, the rate of real economic growth, the unemployment rate, program caseloads, and pay increases.

Estimated outlays and proposed budget authority; submittal to Congress by President.
31 USC 11a.
Ante, p. 324.

(b) The Joint Economic Committee shall review the estimated outlays and proposed budget authority so submitted, and shall submit to the Committees on the Budget of both Houses an economic evaluation thereof on or before December 31 of each year.

Evaluation, submittal to Budget committees.

STUDY OF OFF-BUDGET AGENCIES

SEC. 606. The Committees on the Budget of the House of Representatives and the Senate shall study on a continuing basis those provisions of law which exempt agencies of the Federal Government, or any of their activities or outlays, from inclusion in the Budget of the United States Government transmitted by the President under section 201 of the Budget and Accounting Act, 1921. Each committee shall, from time to time, report to its House its recommendations for terminating or modifying such provisions.

31 USC 11b.

Periodic reports to Congress.

YEAR-AHEAD REQUESTS FOR AUTHORIZATION OF NEW BUDGET AUTHORITY

SEC. 607. Notwithstanding any other provision of law, any request for the enactment of legislation authorizing the enactment of new budget authority to continue a program or activity for a fiscal year (beginning with the fiscal year commencing October 1, 1976) shall be submitted to the Congress not later than May 15 of the year preceding the year in which such fiscal year begins. In the case of a request for the enactment of legislation authorizing the enactment of new budget authority for a new program or activity which is to continue for more than one fiscal year, such request shall be submitted for at least the first 2 fiscal years.

31 USC 11c.

TITLE VII—PROGRAM REVIEW AND EVALUATION

REVIEW AND EVALUATION BY STANDING COMMITTEES

SEC. 701. Section 136(a) of the Legislative Reorganization Act of 1946 (2 U.S.C. 190d) is amended by adding at the end thereof the following new sentences: "Such committees may carry out the required analysis, appraisal, and evaluation themselves, or by contract, or may require a Government agency to do so and furnish a report thereon to the Congress. Such committees may rely on such techniques as pilot testing, analysis of costs in comparison with benefits, or provision for evaluation after a defined period of time."

85 Stat. 376.

Report to Congress.

Pub. Law 93-344   July 12, 1974

88 STAT. 326

REVIEW AND EVALUATION BY THE COMPTROLLER GENERAL

84 Stat. 1168.

SEC. 702. (a) Section 204 of the Legislative Reorganization Act of 1970 (31 U.S.C. 1154) is amended to read as follows:

"REVIEW AND EVALUATION

"SEC. 204. (a) The Comptroller General shall review and evaluate the results of Government programs and activities carried on under existing law when ordered by either House of Congress, or upon his own initiative, or when requested by any committee of the House of Representatives or the Senate, or any joint committee of the two Houses, having jurisdiction over such programs and activities.

"(b) The Comptroller General, upon request of any committee of either House or any joint committee of the two Houses, shall—

"(1) assist such committee or joint committee in developing a statement of legislative objectives and goals and methods for assessing and reporting actual program performance in relation to such legislative objectives and goals. Such statements shall include, but are not limited to, recommendations as to methods of assessment, information to be reported, responsibility for reporting, frequency of reports, and feasibility of pilot testing; and

"(2) assist such committee or joint committee in analyzing and assessing program reviews or evaluation studies prepared by and for any Federal agency.

Copies.

Upon request of any Member of either House, the Comptroller General shall furnish to such Member a copy of any statement or other material compiled in carrying out paragraphs (1) and (2) which has been released by the committee or joint committee for which it was compiled.

"(c) The Comptroller General shall develop and recommend to the Congress methods for review and evaluation of Government programs and activities carried on under existing law.

Office of Program Review and Evaluation, establishment.

"(d) In carrying out his responsibilities under this section, the Comptroller General is authorized to establish an Office of Program Review and Evaluation within the General Accounting Office. The Comptroller General is authorized to employ not to exceed ten experts on a permanent, temporary, or intermittent basis and to obtain services as authorized by section 3109 of title 5, United States Code, but in either case at a rate (or the daily equivalent) for individuals not to exceed that prescribed, from time to time, for level V of the Executive Schedule under section 5316 of title 5, United States Code.

80 Stat. 416;
83 Stat. 863.

"(e) The Comptroller General shall include in his annual report to the Congress a review of his activities under this section, including his recommendations of methods for review and evaluation of Government programs and activities under subsection (c)."

(b) Item 204 in the table of contents of such Act is amended to read as follows:

"Sec. 204. Review and evaluation."

CONTINUING STUDY OF ADDITIONAL BUDGET REFORM PROPOSALS

31 USC 1303.

SEC. 703. (a) The Committees on the Budget of the House of Representatives and the Senate shall study on a continuing basis proposals designed to improve and facilitate methods of congressional budgetmaking. The proposals to be studied shall include, but are not limited to, proposals for—

(1) improving the information base required for determining the effectiveness of new programs by such means as pilot testing, survey research, and other experimental and analytical techniques;

(2) improving analytical and systematic evaluation of the effectivness of existing programs;

(3) establishing maximum and minimum time limitations for program authorization; and

(4) developing techniques of human resource accounting and other means of providing noneconomic as well as economic evaluation measures.

(b) The Committee on the Budget of each House shall, from time to time, report to its House the results of the study carried on by it under subsection (a), together with its recommendations.   *Periodic reports to Congress.*

(c) Nothing in this section shall preclude studies to improve the budgetary process by any other committee of the House of Representatives or the Senate or any joint committee of the Congress.

TITLE VIII—FISCAL AND BUDGETARY INFORMATION AND CONTROLS

AMENDMENT TO LEGISLATIVE REORGANIZATION ACT OF 1970

SEC. 801. (a) So much of title II of the Legislative Reorganization Act of 1970 (31 U.S.C. chapter 22) as precedes section 204 thereof is amended to read as follows: *84 Stat. 1167. 31 USC 1151.*

"TITLE II—FISCAL AND BUDGETARY INFORMATION AND CONTROLS

"PART 1—FISCAL, BUDGETARY, AND PROGRAM-RELATED DATA AND INFORMATION

"FEDERAL FISCAL, BUDGETARY, AND PROGRAM-RELATED DATA AND INFORMATION SYSTEMS

"SEC. 201. The Secretary of the Treasury and the Director of the Office of Management and Budget, in cooperation with the Comptroller General of the United States, shall develop, establish, and maintain, for use by all Federal agencies, standardized data processing and information systems for fiscal, budgetary, and program-related data and information. The development, establishment, and maintenance of such systems shall be carried out so as to meet the needs of the various branches of the Federal Government and, insofar as practicable, of governments at the State and local level.

"STANDARDIZATION OF TERMINOLOGY, DEFINITIONS, CLASSIFICATIONS, AND CODES FOR FISCAL, BUDGETARY, AND PROGRAM-RELATED DATA AND INFORMATION

"SEC. 202. (a) (1) The Comptroller General of the United States, in cooperation with the Secretary of the Treasury, the Director of the Office of Management and Budget, and the Director of the Congressional Budget Office, shall develop, establish, maintain, and publish standard terminology, definitions, classifications, and codes for Federal fiscal, budgetary, and program-related data and information. The authority contained in this section shall include, but not be limited to, data and information pertaining to Federal fiscal policy, revenues,

202

88 STAT. 328   Pub. Law 93-344   July 12, 1974

receipts, expenditures, functions, programs, projects, and activities.
Such standard terms, definitions, classifications, and codes shall be
used by all Federal agencies in supplying to the Congress fiscal,
budgetary, and program-related data and information.

Report to Con-
gress.

"(2) The Comptroller General shall submit to the Congress, on or
before June 30, 1975, a report containing the initial standard terminology, definitions, classifications, and codes referred to in paragraph (1),
and shall recommend any legislation necessary to implement them.

Additional re-
ports to Con-
gress; legisla-
tion recommen-
dations.

After June 30, 1975, the Comptroller General shall submit to the Congress additional reports as he may think advisable, including any
recommendations for any legislation he may deem necessary to further
the development, establishment, and maintenance, modification, and
executive implementation of such standard terminology, definitions,
classifications, and codes.

"(b) In carrying out this responsibility, the Comptroller General
of the United States shall give particular consideration to the needs of
the Committees on the Budget of the House and Senate, the Committees on Appropriations of the House and Senate, the Committee on
Ways and Means of the House, the Committee on Finance of the
Senate, and the Congressional Budget Office.

"(c) The Comptroller General of the United States shall conduct a
continuing program to identify and specify the needs of the committees and Members of the Congress for fiscal, budgetary, and program-
related information to support the objectives of this part.

"(d) The Comptroller General shall assist committees in developing
their information needs, including such needs expressed in legislative
requirements, and shall monitor the various recurring reporting
requirements of the Congress and committees and make recommendations to the Congress and committees for changes and improvements
in their reporting requirements to meet congressional information
needs ascertained by the Comptroller General, to enhance their usefulness to the congressional users and to eliminate duplicative or
unneeded reporting.

Report to Con-
gress.

"(e) On or before September 1, 1974, and each year thereafter, the
Comptroller General shall report to the Congress on needs identified
and specified under subsection (c); the relationship of these needs to
the existing reporting requirements; the extent to which the executive
branch reporting presently meets the identified needs; the specification
of changes to standard classifications needed to meet congressional
needs; the activities, progress and results of his activities under subsection (d); and the progress that the executive branch has made
during the past year.

Report to Con-
gress.

"(f) On or before March 1, 1975, and each year thereafter, the
Director of the Office of Management and Budget and the Secretary
of the Treasury shall report to the Congress on their plans for address-
ing the needs identified and specified under subsection (c), including
plans for implementing changes to classifications and codes to meet
the information needs of the Congress as well as the status of prior
year system and classification implementations.

"AVAILABILITY TO AND USE BY THE CONGRESS AND STATE AND LOCAL GOV-
ERNMENTS OF FEDERAL FISCAL, BUDGETARY, AND PROGRAM-RELATED DATA
AND INFORMATION

"Sec. 203. (a) Upon request of any committee of either House, of
any joint committee of the two Houses, of the Comptroller General,
or of the Director of the Congressional Budget Office, the Secretary of
the Treasury, the Director of the Office of Management and Budget,
and the heads of the various executive agencies shall—

"(1) furnish to such committee or joint committee, the Comptroller General, or the Director of the Congressional Budget Office information as to the location and nature of available fiscal, budgetary, and program-related data and information;

"(2) to the extent practicable, prepare summary tables of such data and information and any related information deemed necessary by such committee or joint committee, the Comptroller General, or the Director of the Congressional Budget Office; and

"(3) furnish to such committee or joint committee, the Comptroller General, or the Director of the Congressional Budget Office any program evaluations conducted or commissioned by any executive agency.

"(b) The Comptroller General, in cooperation with the Director of the Congressional Budget Office, the Secretary of the Treasury, and the Director of the Office of Management and Budget, shall—

"(1) develop, establish, and maintain an up-to-date inventory and directory of sources and information systems containing fiscal, budgetary, and program-related data and information and a brief description of their content;

"(2) provide, upon request, assistance to committees, joint committees, and Members of Congress in securing Federal fiscal, budgetary, and program-related data and information from the sources identified in such inventory and directory; and

"(3) furnish, upon request, assistance to committees and joint committees of Congress and, to the extent practicable, to Members of Congress in appraising and analyzing fiscal, budgetary, and program-related data and information secured from the sources identified in such inventory and directory.

"(c) The Comptroller General and the Director of the Congressional Budget Office shall, to the extent they deem necessary, develop, establish, and maintain a central file or files of the data and information required to carry out the purposes of this title. Such a file or files shall be established to meet recurring requirements of the Congress for fiscal, budgetary, and program-related data and information and shall include, but not be limited to, data and information pertaining to budget requests, congressional authorizations to obligate and spend, apportionment and reserve actions, and obligations and expenditures. Such file or files and their indexes shall be maintained in such a manner as to facilitate their use by the committees of both Houses, joint committees, and other congressional agencies through modern data processing and communications techniques.

Central data files, development.

"(d) The Director of the Office of Management and Budget, in cooperation with the Director of the Congressional Budget Office, the Comptroller General, and appropriate representatives of State and local governments, shall provide, to the extent practicable, State and local governments such fiscal, budgetary, and program-related data and information as may be necessary for the accurate and timely determination by these governments of the impact of Federal assistance upon their budgets."

Information to State and local governments.

(b) The table of contents of the Legislative Reorganization Act of 1970 is amended by striking out—

"TITLE II—FISCAL CONTROLS

"PART 1—BUDGETARY AND FISCAL INFORMATION AND DATA

"Sec. 201. Budgetary and fiscal data processing system.
"Sec. 202. Budget standard classifications.
"Sec. 203. Availability to Congress of budgetary, fiscal, and related data."

and inserting in lieu thereof—

204

Pub. Law 93-344   July 12, 1974

"TITLE II—FISCAL AND BUDGETARY INFORMATION AND CONTROLS

"PART 1—FISCAL, BUDGETARY, AND PROGRAM-RELATED DATA AND INFORMATION

"Sec. 201. Federal fiscal, budgetary, and program-related data and information
systems.
"Sec. 202. Standardization of terminology, definitions, classifications, and codes
for fiscal, budgetary, and program-related data and information.
"Sec. 203. Availability to and use by the Congress and State and local governments of Federal fiscal, budgetary, and program-related data and
information."

CHANGES IN FUNCTIONAL CATEGORIES

31 USC 11d.

Ante, p. 324.

SEC. 802. Any change in the functional categories set forth in the
Budget of the United States Government transmitted pursuant to
section 201 of the Budget and Accounting Act, 1921, shall be made
only in consultation with the Committees on Appropriations and the
Budget of the House of Representatives and Senate.

TITLE IX—MISCELLANEOUS PROVISIONS; EFFECTIVE
DATES

AMENDMENTS TO RULES OF THE HOUSE

Ante, p. 299.

SEC. 901. (a) Rule XI of the Rules of the House of Representatives
(as amended by section 101(c) of this Act) is amended by inserting
immediately after clause 22 the following new clause:
"22A. The respective areas of legislative jurisdiction under this rule
are modified by title I of the Congressional Budget Act of 1974."
(b) Paragraph (c) of clause 29 of Rule XI of the Rules of the
House of Representatives (as redesignated by section 101(c) of this
Act) is amended by inserting "the Committee on the Budget," immediately after "the Committee on Appropriations,".
(c) Subparagraph (5) of paragraph (a) of clause 30 of Rule XI
of the Rules of the House of Representatives (as so redesignated) is
amended by inserting "and the Committee on the Budget" immediately before the period at the end thereof.
(d) Subparagraph (4) of paragraph (b) of clause 30 of Rule XI
of the Rules of the House of Representatives (as so redesignated) is
amended by inserting "and the Committee on the Budget" immediately before the period at the end hereof.
(e) Paragraph (d) of clause 30 of Rule XI of the Rules of the
House of Representatives (as so redesignated) is amended by striking
out "the Committee on Appropriations may appoint" and inserting in
lieu thereof "the Committee on Appropriations and the Committee on
the Budget may each appoint".
(f) Clause 32 of Rule XI of the Rules of the House of Representatives (as so redesignated) is amended by inserting "the Committee on
the Budget," immediately after "the Committee on Appropriations,".
(g) Paragraph (a) of clause 33 of Rule XI of the Rules of the
House of Representatives (as so redesignated) is amended by inserting "and the Committee on the Budget" immediately after "the Committee on Appropriations".

CONFORMING AMENDMENTS TO STANDING RULES OF THE SENATE

SEC. 902. Paragraph 1 of rule XXV of the Standing Rules of the
Senate is amended—
(1) by striking out "Revenue" in subparagraph (h)1 and
inserting in lieu thereof "Except as provided in the Congressional
Budget Act of 1974, revenue";

205

July 12, 1974 Pub. Law 93-344 88 STAT. 331

(2) by striking out "The" in subparagraph (h)2 and inserting in lieu thereof "Except as provided in the Congressional Budget Act of 1974, the"; and
(3) by striking out "Budget" in subparagraph (j)(1)(A) and inserting in lieu thereof "Except as provided in the Congressional Budget Act of 1974, budget".

AMENDMENTS TO LEGISLATIVE REORGANIZATION ACT OF 1946

SEC. 903. (a) Section 134(c) of the Legislative Reorganization Act of 1946 (2 U.S.C. 190b(b)) is amended by inserting "or the Committee on the Budget" after "Appropriations". 84 Stat. 1155, 1440.
(b) Section 136(c) of such Act (2 U.S.C. 190d(c)) is amended by striking out "Committee on Appropriations of the Senate and the Committees on Appropriations," and inserting in lieu thereof "Committees on Appropriations and the Budget of the Senate and the Committees on Appropriations, the Budget,". 85 Stat. 376.

EXERCISE OF RULEMAKING POWERS

SEC. 904. (a) The provisions of this title (except section 905) and of titles I, III, and IV and the provisions of sections 606, 701, 703, and 1017 are enacted by the Congress— 31 USC 1301 note.
(1) as an exercise of the rulemaking power of the House of Representatives and the Senate, respectively, and as such they shall be considered as part of the rules of each House, respectively, or of that House to which they specifically apply, and such rules shall supersede other rules only to the extent that they are inconsistent therewith; and
(2) with full recognition of the constitutional right of either House to change such rules (so far as relating to such House) at any time, in the same manner, and to the same extent as in the case of any other rule of such House.
(b) Any provision of title III or IV may be waived or suspended in the Senate by a majority vote of the Members voting, a quorum being present, or by the unanimous consent of the Senate. Waiver. Ante, pp. 306, 317.
(c) Appeals in the Senate from the decisions of the Chair relating to any provision of title III or IV or section 1017 shall, except as otherwise provided therein, be limited to 1 hour, to be equally divided between, and controlled by, the mover and the manager of the resolution, concurrent resolution, reconciliation bill, or rescission bill, as the case may be. Appeals.

EFFECTIVE DATES

SEC. 905. (a) Except as provided in this section, the provisions of this Act shall take effect on the date of its enactment. 31 USC 1301 note.
(b) Title II (except section 201(a)), section 403, and section 502(c) shall take effect on the day on which the first Director of the Congressional Budget Office is appointed under section 201(a).
(c) Except as provided in section 906, title III and section 402 shall apply with respect to the fiscal year beginning on October 1, 1976, and succeeding fiscal years, and section 401 shall take effect on the first day of the second regular session of the Ninety-fourth Congress.
(d) The amendments to the Budget and Accounting Act, 1921, made by sections 601, 603, and 604 shall apply with respect to the fiscal year beginning on July 1, 1975, and succeeding fiscal years, except that section 201(g) of such Act (as added by section 601) shall apply with respect to the fiscal year beginning on October 1, 1976, and succeeding fiscal years and section 201(i) of such Act (as added by section 601) 42 Stat. 20. 31 USC 1.

Pub. Law 93-344 July 12, 1974

shall apply with respect to the fiscal year beginning on October 1, 1978, and succeeding fiscal years. The amendment to such Act made by section 602 shall apply with respect to the fiscal year beginning on October 1, 1976, and succeeding fiscal years.

APPLICATION OF CONGRESSIONAL BUDGET PROCESS TO FISCAL YEAR 1976

31 USC 1322 note.

Ante, p. 306.

Ante, p. 304.

SEC. 906. If the Committees on the Budget of the House of Representatives and the Senate both agree that it is feasible to report and act on a concurrent resolution on the budget referred to in section 301 (a), or to apply any provision of title III or section 401 or 402, for the fiscal year beginning on July 1, 1975, and submit reports of such agreement to their respective Houses, then to the extent and in the manner specified in such reports, the provisions so specified and section 202(f) shall apply with respect to such fiscal year. If any provision so specified contains a date, such reports shall also specify a substitute date.

Impoundment Control Act of 1974. 31 USC 1401 note.

TITLE X—IMPOUNDMENT CONTROL

PART A—GENERAL PROVISIONS

DISCLAIMER

SEC. 1001. Nothing contained in this Act, or in any amendments made by this Act, shall be construed as—

(1) asserting or conceding the constitutional powers or limitations of either the Congress or the President;

(2) ratifying or approving any impoundment heretofore or hereafter executed or approved by the President or any other Federal officer or employee, except insofar as pursuant to statutory authorization then in effect;

(3) affecting in any way the claims or defenses of any party to litigation concerning any impoundment; or

(4) superseding any provision of law which requires the obligation of budget authority or the making of outlays thereunder.

AMENDMENT TO ANTIDEFICIENCY ACT

Contingency or savings reserves, establishment.

42 Stat. 20. 31 USC 1.

SEC. 1002. Section 3679(c)(2) of the Revised Statutes, as amended (31 U.S.C. 665), is amended to read as follows:

"(2) In apportioning any appropriation, reserves may be established solely to provide for contingencies, or to effect savings whenever savings are made possible by or through changes in requirements or greater efficiency of operations. Whenever it is determined by an officer designated in subsection (d) of this section to make apportionments and reapportionments that any amount so reserved will not be required to carry out the full objectives and scope of the appropriation concerned, he shall recommend the rescission of such amount in the manner provided in the Budget and Accounting Act, 1921, for estimates of appropriations. Except as specifically provided by particular appropriations Acts or other laws, no reserves shall be established other than as authorized by this subsection. Reserves established pursuant to this subsection shall be reported to the Congress in accordance with the Impoundment Control Act of 1974."

REPEAL OF EXISTING IMPOUNDMENT REPORTING PROVISION

87 Stat. 7. 31 USC 581c-1.

SEC. 1003. Section 203 of the Budget and Accounting Procedures Act of 1950 is repealed.

Pub. Law 93-344

88 STAT. 333

PART B—CONGRESSIONAL CONSIDERATION OF PROPOSED RESCISSIONS, RESERVATIONS, AND DEFERRALS OF BUDGET AUTHORITY

DEFINITIONS

SEC. 1011. For purposes of this part— 31 USC 1401.
  (1) "deferral of budget authority" includes—
    (A) withholding or delaying the obligation or expenditure of budget authority (whether by establishing reserves or otherwise) provided for projects or activities; or
    (B) any other type of Executive action or inaction which effectively precludes the obligation or expenditure of budget authority, including authority to obligate by contract in advance of appropriations as specifically authorized by law;
  (2) "Comptroller General" means the Comptroller General of the United States;
  (3) "rescission bill" means a bill or joint resolution which only rescinds, in whole or in part, budget authority proposed to be rescinded in a special message transmitted by the President under section 1012, and upon which the Congress completes action before the end of the first period of 45 calendar days of continuous session of the Congress after the date on which the President's message is received by the Congress;
  (4) "impoundment resolution" means a resolution of the House of Representatives or the Senate which only expresses its disapproval of a proposed deferral of budget authority set forth in a special message transmitted by the President under section 1013; and
  (5) continuity of a session of the Congress shall be considered as broken only by an adjournment of the Congress sine die, and the days on which either House is not in session because of an adjournment of more than 3 days to a day certain shall be excluded in the computation of the 45-day period referred to in paragraph (3) of this section and in section 1012, and the 25-day periods referred to in sections 1016 and 1017(b)(1). If a special message is transmitted under section 1012 during any Congress and the last session of such Congress adjourns sine die before the expiration of 45 calendar days of continuous session (or a special message is so transmitted after the last session of the Congress adjourns sine die), the message shall be deemed to have been retransmitted on the first day of the succeeding Congress and the 45-day period referred to in paragraph (3) of this section and in section 1012 (with respect to such message) shall commence on the day after such first day.

Congressional session continuity.

RESCISSION OF BUDGET AUTHORITY

SEC. 1012. (a) TRANSMITTAL OF SPECIAL MESSAGE.—Whenever the 31 USC 1402.
President determines that all or part of any budget authority will not be required to carry out the full objectives or scope of programs for which it is provided or that such budget authority should be rescinded for fiscal policy or other reasons (including the termination of authorized projects or activities for which budget authority has been provided), or whenever all or part of budget authority provided for only one fiscal year is to be reserved from obligation for such fiscal year, the President shall transmit to both Houses of Congress a special message specifying—

68 STAT. 334

(1) the amount of budget authority which he proposes to be rescinded or which is to be so reserved;

(2) any account, department, or establishment of the Government to which such budget authority is available for obligation, and the specific project or governmental functions involved;

(3) the reasons why the budget authority should be rescinded or is to be so reserved;

(4) to the maximum extent practicable, the estimated fiscal, economic, and budgetary effect of the proposed rescission or of the reservation; and

(5) all facts, circumstances, and considerations relating to or bearing upon the proposed rescission or the reservation and the decision to effect the proposed rescission or the reservation, and to the maximum extent practicable, the estimated effect of the proposed rescission or the reservation upon the objects, purposes, and programs for which the budget authority is provided.

(b) REQUIREMENT TO MAKE AVAILABLE FOR OBLIGATION.—Any amount of budget authority proposed to be rescinded or that is to be reserved as set forth in such special message shall be made available for obligation unless, within the prescribed 45-day period, the Congress has completed action on a rescission bill rescinding all or part of the amount proposed to be rescinded or that is to be reserved.

DISAPPROVAL OF PROPOSED DEFERRALS OF BUDGET AUTHORITY

31 USC 1403.

SEC. 1013. (a) TRANSMITTAL OF SPECIAL MESSAGE.—Whenever the President, the Director of the Office of Management and Budget, the head of any department or agency of the United States, or any officer or employee of the United States proposes to defer any budget authority provided for a specific purpose or project, the President shall transmit to the House of Representatives and the Senate a special message specifying—

(1) the amount of the budget authority proposed to be deferred;

(2) any account, department, or establishment of the Government to which such budget authority is available for obligation, and the specific projects or governmental functions involved;

(3) the period of time during which the budget authority is proposed to be deferred;

(4) the reasons for the proposed deferral, including any legal authority invoked by him to justify the proposed deferral;

(5) to the maximum extent practicable, the estimated fiscal, economic, and budgetary effect of the proposed deferral; and

(6) all facts, circumstances, and considerations relating to or bearing upon the proposed deferral and the decision to effect the proposed deferral, including an analysis of such facts, circumstances, and considerations in terms of their application to any legal authority and specific elements of legal authority invoked by him to justify such proposed deferral, and to the maximum extent practicable, the estimated effect of the proposed deferral upon the objects, purposes, and programs for which the budget authority is provided.

Time limitation.

A special message may include one or more proposed deferrals of budget authority. A deferral may not be proposed for any period of time extending beyond the end of the fiscal year in which the special message proposing the deferral is transmitted to the House and the Senate.

July 12, 1974   Pub. Law 93-344
88 STAT. 335

(b) REQUIREMENT TO MAKE AVAILABLE FOR OBLIGATION.—Any amount of budget authority proposed to be deferred, as set forth in a special message transmitted under subsection (a), shall be made available for obligation if either House of Congress passes an impoundment resolution disapproving such proposed deferral.

(c) EXCEPTION.—The provisions of this section do not apply to any budget authority proposed to be rescinded or that is to be reserved as set forth in a special message required to be transmitted under section 1012.

TRANSMISSION OF MESSAGES; PUBLICATION

SEC. 1014. (a) DELIVERY TO HOUSE AND SENATE.—Each special message transmitted under section 1012 or 1013 shall be transmitted to the House of Representatives and the Senate on the same day, and shall be delivered to the Clerk of the House of Representatives if the House is not in session, and to the Secretary of the Senate if the Senate is not in session. Each special message so transmitted shall be referred to the appropriate committee of the House of Representatives and the Senate. Each such message shall be printed as a document of each House.

31 USC 1404.

Printing as House or Senate document.

(b) DELIVERY TO COMPTROLLER GENERAL.—A copy of each special message transmitted under section 1012 or 1013 shall be transmitted to the Comptroller General on the same day it is transmitted to the House of Representatives and the Senate. In order to assist the Congress in the exercise of its functions under sections 1012 and 1013, the Comptroller General shall review each such message and inform the House of Representatives and the Senate as promptly as practicable with respect to—

Copy.

Review.

> (1) in the case of a special message transmitted under section 1012, the facts surrounding the proposed rescission or the reservation of budget authority (including the probable effects thereof); and
>
> (2) in the case of a special message transmitted under section 1013, (A) the facts surrounding each proposed deferral of budget authority (including the probable effects thereof) and (B) whether or not (or to what extent), in his judgment, such proposed deferral is in accordance with existing statutory authority.

(c) TRANSMISSION OF SUPPLEMENTARY MESSAGES.—If any information contained in a special message transmitted under section 1012 or 1013 is subsequently revised, the President shall transmit to both Houses of Congress and the Comptroller General a supplementary message stating and explaining such revision. Any such supplementary message shall be delivered, referred, and printed as provided in subsection (a). The Comptroller General shall promptly notify the House of Representatives and the Senate of any changes in the information submitted by him under subsection (b) which may be necessitated by such revision.

Notification of Congress.

(d) PRINTING IN FEDERAL REGISTER.—Any special message transmitted under section 1012 or 1013, and any supplementary message transmitted under subsection (c), shall be printed in the first issue of the Federal Register published after such transmittal.

(e) CUMULATIVE REPORTS OF PROPOSED RESCISSIONS, RESERVATIONS, AND DEFERRALS OF BUDGET AUTHORITY.—

> (1) The President shall submit a report to the House of Representatives and the Senate, not later than the 10th day of each month during a fiscal year, listing all budget authority for that fiscal year with respect to which, as of the first day of such month—

(A) he has transmitted a special message under section 1012 with respect to a proposed rescission or a reservation; and

(B) he has transmitted a special message under section 1013 proposing a deferral.

Such report shall also contain, with respect to each such proposed rescission or deferral, or each such reservation, the information required to be submitted in the special message with respect thereto under section 1012 or 1013.

Publication in
Federal Register.

(2) Each report submitted under paragraph (1) shall be printed in the first issue of the Federal Register published after its submission.

REPORTS BY COMPTROLLER GENERAL

31 USC 1405.

SEC. 1015. (a) FAILURE TO TRANSMIT SPECIAL MESSAGE.—If the Comptroller General finds that the President, the Director of the Office of Management and Budget, the head of any department or agency of the United States, or any other officer or employee of the United States—

(1) is to establish a reserve or proposes to defer budget authority with respect to which the President is required to transmit a special message under section 1012 or 1013; or

(2) has ordered, permitted, or approved the establishment of such a reserve or a deferral of budget authority;

Report to Congress.

and that the President has failed to transmit a special message with respect to such reserve or deferral, the Comptroller General shall make a report on such reserve or deferral and any available information concerning it to both Houses of Congress. The provisions of this part shall apply with respect to such reserve or deferral in the same manner and with the same effect as if such report of the Comptroller General were a special message transmitted by the President under section 1012 or 1013, and, for purposes of this part, such report shall be considered a special message transmitted under section 1012 or 1013.

(b) INCORRECT CLASSIFICATION OF SPECIAL MESSAGE.—If the President has transmitted a special message to both Houses of Congress in accordance with section 1012 or 1013, and the Comptroller General believes that the President so transmitted the special message in accordance with one of those sections when the special message should have been transmitted in accordance with the other of those sections,

Report to Congress.

the Comptroller General shall make a report to both Houses of the Congress setting forth his reasons.

SUITS BY COMPTROLLER GENERAL

31 USC 1406.

SEC. 1016. If, under section 1012(b) or 1013(b), budget authority is required to be made available for obligation and such budget authority is not made available for obligation, the Comptroller General is hereby expressly empowered, through attorneys of his own selection, to bring a civil action in the United States District Court for the District of Columbia to require such budget authority to be made available for obligation, and such court is hereby expressly empowered to enter in such civil action, against any department, agency, officer, or employee of the United States, any decree, judgment, or order which may be necessary or appropriate to make such budget authority available for

Precedence.

obligation. The courts shall give precedence to civil actions brought under this section, and to appeals and writs from decisions in such actions, over all other civil actions, appeals, and writs. No civil action *Civil actions;* shall be brought by the Comptroller General under this section until *25-day waiting* the expiration of 25 calendar days of continuous session of the Con- *period.* gress following the date on which an explanatory statement by the *Statement,* Comptroller General of the circumstances giving rise to the action *filing.* contemplated has been filed with the Speaker of the House of Representatives and the President of the Senate.

PROCEDURE IN HOUSE AND SENATE

SEC. 1017. (a) REFERRAL.—Any rescission bill introduced with *31 USC 1407.* respect to a special message or impoundment resolution introduced with respect to a proposed deferral of budget authority shall be referred to the appropriate committee of the House of Representatives or the Senate, as the case may be.

(b) DISCHARGE OF COMMITTEE.—

(1) If the committee to which a rescission bill or impoundment resolution has been referred has not reported at the end of 25 calendar days of continuous session of the Congress after its introduction, it is in order to move either to discharge the committee from further consideration of the bill or resolution or to discharge the committee from further consideration of any other rescission bill with respect to the same special message or impoundment resolution with respect to the same proposed deferral, as the case may be, which has been referred to the committee.

(2) A motion to discharge may be made only by an individual favoring the bill or resolution, may be made only if supported by one-fifth of the Members of the House involved (a quorum being present), and is highly privileged in the House and privileged in the Senate (except that it may not be made after the committee has reported a bill or resolution with respect to the same special message or the same proposed deferral, as the case may be); and debate thereon shall be limited to not more than 1 hour, the time to be divided in the House equally between those favoring and those opposing the bill or resolution, and to be divided in the Senate equally between, and controlled by, the majority leader and the minority leader or their designees. An amendment to the motion is not in order, and it is not in order to move to reconsider the vote by which the motion is agreed to or disagreed to.

(c) FLOOR CONSIDERATION IN THE HOUSE.—

(1) When the committee of the House of Representatives has reported, or has been discharged from further consideration of, a rescission bill or impoundment resolution, it shall at any time thereafter be in order (even though a previous motion to the same effect has been disagreed to) to move to proceed to the consideration of the bill or resolution. The motion shall be highly privileged and not debatable. An amendment to the motion shall not be in order, nor shall it be in order to move to reconsider the vote by which the motion is agreed to or disagreed to.

(2) Debate on a rescission bill or impoundment resolution shall *Debate, time* be limited to not more than 2 hours, which shall be divided *limitation.* equally between those favoring and those opposing the bill or resolution. A motion further to limit debate shall not be debatable. In the case of an impoundment resolution, no amendment to, or motion to recommit, the resolution shall be in order. It shall not be in order to move to reconsider the vote by which a rescission bill or impoundment resolution is agreed to or disagreed to.

212

88 STAT. 338

Pub. Law 93-344   July 12, 1974

Postponement
motions.

(3) Motions to postpone, made with respect to the consideration of a rescission bill or impoundment resolution, and motions to proceed to the consideration of other business, shall be decided without debate.

Appeals.

(4) All appeals from the decisions of the Chair relating to the application of the Rules of the House of Representatives to the procedure relating to any rescission bill or impoundment resolution shall be decided without debate.

(5) Except to the extent specifically provided in the preceding provisions of this subsection, consideration of any rescission bill or impoundment resolution and amendments thereto (or any conference report thereon) shall be governed by the Rules of the House of Representatives applicable to other bills and resolutions, amendments, and conference reports in similar circumstances.

(d) FLOOR CONSIDERATION IN THE SENATE.—

Debate, time
limitation.

(1) Debate in the Senate on any rescission bill or impoundment resolution, and all amendments thereto (in the case of a rescission bill) and debatable motions and appeals in connection therewith, shall be limited to not more than 10 hours. The time shall be equally divided between, and controlled by, the majority leader and the minority leader or their designees.

(2) Debate in the Senate on any amendment to a rescission bill shall be limited to 2 hours, to be equally divided between, and controlled by, the mover and the manager of the bill. Debate on any amendment to an amendment, to such a bill, and debate on any debatable motion or appeal in connection with such a bill or an impoundment resolution shall be limited to 1 hour, to be equally divided between, and controlled by, the mover and the manager of the bill or resolution, except that in the event the manager of the bill or resolution is in favor of any such amendment, motion, or appeal, the time in opposition thereto, shall be controlled by the minority leader or his designee. No amendment that is not germane to the provisions of a rescission bill shall be received. Such leaders, or either of them, may, from the time under their control on the passage of a rescission bill or impoundment resolution, allot additional time to any Senator during the consideration of any amendment, debatable motion, or appeal.

(3) A motion to further limit debate is not debatable. In the case of a rescission bill, a motion to recommit (except a motion to recommit with instructions to report back within a specified number of days, not to exceed 3, not counting any day on which the Senate is not in session) is not in order. Debate on any such motion to recommit shall be limited to one hour, to be equally divided between, and controlled by, the mover and the manager of the concurrent resolution. In the case of an impoundment resolution, no amendment or motion to recommit is in order.

Conference reports.

(4) The conference report on any rescission bill shall be in order in the Senate at any time after the third day (excluding Saturdays, Sundays, and legal holidays) following the day on which such a conference report is reported and is available to Members of the Senate. A motion to proceed to the consideration of the conference report may be made even though a previous motion to the same effect has been disagreed to.

July 12, 1974   Pub. Law 93-344

(5) During the consideration in the Senate of the conference Debate, time
report on any rescission bill, debate shall be limited to 2 hours, to limitation.
be equally divided between, and controlled by, the majority leader
and minority leader or their designees. Debate on any debatable
motion or appeal related to the conference report shall be limited
to 30 minutes, to be equally divided between, and controlled by,
the mover and the manager of the conference report.

(6) Should the conference report be defeated, debate on any
request for a new conference and the appointment of conferees
shall be limited to one hour, to be equally divided between, and
controlled by, the manager of the conference report and the minority leader or his designee, and should any motion be made to
instruct the conferees before the conferees are named, debate on
such motion shall be limited to 30 minutes, to be equally divided
between, and controlled by, the mover and the manager of the
conference report. Debate on any amendment to any such instructions shall be limited to 20 minutes, to be equally divided between,
and controlled by, the mover and the manager of the conference
report. In all cases when the manager of the conference report is
in favor of any motion, appeal, or amendment, the time in opposition shall be under the control of the minority leader or his
designee.

(7) In any case in which there are amendments in disagreement, time on each amendment shall be limited to 30 minutes, to be
equally divided between, and controlled by, the manager of the
conference report and the minority leader or his designee. No
amendment that is not germane to the provisions of such amendments shall be received.

Approved July 12, 1974.

LEGISLATIVE HISTORY:

HOUSE REPORTS: No. 93-658 (Comm. on Rules) and No. 93-1101 (Comm.
                  of Conference).
SENATE REPORTS: No. 93-579 accompanying S. 1541 (Comm. on
                  Government Operations) and No. 93-688 accom-
                  panying S. 1541 (Comm. on Rules and Administra-
                  tion) and No. 93-924 (Comm. of Conference).
CONGRESSIONAL RECORD:
    Vol. 119 (1973): Dec. 4, 5, considered and passed House.
    Vol. 120 (1974): Mar. 13, 19-21, S. 1541 considered in
                      Senate.
                      Mar. 22, considered and passed Senate,
                      amended, in lieu of S. 1541.
                      June 18, House agreed to conference
                      report.
                      June 21, Senate agreed to conference
                      report.
WEEKLY COMPILATION OF PRESIDENTIAL DOCUMENTS:
    Vol. 10, No. 28 (1974): July 12, Presidential statement.

O

Selected Bibliography

There are many primary and secondary materials available on the budget process, and the scholarly literature is rapidly growing. Two useful sources on the budget process are the *National Journal* and *Congressional Quarterly Weekly Reports*. Government documents dealing with the budget are indeed voluminous, particularly from the Office of Management and Budget (OMB) and the executive branch. Concentrating on congressional sources, a number of relevant research materials are published regularly by Congress. Beginning with the *Congressional Record*, the list includes documents published by the House Budget Committee (Task Force reports, hearings, reports to accompany first and second concurrent resolutions, and views and estimates of the standing committees), the Senate Budget Committee (hearings, resolutions and accompanying reports, and scorekeeping reports), Congressional Budget Office (annual reports, background papers, technical analysis papers, and budget issue papers). Both Budget committees and CBO issue complete lists of publications that may be requested by mail. The Congressional Research Service publishes a variety of materials of direct interest to congressional budgeting.

A number of books, special reports, studies, and hearings have been published on Congress and the budget. Some of the most useful ones are listed here.

Bledsoe, Robert, and Handberg, Roger. "Congressional Decision-Making in the Post-Vietnam Era: Continuity or Change Concerning the Defense Budget." Paper delivered at the Southwestern Political Science Association, Dallas, Texas, March 30-April 2, 1977.

Brookings Institution. *Setting National Priorities: The (1970-1980) Budget*. Washington. Published annually.

Brundage, Percival F. *The Bureau of the Budget*. New York: Praeger, 1970.

Buchanan, James M., and Wagner, Richard E. *Democracy in Deficit*. New York: Academic Press, 1977.

Burkhead, Jesse. "Federal Budgetary Developments: 1947-48." *Public Administration Review* 8 (Autumn 1948): 267-274.

Burkhead, Jesse. *Government Budgeting*. New York: Wiley, 1956.

Clark, Joseph S. *The Senate Establishment.* New York: Hill and Wang, 1963.

Congressional Budget Office. *Advance Budgeting: A Report to the Congress.* 95th Congress, 1st Sess., February 24, 1977.

Davis, Otto; Dempster, Michael; and Wildavsky, Aaron. "A Theory of the Budgetary Process." *American Political Science Review* 60 (September 1966): 529.

Derthick, Martha. *Uncontrollable Spending For Social Services Grants.* Washington, D.C.: Brookings Institution, 1975.

Ellwood, John W., and Taylor, Marcia. "The Impact of Sequencing of Congressional Budget Decisions on the Policy Output." Paper delivered at the Midwest Political Science Association, Chicago, Ill., April 21-23, 1977.

Ellwood, John W., and Thurber, James A. "The New Congressional Budget Process: Its Causes, Consequences and Possible Success." In *Legislative Reform and Public Policy,* edited by Susan Welch and John Peters. New York: Praeger, 1977.

Ellwood, John W., and Thurber, James A. "The New Congressional Budget Process: The Hows and Whys of House-Senate Differences." In *Congress Reconsidered,* edited by Lawrence Dodd and Bruce Oppenheimer. New York: Praeger, 1977.

Ellwood, John W., and Thurber, James A. "Some Implications of the Congressional Budget and Impoundment Control Act for the Senate." Paper delivered at the American Political Science Association, Chicago, Ill., September 1-5, 1976.

Fenno, Richard. *Congressmen in Committee.* Boston: Little, Brown, 1973.

Fenno, Richard. "The House Appropriations Committee as a Political System: The Problem of Integration." *American Political Science Review* 56 (June 1962): 310-324.

Fenno, Richard. *The Power of the Purse.* Boston: Little, Brown, 1966.

Ferejohn, John. *Porkbarrel Politics.* Stanford: Stanford University Press, 1974.

Finley, James. "The 1974 Congressional Initiative in Budget Making." *Public Administration Review* 35, no. 3 (May/June 1975): 270-278.

Fiorina, Morris. *Congress: Keystone of the Washington Establishment.* New Haven: Yale University Press, 1977.

Fisher, Louis. "Congressional Budget Reform: Committee Conflicts." Paper delivered at the Midwest Political Science Association, Chicago, Ill., April 21-23, 1977.

Fisher, Louis. "Congressional Budget Reform: The First Two Years." *Harvard Journal on Legislation* 14 (April 1977): 413-457.

Fisher, Louis. *Court Cases on Impoundment of Funds: A Public Policy Analysis.* Washington: Congressional Research Service, March 15, 1974.

Fisher, Louis. "The Politics of Impounded Funds." *Administration Science Quarterly* 15 (September 1970): 361-377.

Fisher, Louis. *Presidential Spending Power.* Princeton: Princeton University Press, 1975.

Fisher, Louis. "Supplemental Appropriations, Fiscal Years 1964-1968." Paper delivered at the Midwest Political Science Association, Chiacgo, Ill., April 20, 1979.

Havemann, Joel. *Congress and the Budget.* Bloomington: Indiana University Press, 1978.

Joint Study Committee on Budget Control. *Recommendations for Improving Congressional Control Over Budgetary Outlay and Receipt Totals.* 93rd Congress, 1st Sess., April 18, 1973.

Kanter, Arnold. "Congress and the Defense Budget: 1960-1970." *American Political Science Review* 66 (March 1972): 129-143.

Key, V. O. "The Lack of a Budgetary Theory." *American Political Science Review* 34 (December 1940): 1137-1144.

Leiserson, Avery. "Coordination of Federal Budgetary and Appropriation Procedures Under the Legislative Reorganization Act of 1946." *National Tax Journal* 1 (June 1948): 118-126.

LeLoup, Lance T. *Budgetary Politics.* 2nd ed. Brunswick, Ohio: Kings Court, 1980.

LeLoup, Lance T. "Budgeting in the Senate." Paper delivered at the Midwest Political Science Association, Chicago, Ill., April 20, 1979.

LeLoup, Lance T. "Discretion in National Budgeting: Controlling the Controllables." *Policy Analysis* 4 (Fall 1978): 455-475.

LeLoup, Lance T. "The Myth of Incrementalism: Analytic Choices in Budgetary Theory." *Polity* 10 (Summer 1978): 488-509.

LeLoup, Lance T. "Process Versus Policy: The U.S. House Budget Committee." *Legislative Studies Quarterly* 4 (May 1979): 227-254.

LeLoup, Lance T., and Moreland, William. "Agency Strategies and Executive Review: The Hidden Politics of Budgeting." *Public Administration Review* 38 (May/June 1978): 232-239.

Mahew, David. *The Electoral Connection.* New Haven: Yale University Press, 1974.

Manley, John F. *The Politics of Finance.* Boston: Little, Brown, 1970.

Masters, Nicholas. "Committee Assignments." In *New Perspectives on the House of Representatives,* edited by Robert Peabody and Nelson Polsby. New York. Rand McNally, 1969.

Matthews, Donald. *U.S. Senators and their World.* Chapel Hill: University of North Carolina Press, 1960.

McAllister, Eugene J. *Congress and the Budget: Evaluating the Process.* Washington, D.C.: Heritage Foundations, 1979.

Morrow, William. *Congressional Committees.* New York: Scribners, 1969.

Nathan, Richard, and Adams, Charles. *Revenue Sharing: The Second Round.* Washington: Brookings Institution, 1977.

Ornstein, Norman; Peabody, Robert; and Rohde, David. "The Changing Senate: From the 1950s to the 1970s." In *Congress Reconsidered,* edited by Lawrence Dodd and Bruce Oppenheimer, pp. 3-20. New York: Praeger, 1977.

Ott, David J., and Ott, Attiat F. *Federal Budget Policy.* Washington: Brookings Institution, 1965.

Pfiffner, James P. "Congressional Budget Reform, 1974: Initiative and Reaction." Paper delivered at the American Political Science Association, San Francisco, Calif., September 2-5, 1975.

Pfiffner, James. "Executive Control and the Congressional Budget." Paper delivered at the Midwest Political Science Association, Chicago, Ill., April 21-23, 1977.

Pfiffner, James. *The President, The Budget and Congress: Impoundment and the 1974 Budget Act.* (Boulder: Westview, 1979).

Pressman, Jeffrey L. *House versus Senate*. New Haven: Yale University Press, 1966.

Ripley, Randall B. *Congress: Process and Policy*. New York: Norton, 1975.

Ripley, Randall B. *Power in the Senate*. New York: St. Martin's, 1969.

Rudder, Catherine. "Committee Reform and the Revenue Process." In *Congress Reconsidered*, edited by Lawrence Dodd and Bruce Oppenheimer, pp. 117-139. New York: Praeger, 1977.

Saloma, John S. III. "Legislative Effectiveness: Control and Investigation." In *Congress and the President: Allies and Adversaries*, edited by Ronald C. Moe. Pacific Palisades, Calif.: Goodyear, 1971.

Schick, Allen. "The Battle of the Budget." *Proceedings of the Academy of Political Science* 32 (1975): 51-70.

Schick, Allen. "The Budget Bureau That Was: Thoughts on the Rise, Decline, and Future of a Presidential Agency." *Law and Contemporary Problems* 35 (Summer 1970): pp. 519-539.

Schick, Allen. "Budget Reform Legislation: Reorganizing Congressional Centers of Fiscal Power." *Harvard Journal on Legislation* 11 (February 1974): 303-350.

Schick, Allen. *The Congressional Budget and Impoundment Act: A Summary of Its Provisions*. Washington: Congressional Research Service (February 5, 1975): 75-335.

Schick, Allen. *The Congressional Budget Act of 1974: Legislative History and Analysis*. Washington: Congressional Research Service (February 26, 1975): 75-945.

Schick, Allen. "Congressional Control of Expenditures." U.S. House Budget Committee 95th Congress, 1st Sess., January 1977.

Schick, Allen. *The First Years of the Congressional Budget Process*. Washington: Congressional Research Service (June 30, 1976): 76-1215.

Schick, Allen. *The Impoundment Control Act of 1974: Legislative History and Implementation*. Washington: Congressional Research Service (February 27, 1976): 76-455.

Shull, Steven A. "An Agency's Best Friend: The President or Congress." In *The Presidency: Studies in Public Policy*, edited by Steven A. Shull and Lance T. LeLoup, pp. 219-238. Brunswick, Ohio: Kings Court, 1979.

Shull, Steven A. "Presidential-Congressional Support for Agencies and for Each Other." *Journal of Politics* 40 (August, 1978): 753-760.

Smithies, Arthur. *The Budgetary Process in the United States*. New York: McGraw-Hill, 1955.

Thurber, James A. "Congressional Budget Reform and New Demands for Policy Analysis." *Policy Analysis* 2, no. 4 (Spring 1976): 197-214.

U.S. House Budget Committee. *Oversight of the Congressional Budget Process*. Hearings, 95th Congress, 1st Sess., October 5-6, 1977.

U.S. House Commission on Information and Facilities. *Congressional Budget Office: A Study of its Organizational Effectiveness*. 95th Congress, 1st Session, January 4, 1977.

U.S. House Committee on Rules. *Hearings on Budget Control Act of 1973*. 93rd Congress, 1st Sess., 1973.

U.S. Office of Management and Budget. *Budget of the United States Government.* Washington: U.S. Government Printing Office.

U.S. Senate Budget Committee. *Can Congress Control the Power of the Purse?* Hearings, 95th Congress, 2nd Sess., March 6, 1978.

U.S. Senate Budget Committee. *Tax Expenditures.* 94th Congress, 2nd Sess., March 17, 1976.

U.S. Senate Commission on the Operation of the Senate. *Congressional Support Agencies.* 94th Congress, 2nd Sess., 1976.

U.S. Senate Committee on Governmental Affairs. *Sunset Act of 1977.* Hearings, 95th Congress, 2nd Sess., 1978.

U.S. Senate Committee on Government Operations. *Improving Congressional Control Over the Budget: A Compendium of Materials.* 93rd Congress, 1st Sess., March 27, 1973.

U.S. Senate Committee on Rules and Administration. *The Program Evaluation Act of 1977 and Federal Spending Control Act of 1977.* 95th Congress, 2nd Sess., 1978. (A useful compendium of materials on sunset legislation.)

Wallace, Robert. *Congressional Control of Federal Spending.* Detroit: Wayne State University Press, 1960.

Weidenbaum, Murray. "Institutional Obstacles to Relocating Government Expenditures." In *Public Expenditures and Policy Analysis,* edited by R. Havemann and J. Margoles, pp. 232-245. Chicago: Markham, 1970.

Wildavsky, Aaron. *The Politics of the Budgetary Process.* 2nd ed. Boston: Little, Brown, 1974.

Wildavsky, Aaron. *Budgeting.* Boston: Little, Brown, 1975.

Index

ABOUT THE AUTHOR

Lance T. LeLoup is a member of the faculty of the Political Science Department at the University of Missouri at St. Louis. His earlier publications include *Budgetary Politics* and *The Presidency: Studies in Policy-Making* (with Steven A. Shull).